SERVANTS OF THE SUPERNATURAL

Antonio Melechi is a Visiting Fellow at the University of York and the author of *Fugitive Minds*.

Praise for *Servants of the Supernatural*:

'*Servants of the Supernatural* picks its way through the history of spiritualism in the Victorian era carefully and with an understated wit.' *Financial Times*

'It tells the story of the Victorian obsession with séances, spirit writing, communing with the dead and all the showmanship that went with it . . . Melechi tells it well and wittily.'
Daily Express

'In his fascinating book, *Servants of the Supernatural*, Antonio Melechi brings to life the wonderfully flamboyant cheats and frauds of the 19th century medium trade.'
Deborah Blum, author of *Ghost Hunters*

'[A] lustrous new book – a history of the heyday of the Victorian séance in all its table-trembling, tambourine-tapping glory.' *Word*

Also by Antonio Melechi

Fugitive Minds

ANTONIO MELECHI

SERVANTS OF THE SUPERNATURAL

THE NIGHT SIDE OF THE VICTORIAN MIND

arrow books

Published by Arrow Books 2009

4 6 8 10 9 7 5

Copyright © Antonio Melechi 2008

Antonio Melechi has asserted his right under the Copyright, Designs
and Patents Act 1988 to be identified as the author of this work

This book is sold subject to the condition that it shall not, by way of trade or
otherwise, be lent, resold, hired out, or otherwise circulated without the
publisher's prior consent in any form of binding or cover other than that
in which it is published and without a similar condition, including
this condition, being imposed on the subsequent purchaser

First published in Great Britain in 2008 by
William Heinemann

Arrow Books
Random House, 20 Vauxhall Bridge Road,
London SW1V 2SA

www.rbooks.co.uk

Addresses for companies within The Random House Group Limited can be found at:
www.randomhouse.co.uk/offices.htm

The Random House Group Limited Reg. No. 954009

A CIP catalogue record for this book
is available from the British Library

ISBN: 9780099478867

**Penguin Random House is committed to a sustainable future for
our business, our readers and our planet. This book is made from
Forest Stewardship Council® certified paper.**

Printed and bound in Great Britain by Clays Ltd, St Ives plc

Typeset by SX Composing DTP, Rayleigh, Essex

For Julie, Silvie, Tilly and Lana – my foreverloves

There is another world, but it is inside this one

Paul Eluard

Contents

List of illustrations — xi
Introduction   A Séance for Sceptics — 1
Chapter One   Bodies Electric — 7
Chapter Two   Magnetic Mockeries — 35
Chapter Three   London Trance — 75
Chapter Four   'Lecture Mania' — 99
Chapter Five   The Infidel in Petticoats — 121
Chapter Six   News from Nowhere — 137
Chapter Seven   Tea and Table Moving — 161
Chapter Eight   Dark Employments — 179
Chapter Nine   'Conjurers in Disguise' — 207
Chapter Ten   Mental Notes — 233

Epilogue 261

Select Bibliography 267

Acknowledgements 277

Index 279

List of Illustrations

1. Mesmer's *baquet* (Oxford Science Archive/Heritage Images)
2. University College Hospital (English Heritage/Heritage Images)
3. John Elliotson (Wellcome Library, London)
4. Thomas Wakley (Mary Evans Picture Library)
5. Mesmeric chapbook (Wellcome Library, London)
6. Elliotson in *Punch* (Mary Evans Picture Library)
7. Thomas Macaulay (Mary Evans Picture Library)
8. Alexis Didier, from frontispiece of *Le Someil Magnetique* (British Library © The British Library Board)
9. Sir John Franklin (Anne Ronan/Heritage Images)
10. Valentine Greatrakes (Mary Evans Picture Library)
11. Harriet Martineau (British Library © The British Library Board)
12. The Fox Sisters (Mary Evans Picture Library)
13. A table moving séance (Mary Evans Picture Library)
14. Daniel Dunglas Home (Society for Psychical Research/

Mary Evans Picture Library)
15. The prosecution of Henry Slade, from *The Graphic* (Mary Evans Picture Library)
16. Michael Faraday (Oxford Science Archive/Heritage Images)
17. The Rev. William Stainton Moses (Mary Evans Picture Library)
18. Alfred Russel Wallace & Spirit (College of Psychic Studies Collection/Mary Evans Picture Library)
19. Mrs Piper (Mary Evans Picture Library)
20. Davenport Brothers' Playbill (Mary Evans Picture Library)
21. John Nevil Maskelyne's *Modern Spiritualism* (Harry Price Library of Magical Literature, University of London/Mary Evans Picture Library)
22. Florence Cook unmasked, from *The Graphic* (Anne Ronan/Heritage Images)

Introduction

A Séance for Sceptics

Crouching behind the glass-fronted cabinet, I steadied my breath and waited to catch a glimpse of our Latvian neighbour – the lady who'd promised that spirits would help find my aunt's 'stolen' purse. Shuffling backwards, my knees knocked the cabinet's splintering underside, sending a bottle of Sambuca rolling into a plumed Sicilian carriage. Cornered in my hideaway, I saw a large handbag appear at the doorway, followed by a pale, austere-looking woman in a flowery kaftan. 'No, no, no – no children,' she muttered gravely, before asking that the table be moved away from the window and that I be sent out to play.

Later that evening I learned that our local medium's description of the 'thief' had confirmed my aunt's suspicions. My mother, thinking otherwise, enlisted my help on a Sunday morning search of house and garden. Sure enough, we eventually found the purse in a laundry basket, swaddled in a pile of folded tea towels. Clicking it open, my aunt lingered over its contents. Notes. Coins. House keys. Photographs.

Wage slips. Co-op stamps. A small laminated print of Padre Pio – it was all there, she nodded, clasping her hands and looking heavenwards as she thanked St Anthony for its safe return.

Many years later, on reading Arthur Conan Doyle's *History of Spiritualism*, I was reminded of *the affair of the missing purse*. Though Conan Doyle accepted that mediums might sometimes resort to trickery and dissemblance in the séance room, skilfully pilfering information from their sitters, his faith in spiritualism – 'the most important [movement] in the history of the world since the Christ episode' – was almost entirely at odds with the methods of my childhood hero, the long-time occupier of 221b Baker Street. For Conan Doyle, testimony to séance-room miracles was tantamount to cast-iron evidence if attested by 'men of honour and repute, who were willing afterwards to take their oath upon it'. Following this rule of thumb, his account of the early history of spiritualism found in favour of almost every reported manifestation, from human levitation to spiritual materialisation, giving credence to the questionable powers of Daniel Dunglas Home, the Davenport brothers, Henry Slade and other well-known nineteenth-century mediums.

It was in the mid 1880s, while establishing himself in private practice in Southsea, near Portsmouth, that Conan Doyle had attended his first séances. Before then he had dismissed all spiritual phenomena as 'the greatest nonsense upon earth', finding it difficult to imagine that 'any sane man could believe such things'. Yet after visiting various mediums with his friend General Drayson, he erred: the messages that were conveyed seemed to suggest that life beyond the grave was more than a hopeful delusion. On joining the Society for Psychical Research in 1891, Conan Doyle continued to look into these 'bewildering and more or less unrelated facts', yet he remained shy of any public declaration of faith. It was only after his son

Kinsley died on the Somme that he confessed that 'this subject with which I had so long dallied was not merely a study of a force outside the rules of science', but 'a direct undeniable message from beyond, a call of hope and guidance to the human race at the time of its deepest affliction'. From now on, Sherlock Holmes's creator would surrender pen, royalties and common sense to the spiritualist cause.

The idea for this book came while I was researching the history of madness and visionary states for *Fugitive Minds* (2003). Working my way through nineteenth-century journals, diaries and reportage, I found that mediums, psychics and somnambules had been investigated by scientific grandees such as Faraday, Darwin and Huxley, and that their performances had, while underwriting a whole new mythology of the supernatural, been imitated and exposed by stage magicians, denounced by clerics and mercilessly satirised by the wags at *Punch*. The golden age of the Victorian séance seemed far more arresting and intriguing than Conan Doyle's dutiful survey had grasped.

Britain's first séances were trials of mesmerism, a hands-on therapy that had been hawked around the European academies with limited success since the 1770s. Aptly defined in Ambrose Pierce's *Devil's Dictionary* as 'Hypnotism before it wore good clothes, kept a carriage and asked Incredulity to dinner', mesmerism found its first plausible English champion in Dr John Elliotson – the template for Julian Faber in Edward Bulwer-Lytton's *Strange Story*, and Dr Goodenough in Thackeray's *Pendennis*. Elliotson's experiments at University College Hospital in the late 1830s roused widespread interest in the curative effects of the magnetic effluvia he claimed to have harnessed, prompting journeyman lecturers to undertake demonstrations of this ethereal force at temperance halls and mechanics' institutes, the likes of Harriet Martineau to submit herself to mesmeric treatment and the ever-curious Dickens to try his hand at a spot of lay healing.

Over the coming decades the séance would assume a myriad of unexpected forms, serving as a platform where entranced maids extemporised on politics, theology and the cosmography of the spirit world, society clairvoyants gave notice of stolen property and missing persons, spirits rapped out messages and dispatched letters, spectral arms tugged at unsuspecting sleeves, ghostly shapes materialised from darkened cabinets, furniture danced, and dew-dappled fruit and flowers fell from heaven's orchard. It was this array of mental and physical oddities that helped convince a significant number of Victorian intellectuals (and an even greater number of nameless artisans) that the Enlightenment *philosophes* had been much too hasty in dismissing the miracles and prodigies of old as fable and hearsay.

A New Age was under way. By the 1840s ghosts, spectres and doubles had begun their long march through the penny dreadfuls, and into the creaking stairwells of mainstream fiction and theatre. Works of medicine and psychology profiled the exalted powers of somnambulists and trance mediums. Dreams, reveries and the manifold forms of 'unconscious cerebration' were laid bare in popular periodicals. As Catherine Crowe observed in her popular miscellany *The Night Side of Nature* (1848), all these manifestations appeared to 'bring the mysterious within the bounds of science'.

Traversing this book are three sciences – mesmerism, spiritualism and psychical research – that have been long regarded as 'epidemic delusions' or 'marginal cults'. Though I would not entirely dispute their fringe status, it would be fair to say that the cultural and psychological significance of these (pseudo)-sciences remains underappreciated. Few social historians have acknowledged the extent to which religious doubt and scientific fervour were conjoined in the Victorian séance room, and fewer still that its procession of strange manifestations, while renewing belief in the afterlife, also fanned the flames of materialism and infidelity.

For every heartfelt avowal of faith in a séance-room manifestation one can find a corresponding accusation of legerdemain, or an exasperated admission of complete uncertainty on the part of a sitter. While recent scholarship has tended to suspend judgement on the reality of the physical and mental phenomena that the séance gave birth to, foregrounding the motives of the disenchanted Victorians who found succour in its catalogue of wonders, this tells us little about the psychology of mediumship, and all but ignores the forms of deception and scepticism that it generated. Eschewing this open verdict, I have, wherever possible, tried to shed some light on the manufacturing of supernatural events, giving doubtful observers who have been rarely called upon their time in the witness box.

This book is by no means a comprehensive or in-depth history of the séance. Amateur mediums and mesmerists who were not patronised by literate investigators are, for understandable reasons, absent in the following pages. I have hardly touched upon experiments with telepathy and spirit photography, and said little about the medicalisation of mediumship or the séance room's affinity with hydropathy, Swedenborgianism, occultism and radical Socialism. Instead, I have attempted to assemble a gallery of contrasting thumbnail portraits, focusing on a fairly wide cross-section of Victorians – and some notable 'magnetic' forebears – whose appetite for 'curious facts' transformed them into servants of the supernatural.

Sham miracles and profound insights abound in the séance room. 'The difficulty', as Holmes reminded Watson in *The Adventure of Silver Blaze*, 'is to detach the framework of fact – of absolute undeniable fact – from the embellishments of theorists and reporters.' Only then can we begin to approach 'the special points upon which the whole mystery turns'.

Chapter One

Bodies Electric

Sleep, sleep on, forget thy pain –
My hand is on thy brow,
My spirit on thy brain,
My pity on thy heart, poor friend

     Percy Bysshe Shelley, 'The Magnetic Lady to
          Her Patient', 1822

On a cloudy August afternoon in 1837 a 'small, spare man, with a pale, intellectual face' walked quickly down Gower Street and into the gloomy interior of University College Hospital. Making his way up to the Women's Ward, Baron Jules Dupotet de Sennevoy found a horseshoe of visiting doctors and invited gentlemen awaiting him. With a brief introduction from the senior physician, Dr John Elliotson, the soi-disant baron began to demonstrate a 'new and mysterious science' upon a young epileptic patient. Drawing his hand towards the young woman, who was seated in an armchair in the centre of the ward,

Dupotet stared intently at her downturned eyes and began to make slow downwards movements before her, 'as if he was intending to keep up an electrical communication'.

Colonel Peyronnet Thompson, the recently ousted MP for Hull, was in no mood to be taken in by humbug or imposture. Avoiding the main semicircle of onlookers, he remained standing by the stairwell at the back of the ward. Colonel Thompson had received an unfavourable report on Dupotet from his daughter, who had seen him perform in Paris some years previously. Yet, having recently 'gathered much interesting information on the power of the imagination over epileptic afflictions', this 'professed unbeliever' welcomed the opportunity to witness what effects Dupotet's magnetic treatment might yield. First impressions were not encouraging. When the first trial was terminated, with the patient declaring herself no more than 'a little sleepy', Thompson was convinced that he would remain an 'infidel before whom nothing was fated to be seen'.

A new patient was led to the chair. The young woman was 'about seventeen years of age, with fair complexion and a profusion of flaxen ringlets', which hung over a horsehair seton that was threaded through the back of her neck. Guessing that she was neither servant-girl nor seamstress, but probably the daughter of an artisan or tradesman, Thompson watched Dupotet perform exactly the same procedure. Within a few minutes the young woman stood up, took a sharp intake of breath and fell back into the chair with a swooning sigh. Thompson moved closer and found that the patient 'presented the appearance of a recent corpse'. When Dr Elliotson invited his medical colleagues to pull on the young woman's arms and legs, her limbs were easily contorted and fixed into different poses. When the same physicians were invited to pinch her hands and to force snuff up her nostrils, each of them failed to produce any token of sensibility.

It was only after being vigorously shaken and shouted at that the patient appeared to partially wake. 'O why should blushes dye my cheek?' she asked dreamily. Shaken again, she insisted that she would not be 'turned out, as I was before, for the servants to laugh at'. Dupotet now announced that he would bring the patient back to her senses by moving to the far side of the ward. The procedure failed. 'What he did this time', Thompson observed, 'appeared to consist in bringing his two hands within a foot of her face, and waving them two or three times across the face, from the nose outwards ... saying at the same time, with as much English pronunciation as he could muster, "Get up." The patient immediately rose, and with the same winking and embarrassed air as before ... disappeared in the matron's room.'

Colonel Thompson had seen enough. Collusion or dissemblance could not explain this patient's insensibility; besides, the girl was 'much too pretty and light-hearted to be the instrument of a cold-blooded and painful fraud'. As he boarded his carriage and turned away from Russell Square, Thompson reflected on the strange, sleep-like state that Dupotet had ushered the young woman into. What agency, he wondered, could cause volition to be suspended, the senses to be muted, and the body to be so grossly puppeteered? Was there, after all, a subtle force, a vital power, that had eluded all of nature's philosophers?

Later that evening, as he drafted an eyewitness report for the *Lancet*, the leading medical journal of the day, Thompson wondered if the waving action of Dupotet's hands might have been sufficient to induce dizziness and trigger an epileptic fit. The 'diminution of language' that the patient had demonstrated was, to Thompson's mind, clear evidence that she had been in the grip of some form of 'cerebral irritation'. Whether these 'artificial fits' might have a remedial effect on epilepsy and other diseases remained to be seen. The careful scrutiny that would be required to establish the true efficacy of animal magnetism was, he lamented, clearly absent among the *gobe-mouche* physicians who had been present at Dupotet's demonstration:

> ... some of the questions they asked were in the highest degree unwise; not only as implying the expectation of supernatural or extra-natural response, but as having a direct tendency to act as what counsel call 'leading questions'. Take for example, 'How many times must you be magnetised before you are able to see with your eyes shut?' ... My hope therefore is, that some medical person will take up the question with the advantages of professional knowledge, and will steer a just course between credulity on one hand, and a sickly dread of discovering new truths on the other, though concealed under any imaginable mass of the fantastic and the unsound.

The *Lancet*'s decision to publish Thompson's anonymous report on Dupotet's demonstrations of animal magnetism at University College Hospital took its rival journals by surprise. The medical press had for many years collectively scoffed at the progress of animal magnetism in France and Germany. Dismissing the 'mystic art' as more unbelievable than anything Baron Munchausen could have dreamed of, most popular encyclopaedias had relegated animal magnetism to a bit part in the history of 'juggling' and its motley procession of oracles, fire breathers and talking automata. According to the *British Cyclopaedia*, animal magnetism was a 'long-exploded doctrine' that the French academies had emphatically dismissed. Its originator, Franz Anton Mesmer (1734–1815), had feigned discovery of an invisible force – 'a medium of reciprocal influence between celestial bodies, the earth and living things' – that he deemed capable of 'curing directly all disorders of the nervous system, and indirectly all other maladies'. Mesmer was, in short, a 'fraud' and a 'charlatan' who had 'the impudence to demand from the French government the gift of a castle and estate if he would establish a magnetic clinic'.

Though widely caricatured as 'a vain boastful pretender to physic' (Samuel Johnson's *Dictionary* definition of the age-old 'quack') Mesmer was no fairground mountebank. The son of a Swabian gamekeeper from the western side of Lake Constance, Mesmer was educated for the priesthood at the Universities of Dillingen and Ingolstadt before beginning his medical studies at the University of Vienna. After marrying a wealthy widow, Mesmer renewed his research into 'animal gravity', the subject of his 1766 dissertation, *The Influence of the Planets on the Human Body*. Experimenting with variously shaped magnets, used in conjunction with an iron-based tonic, Mesmer found that, by careful placement of the magnets on specific parts of the body, he was able to restore dramatically the balance of 'animal gravity' in numerous patients.

Mesmer's magnets had come from the workshop of Maximillian Hell, a Jesuit professor of astronomy, who proceeded to take credit for perfecting their design. Aggrieved that Hell should blatantly have stolen priority for his discovery, Mesmer attempted to outmanoeuvre his adversary. The magnets had, he insisted, been merely conductors to an ethereal fluid, 'an essentially different agent' from that described by Hell. This substance, which he named 'animal magnetism', which resided in all healthy bodies and could be transmitted by touch to virtually any material. A bath in 'magnetised water' would have the same effect as magnets. Indeed, by merely touching or stroking with his fingertips, or wafting an iron wand, Mesmer found that he could relieve many physical and nervous afflictions through a simple transfusion of animal magnetism.

Amassing an impressive catalogue of cures by way of this 'artificial tide', Mesmer travelled to Hungary, Switzerland and Bavaria, where his methods earned him a glittering reputation as a healer and miracle worker. Vienna's medical faculty was less than impressed by the reports it had received, but Mesmer was presented an ideal opportunity to win over the faculty sceptics when he began to treat the blind daughter of Joseph Anton von Paradis, the empress's court councillor. A talented singer and pianist, Maria Theresia had excelled under the tutelage of Leopold Kuzeluch and Antonio Salieri, and was now, at the age of eighteen, a much sought-after performer in the salons and concert halls of Vienna. Since losing her sight at the age of three, Miss Paradis had endured countless consultations and serial therapies, including a year-long course of electric shocks, which had caused her eyes to become grossly swollen and misaligned. Though there was no damage to the optic nerve, experts believed that Miss Paradis's hysterical blindness was incurable.

Refusing to give up hope of a cure, Maria Theresia's parents paid the first of many visits to Mesmer's Landstrasse clinic in January 1777. Mesmer believed that Maria Theresia's 'complete amaurosis attended by spasms in the eyes' was connected to acute melancholy, a 'deep sadness' that had periodically 'caused her to go into transports of delirium bad enough to make her think she was losing her mind'. Promising that he would, at the very least, be able to realign her eyes, Mesmer privately held high hopes for an outright cure. During her first treatment Maria Theresia was thrown into convulsions, her head tilting violently backwards, her arms and legs shaking uncontrollably. On the following day Herr Paradis was present to observe the first signs of improvement: 'As he sat beside his patient, he pointed his wand at the reflection of her face in the mirror. Then, as he moved the wand, she moved her head to follow it. She was even able to describe the movements of the wand.' A few weeks later Mesmer made his first attempts to make her see faces. 'The sight of the human face disconcerted her: she thought the nose was ridiculous, and for several days she could not look at it without laughing.'

Mesmer took care to expose Maria Theresia to light in a semi-darkened room, allowing her wasted eye muscles time to master control of her gaze and depth of vision. In the meantime he continued with his daily ministration of magnetic fluid, making downwards passes from the forehead and gentle circular motions round the eyes with his thumbs. When a deputation from the medical faculty agreed to examine Miss Paradis, it confirmed that her vision had been successfully restored, prompting Professor von Stoerk to acknowledge openly Mesmer's 'extraordinary cure'. This was the ringing endorsement that Mesmer had hoped for. The future appeared bright – for doctor and patient.

The case of Maria Theresia von Paradis turned quickly to scandal. As the young pianist struggled to navigate her way through the barrage of new forms and shapes, her eyes constantly prickled, her head spun and her prodigious memory for music seemed to elude her fingertips. Herr and Frau von Paradis, having initially been overjoyed at their daughter's progress, became anxious about Maria Theresia's welfare, her career and the whispers of imposture that surrounded Mesmer's 'extraordinary cure'. A dramatic confrontation occurred when Maria Theresia's mother called to announce her intention immediately to remove her daughter from Mesmer's care. Overhearing Mesmer express his concerns that her health might suffer if the treatment was terminated prematurely, Maria Theresia insisted that she wished to remain exactly where she was. Shrieking insults at Mesmer, Frau von Paradis grabbed her daughter and flung her against a wall. According to Mesmer, it was at this point that Herr von Paradis came storming into the room brandishing a sword. While Mesmer and his servant set about disarming the 'madman', who 'rushed from the house calling down maledictions on one and all', Frau von Paradis lost consciousness and her delirious daughter relapsed into blindness.

Lambasted by Professor Stoerk and his faculty colleagues, blackballed by society ladies who gave credence to rumours of seduction and necromancy, Mesmer believed that the Paradis affair had been especially contrived to deprive animal magnetism of due recognition. There was no future for him in Vienna. In February 1778 Mesmer and his footman journeyed north, to a city that was rediscovering its pre-enlightened appetite for miracles.

Paris was in thrall of scientific wonders and occult secrets. While the newspapers reported balloon flights and electrical demonstrations, there was a lively trade in amulets and sympathetic powders, and a myriad of faith healers and fortune tellers. Intent on gaining official endorsement for a discovery which was, to his mind, equal to those of Galileo and Newton, Mesmer took rooms on the Place Vendôme and began to minister to the dropsied, the palsied and the blind, waiving fees for his poorest patients by attending to the well-heeled regulars who came to have 'convulsions at ten louis a month'.

On moving to more opulent rooms at the Hôtel Bulliôn in the rue Coq Héron, Mesmer devised a method of collective treatment known as the *baquet*. This enclosed wooden tub filled with 'magnetised water' was able to accommodate twenty patients, who would sit around its periphery holding on to the iron rods that were fed, at right angles, into the tub. A rope fastened to the *baquet* was at the same time held by each patient. As a lilac-cloaked Mesmer circled the *baquet* he would augment the flow of magnetic fluid by a quick wave of his hand, or ease his patients' paroxysms with a spine-tingling refrain from his much-loved glass harmonica.

Mesmer tended to reserve his personal attention for 'ladies of breeding', such as the Comtesse de la Malmaison and Madame de Berny, who were respectively cured of paralysis and clouded vision. These ladies would sit at his best *baquet*, being ushered promptly into one of the finely furnished *chambres des crises* when overcome by infusions of magnetic fluid. One free *baquet* was also made available to the poor, but when demand became impossible to meet, Mesmer directed his needier patients to a large oak tree at the end of rue Bondy. The tree, which he had personally magnetised, became the site of a makeshift infirmary, accommodating up to a hundred rope-tied patients at any one time.

While Henri Ellenberger, historian of the medical unconscious, has claimed that Mesmer provided a touchstone for the development of modern psychiatry, the healing drama he choreographed in the Hôtel Bulliôn's *salles aux baquets* was testament to his growing sense of personal charisma and mystagogy. Evolving few insights into the psychological aspects of nervous disease, Mesmer was essentially a *bricoleur*, a scientific magpie who pilfered the language and symbolism of Newton's gravity and Franklin's electricity to postulate the existence of an occult force 'propagated by intermediary bodies in the same ways as is electrical fluid'. What others before him had termed 'sympathy' was now transformed into a material agent, an invisible fluid that could be dispensed according to the principles of electricity.

The electrical experiments that anticipated and informed Mesmer's use of the *baquet* began in Leyden, in 1746, when the Dutch physicist Pieter van Musschenbroek became the unwitting victim of a 'terrible experiment'. Attempting to gauge the strength of electrical charge produced when a glass globe was turned rapidly on its axis, van Musschenbroek received 'a shock of such violence that my whole body was shaken as by a lightning stroke'. The sparks of van Musschenbroek's experiments travelled far and wide. Across Europe and America, medical electricians seized upon this source of portable lightning, reporting success in the treatments of rheumatism, fever, plague, lameness and palsy. Faith in the healing powers of electricity – which was generally believed to relieve a raft of maladies and disorders by improving circulation – was carried into all corners of European society. The enthusiasm with which the Methodist preacher John Wesley embraced this 'universal medicine' was not unusual. After taking delivery of his first static machine in 1756, Wesley proceeded to electrify hundreds of troubled souls around Southwark and Moorfields, becoming an unflagging champion of electrical experiments. When the *London Magazine* asked, 'Why do you meddle with electricity?' Wesley's reply was disarmingly simple: 'to do as much good as I can.'

Mesmer's fervour, his sense of benevolent mission, matched that of any medical electrician. The subtle medium he administered was, he honestly believed, a form of inner electricity or magnetism (the two forces had yet to be distinguished) that could be passed from one nervous system to another. The *baquet*, which he contrived to store and administer his personal supply of animal magnetism, pressed the analogy into service. An oversized travesty of van Musschenbroek's Leyden jar, the *baquet* primed Mesmer's patients to experience remarkably powerful and protracted crises, attended by 'involuntary jerking movements in all limbs, and in the whole body, by contraction of the throat, by twitchings in the hypochondriac and epigastric regions, by dimness of and rolling of the eyes, by piercing cries, tears, hiccoughs, and immoderate laughter'.

These convulsions proved extremely cathartic and it was by no means only 'ladies of breeding' that were returned to health at Mesmer's *baquet*. Charles Deslon, a well-connected court physician, was not only happy to supply personal testimony to the *baquet*'s remarkable effects: on being cured of a long-standing stomach complaint, Deslon became Mesmer's understudy, approaching the faculty of medicine on his behalf. Another vocal ally was Antoine Court de Gébelin, the linguist and antiquary whose nine-volume *Monde Primitif* sought to persuade his fellow *philosophes* 'that the first men were sensible and not idolaters as we think'. Relieved of a serious infection of the legs after a stint at the *baquet*, Gébelin informed his Masonic brethren that Mesmer had, through the wonderful effects of magnetism, unknowingly resurrected the healing art of the Egyptian priests.

By neglecting to prepare detailed reports of his experiments and preventing his patients from being independently examined, Mesmer sabotaged his first attempts to gain recognition for his discovery of animal magnetism from the academies. In 1779 he renewed his bid for scientific respectability with the publication of his *Mémoire sur la découverte du magnétisme animal* – a flimsy pamphlet that trumpeted magnetism as a universal panacea and laid out a twenty-seven-point guide to its properties and principles – but the medical and scientific academies remained impervious to the allure of animal magnetism.

To disseminate the science of animal magnetism, two of Mesmer's acolytes decided on a different strategy. Through the auspices of the Society of Universal Harmony, the secret of animal magnetism was franchised in Masonic branches in the major towns and cities. The first hundred members of the Paris lodge each paid one hundred gold louis to Mesmer for instruction. Having mastered the healing rites of animal magnetism, a diploma recognised their authority to act as independent practitioners.

The cult of animal magnetism was born. The excitement, the sense of office and purpose that the would-be science roused in the idle rich and new bourgeoisie proved remarkably enlivening. When the Comte de Montlosier, a young gentleman who pursued the usual range of scientific divertimenti, witnessed his first mesmeric cure in his home town of Auxerre, a new vocation unfolded before him. 'His instant success inspired him to travel about the countryside, healing peasants and gentlewomen, and to abandon his flirtation with atheism. He had found a deeper, more satisfying kind of science, a science that left room for his religious impulses without excluding his sympathies for philosophy . . . It seemed to Montlosier that mesmerism would "change the face of the world".' Mentlosier's faith was unflagging. Fifty years on, he insisted that: 'No event, not even the revolution, has provided me with such vivid insights as mesmerism.'

Many of the most prominent disciples of mesmerism claimed to have similarly discovered a practical means of restoring moral and political harmony. Supporting Mesmer's challenge to the scientific academies, Jacques-Pierre Brissot, an aspirant *philosophe*, championed mesmerism as an agent of social justice, 'a way to bring social classes together, to make the rich more humane, to make them into real fathers of the poor'. The academicians whom Brissot loudly castigated for ignoring the 'extraordinary facts' of mesmerism were stirred into action in March 1784, when King Louis XVI's government appointed a commission on animal magnetism. A committee of the Académie des Sciences was instructed to work alongside a second body appointed by the Société Royale de Médecine. Mesmer, who previously refused the terms of a royal commission, took no part in the ensuing trials. After attending the clinic of Charles Deslon on numerous occasions, both bodies concluded that there was no evidence of a magnetic fluid and that since some of the seizures had been stimulated by suggestion alone, imagination was mesmerism's effective 'machine of incitement'.

The widespread circulation of the *Académie* report ensured that Mesmer and Deslon were crowned as emperors of a deluded science. As popular ridicule of animal magnetism reached its theatrical acme with *Two Modern Doctors*, a farce Philippe Pinel, one of the pioneers of modern psychiatry, recommended as 'an excellent antidote to melancholy', a forlorn Mesmer left Paris. After a lengthy tour of Europe he returned to Lake Constance where, after continuing to petition medical and scientific societies to endorse animal magnetism, he died at the age of eighty-one.

The Marquis de Puységur, one of the original members of

Mesmer's Society of Universal Harmony, opened a new chapter in the history of the 'medicine of the imagination' in 1784, when he began to magnetise workers on his family estate at Buzancy, near Soissons, in northern France. One of the very first patients Puységur attended to was Victor Race, a twenty-three-year-old peasant who had been confined to his bed with a fever for four days. After seven or eight minutes of touching and stroking, Puységur was surprised 'to see the man go to sleep quietly in my arms, without any convulsions or pain'. Soon, he began to discuss his personal affairs. 'When I thought his ideas might affect him in a disagreeable way, I stopped and tried to inspire more cheerful ones . . . At length, I saw him content, imagining that he was shooting at a target, dancing at a festival, and so on.' Puységur returned the following day to find Victor much recovered but unable to recall his previous visit. In further sessions Puységur found that the shy and diffident peasant began to speak openly about certain private matters that preoccupied him. The rapport that Puységur established with Victor became increasingly intimate, allowing him to convey silent instructions and wordless thoughts to his patient. When magnetised, Victor was as 'profound, prudent and clear sighted' as anyone he had ever known.

Nothing like this had ever been witnessed in Mesmer's *salles aux baquets*. When Puységur's version of magnetism wound its way into Switzerland, Bavaria and the German-speaking states, the dramatic convulsions that Mesmer had routinely provoked in his patients gave way to the 'gentle crisis' and a new battery of somnambulant powers, including the ability to experience a 'community of sensation' with the operator, to perceive clairvoyantly, and to diagnose ailments and prescribe sundry treatments. As these phenomena became recognised as the true signature of 'magnetic sleep', many practitioners followed

Puységur in placing greater emphasis on the will and intentions of the magnetiser (as opposed to Mesmer's purported fluid), who was seen to be chiefly responsible for inducing the 'calm and tranquil state' that would enable a return to health. Though still censured by the academies, Puységur's version of animal magnetism was followed with some interest by physicians who were keen to utilise the medical insights of these 'artificial somnambules' and to explore new methods in the psychological treatment of the insane. By 1812, Pinel was happy to invite the marquis to try out 'the power of magnetic influence' over the madwomen of the Salpêtrière.

A number of English physicians had called on Mesmer at his clinic at the Hôtel Bulliôn, but it was not until 1785, when William Godwin published a full translation of the French Royal Academy of Science's damning report, that the renegade science made its first appearance on British soil. An early torchbearer, John Bell, made a brief and unsuccessful tour of London and the provinces with an eight-foot version of Mesmer's oak *baquet*. Dr Bell was followed by John Benoit de Mainauduc, an Irish 'man-midwife' who, having studied under Mesmer, planned to establish a 'Hygiaean Society' that would provide London society with instruction in magnetism.

Though de Mainauduc never established an institutional base, his public lectures turned animal magnetism into the subject of countless scientific *conversazioni*, provoking a minor panic, and the usual cries of quackery and jugglery, among Georgian medics and ministers. Arriving in the capital in 1787, de Mainauduc found the beau monde happy to part with fifteen guineas for 'full exhibition and treatment'. Those who went 'to hear him with a firm and rational disbelief, expecting to be amused by the folly of his patients, were themselves thrown into what is called *the crisis*: his steady looks and continued gesticulations arrested their attention, made them dizzy, deranged the ordinary functions of the system, and fairly deprived them for a time of all voluntary power, and all perception'. Raising his subscription fee to twenty-five guineas, de Mainauduc soon transferred to Bristol and Bath, where he continued to restore 'dignity to the Art' which he claimed Mesmer had debased through 'superstitious juggling in material things'.

Rejecting Mesmer's claim to have discovered a purely physical medium, de Mainauduc approached animal magnetism as a form of faith healing which utilised the power of 'sympathy' and could be transmitted via atmospherical 'nerves' that placed all bodies in permanent connection with animate matter. Seeking to demonstrate that it was 'in the capacity of everyone to become a perfect master of this most essential science', de Mainauduc's practical demonstrations showed how magnetists could exercise their will to penetrate and cure the diseased body, with or without the convulsions that Mesmer had induced. No knowledge of medicine was required. The physical distance between operator and patient was equally unimportant. Instead, de Mainauduc offered four simple rules for maintaining concentrated attention:

> Be as much *abstracted* as possible; put every thought and idea out of your mind.
> Let your mind be filled with *affection* and *benevolence* towards the subject you are treating.
> Let there be a constant *intention* within you; keep up an idea of the complaint you are to remove.
> Exert the strong internal faculty of volition, or *will*, towards the subject . . . you will find oftentimes a strange connection with those whom you are treating.

After attending to the Duchess of Devonshire, Lady Salisbury and the Princess of Wales – all of whom succumbed, in varying degrees, to his magnetic ministrations – de Mainauduc faced little competition from a new wave of practitioners. By 1788 he could boast a subscription list that included '1 Duke, 1 Duchess, 1 Marchioness, 2 Countesses, 1 Earl, 1 Lord, 3 Ladies, 1 Bishop, 5 Right Honourable Gentlemen and Ladies, 2 Baronets, 7 Members of Parliament, 1 Clergyman, 2 Physicians, 7 Surgeons, exclusive of 92 Gentlemen and Ladies of respectability', each having signed an affidavit that obliged them not 'to discover the secrets of the science in the doctor's natural life'. According to the playwright and bluestocking Hannah More, de Mainauduc had by this time pocketed £100,000 from his 'demoniacal mummery', as much as Mesmer had earned during his Parisian pomp.

De Mainauduc's fame was brief. As Robert Southey tartly observed in his *Letters from England* (1807), London's magnetic messiah 'might have gone on triumphantly, and have made himself head of a sect, or even a religion' had the English not been preoccupied by the fall of the Bastille and the shockwaves of the Revolution. The most enthusiastic of de Mainauduc's supporters belonged to a tight-knit circle of well-heeled Freemasons, cabbalists and illuminists. These 'occult' followers of animal magnetism included de Mainauduc's former assistant, Benedict Chastenier (whose short-lived clinic on Tottenham Court Road promised 'INTELLECTUAL TREATMENT OF DISEASE BY SENSATIONS HITHERTO CALLED ANIMAL MAGNETISM'), the miniaturist Richard Cosway, and the painter and set designer Philip de Loutherbourg.

De Loutherbourg was the most benevolent of converts. The crowds that amassed outside his Hammersmith home on advertising free magnetic therapy in 1789 were more than equal to those that had once flocked to see his *Eidophusikon*, a complete miniature theatre replete with moving scenery, sound effects and mechanical actors. Employing animal magnetism alongside incantations and 'alchemical preparations', de Loutherbourg and his wife Lucy, one-time followers of the great occult charlatan Count Cagliostro, aimed 'to diffuse healing to *all* who have faith in the Lord as mediator, be they Deaf, Dumb, Lame, Halt or Blind'. The fanfare that de Loutherbourg received from Mary Pratt, one of the two thousand or so patients who were apparently cured within six months, caused his reputation to briefly eclipse that of his mentor, de Mainauduc. According to Pratt's feverish account of the daily miracles being performed in Hammersmith, the de Loutherbourgs were the recipients of 'heavenly and divine influx, coming from the radix of *God*'. Pratt took it upon herself to implore the Archbishop of Canterbury to compose a new prayer to speed the news of the de Loutherbourgs' 'divine manundictions' across the nation's churches and chapels, petitioning magistrates and their like to work with de Loutherbourg to build a large hospital, with its own pool of Bethesda. But as the crowds swelled to unmanageable proportions, the de Loutherbourgs left London, leaving the city's debating societies to decide whether 'Animal Magnetism, as practiced by Mr de Loutherbourg' had any philosophical basis.

Compared to the rise of animal magnetism in Paris a decade earlier, the British craze had been a minor affair, with no calls for a royal commission from its more respectable converts, no attempts to establish a collective forum or society to promote it and few broadsides from the medical and scientific academies. The most common charge levelled at the animal magnetists was that the state of suggestibility they produced could be abused by unscrupulous physicians, who might sexually exploit their patients, and by corrupt ministers who might cannily silence their political adversaries by putting them to sleep. Churchly critics of animal magnetism maintained that the rapport that practitioners established with their entranced patients was a kind of mental servitude, an ungodly state tantamount to possession. When Mesmer wrote to the Royal College of Physicians in 1802, begging assistance from the medical fraternity to help bring his discovery into 'the bosom of society', respectable society had turned its back on animal magnetism, dispatching its remaining practitioners into the 'dark alleys and obscure cellars of the metropolis'.

While France and Germany experienced a revival of medical and scientific interest in animal magnetism after 1810, the British intelligentsia would remain stubbornly ill disposed to Mesmer's 'long exploded doctrine'. Samuel Taylor Coleridge, one of the few notable figures to be swayed by the Continental renaissance, had initially poured cold water on the resurgent science, comparing its followers to deluded religious fanatics. The same dismissive attitude was apparent in his 1816 contribution to *An Essay on Scrofula*, which filed animal magnetism together with other bogus therapies, such as the royal touch and Perkins metallic tractors. Then, on reading Johann Blumenbach's *Institutions of Physiology*, Coleridge had a change of heart.

Methodically annotating all the books and periodical literature he was able to procure, and taking every opportunity to discuss animal magnetism with continental visitors and correspondents, Coleridge now urged an 'impartial examination' of the 'mass of evidence supplied by every variety of witness, from almost every part of Europe'. In manuscript notes composed in July 1817 (probably intended for the *Encyclopaedia Metropolitana*) he continued to question the 'contemptuous rejection of animal magnetism'. Stopping short of endorsing the claims made by Kluge, Wolfart and other mystically minded magnetists (whom he accused of seeking 'to replace the dreggy materialism of Mesmer with *Naturphilosophie*'), Coleridge declared that he would remain neutral – until he had the opportunity to try it himself, or see others undertake it. Indeed, Coleridge even contemplated studying under Wolfart in Berlin, and considered writing a 'popular work' on 'the facts of animal Magnetism, the divining rod, etc.'. As always, such plans came to nothing.

Coleridge was led to believe 'that under certain conditions one human Being may so act on the body as well as on the mind of another – as to produce a morbid sleep, from which the brain awakes, while the organs of sense remain in stupor'. The external manipulations employed by most magnetisers were, he suspected, secondary to the will they exercised to achieve sympathetic rapport. Finding many affinities between these methods and the poetic ability to captivate through recitation – a talent that came rather too easily to Coleridge – he guessed that the 'medical effects' of animal magnetism were best compared to a double dose of opium and nitrous oxide.

While Coleridge was left to speculate on the nature and effects of animal magnetism, the poet Percy Bysshe Shelley (1792–1822), abroad in Italy, agreed to allow his cousin Captain Medwin to try to quell the nervous attacks that had afflicted him for the best part of a decade. According to Medwin, 'my hand on his forehead instantaneously put a stop to the spasm, and threw him into a magnetic sleep'. The procedure was repeated on several occasions after 1819, with both Mary and her sister Claire acting as operator (during one séance in Pisa an entranced Shelley is reputed to have spoken and improvised verses in Italian) but magnetism had no lasting grip over the nightmares and hallucinations that consumed him.

The remedial effects of animal magnetism were, by contrast, only of incidental interest to Coleridge. Regarding himself as a purely 'historical critic' of animal magnetism, he traced its antecedence back through demonological accounts of possession and classical accounts of incubation and prophecy. This line of inquiry appeared to throw 'new light on the oracles and mysteries of Greek, Roman, and Egyptian paganism', leading him to think of Mesmer as the reviver of animal magnetism and not its discoverer. The weekly philosophical lectures he began to deliver at the Crown and Anchor tavern in December 1818 provided an outlet for some of these vertiginous speculations. Animal magnetism was, he explained to meagre audiences, a prime example of how 'philosophy, through magic, gradually passed into experimental science'.

Coleridge, still in bondage to opium, returned to the subject of animal magnetism with new vigour and direction in 1821. The commonplace effects of what he now called zoo-magnetism were, he argued, agreed upon by both the opponents and supporters. 'The controversy is confined to the *Solution* of the Facts.' Without calling on the vital powers too readily invoked by Mesmer and his followers, Coleridge noted that these facts could be explained in a number of ways. Friction might increase the sensibility of the nervous system, exciting sympathy between remote organs of the body. The magnetist's attentions might induce the kind of 'sentimental love' or 'sexual inquietude' so often observed in forms of hysteria. The patient's imagination might be stimulated, unintentionally generating any number of bodily sensations, from inflammation to hallucination. Coleridge was open to all these explanations; his one reservation was that the anti-mesmerists had always placed too much emphasis on the imagination, using it as 'a mere x y z or substitute for the whole terra incognita of causation'.

Thus far, Coleridge ignored the advice he had issued all would-be examiners of animal magnetism: 'Viz. Try it yourself.' After almost a decade of research, Coleridge remained exactly where his first reading of Kluge and the German magnetists had brought him. Having neither tried nor observed the operation of animal magnetism at first hand, he could claim no particular insight into its machinations. The facts were, he nevertheless insisted, too strong to allow any candid investigator to claim imposture, 'too fugacious and unfixable to support the existence of a correspondent faculty in the human soul' – as he himself was inclined to.

The nearest Coleridge actually came to trying his hand at mesmerism was late one night in April 1824 when, woken by a loud peal of the night bell, he was confronted by a neighbour who was 'mad with fright' and eager for Dr Gillman to attend to his dying child. Volunteering himself as a locum to the absent doctor, Coleridge ran down to his neighbour's house, finding the child expired and the mother 'like a Tyger-cat – abusing every body round her'. Coleridge's response to the mother was, he confessed, strangely phlegmatic. 'I should not have thought it in my nature to have witnessed a mother's distress with so little sympathy. Had she been a quiet woman ... I should have tried – at least, I felt a vehement impulse to try zoo-magnetism, i.e. to try my hand at resurrection. I felt or fancied a power in me to concentrate my will that I have never felt or fancied before.'

In most European cities it was now possible to attend the lectures and stage demonstrations featuring itinerant 'professors' of mesmerism, to consult with ragged-hemmed somnambules, or pay a hefty premium for magnetic treatment from a society physician. It was in Germany, however, that animal magnetism reached occult heights that Mesmer had never dreamed of. Embraced by the idealist philosopher Friedrich Schelling as a lost bridge between man and the 'soul-world', mesmerism found a substantial number of medico-mystical followers. Altogether less sceptical than the French in their relation to the supernatural, many German mesmerists came to find spiritual sustenance at the sickbed of Friedericke Hauffe, a forester's daughter from the small village of Prevorst in Swabia, who was widely famed for her magnetic transformation into a saintly seeress.

Hauffe was from a very early age 'acquainted with spiritual and supernatural matters' through prophetic dreams and visions. During a long fever in February 1822 she heard and saw the ghost of her grandmother. A year later, after the death of her five-month-old child, she began to speak in verse, to prescribe her own treatments and remedies, and experience yet more visions of the dead. The weaker she became, the more sensitive she was to the magnetic influence of objects and visitors. Finding daylight intolerable, she refused food and was sustained by the 'nervous emanations' of the sitters that came to hold her hands. Hauffe was very quickly convinced that only magnetism would save her. After her first magnetiser, 'Dr B', failed to alleviate her most distressing symptoms – besides constant stomach cramps, she felt a stone lodged in her head – family and friends began to make daily passes. With her health failing and rumours of possession rife, she was finally brought to Weinsberg and deposited at the front door of the city's medical officer Justinus Kerner, who had treated and written about similar cases in his *History of Two Somnambules*.

On first attending to Friederike Hauffe, Kerner showed little of his usual compassion towards this 'somnambule and cramp-sufferer'. Threatening her with punishment and the madhouse, he tried 'to bring her out of her belly-enchantment by restoring the life of her brain'. But Kerner soon concluded that there was no hope for Hauffe. Already 'a picture of death, wasted to a skeleton', she was, in his eyes, fast approaching the Other World. Growing weaker and weaker, Hauffe, now a permanent resident in Kerner's home, became a spiritual commuter, travelling in her sleepwaking state to a 'deeper sphere of the life-orbit'. Sensible of 'electrical influences' near and far, she nurtured an uncanny 'feeling or consciousness of human writing'. To her dilated eyes, people's inner selves were rendered visible. Second sight enabled her to diagnose and prescribe treatments for Kerner's own patients. Most ingenious of all was the 'nerve-tuner' that came to her in one dream. Eventually built according to her own design, the machine apparently provided its moribund inventor with magnetic life support in the weeks before her death.

Kerner's magnetic experiments confirmed and extended Hauffe's supernatural talents. When books were placed on the pit of her stomach she was usually able to read. After secretly magnetising her drinking water, Kerner found that she would invariably break into song. Within a few weeks Hauffe had become more than a patient. On one hand she was a medical curiosity, much like the somnambules who accompanied itinerant lecturers and physicians on their travels through the German cities. On the other she had become Kerner's dark muse, his conduit to the afterlife.

Kerner was not alone in his romantic convictions. After Hauffe had succeeded in curing Countess von Maldeghem of a 'nervous illness' by placing herself *en rapport* with the sickly grandee, Hauffe was increasingly discussed in intellectual circles. Soon, her dimly lit sickroom became a place of pious vigil. After hearing Hauffe speak in tongues, or hearing her solemn discourses on the nature of illness, morality and the spirits, few left disappointed. Even David Strauss, a theologian who would attempt to exorcise all elements of the supernatural from scripture, succumbed to her ethereal charms:

> Her face, full of suffering but of noble and tender build, bathed in heavenly transfiguration; her language the purest German, her diction gentle, slow, solemn, musical . . . its contents of excessive feelings, moving through the soul and melting again like light or dark clouds . . . conversations with or about blessed or unhappy spirits, held with such truth that we could not really doubt having before us a Seeress, blessed with the commerce with a higher world.

Having imbibed a heady brew of *Naturphilosophie*, mesmerism and philosophical idealism, Hauffe's romantic sponsors found the higher worlds to which she was a regular commuter neither strange nor foreign. Even the less well educated, whose learning, like that of Hauffe, extended little beyond Lutheran Protestantism, were able to relate to and understand her 'teachings'. When Hauffe spoke of her magnetic rapport with the higher and lower spirits (the former wore long, flowing and colourful garments; the 'grovelling and low-minded spirits' were condemned to a colourless and grey uniform), revealing what she had learned from these ghostly denizens, her wide-eyed sitters lost sight of this delirious anorexic – all they saw was a holy hierophant.

A few months before Hauffe's death in 1829, a wealthy Irish

mineralogist by the name of Richard Chenevix left Paris for London, hoping to convince his eminent peers that the discovery of mesmerism was 'the most extraordinary event in the whole history of human science'. After an extended trial on the female peasantry at Dublin's Hospital of Incurables, and whirlwind experiments at Wakefield Asylum, St George's Hospital, the Middlesex Infirmary and the hospital of the Coldstream Guards, Chenevix invited several prominent members of the Royal Society to witness experiments on two teenage epileptics at his Old Burlington lodgings. While the chemist and physicist Michael Faraday complained that everything he had seen could be easily feigned by a competent actor, one physician insisted its chief phenomena were devoid of mystery, all being explicable by the principles through which 'a child is lulled to rest by fatiguing its senses with some nursery lullaby, or some gentle and oft-repeated motion'.

Chenevix's London séances failed to excite anything like the reception he had hoped for. The only visitor to be genuinely arrested by his 'odd feats' was a young London doctor whom Coleridge had occasionally badgered for medical advice. Curious to see what effect magnetism might have on patients of his own, Dr. John Elliotson invited Chenevix on to the wards at St Thomas's Hospital. While magnetism did indeed appear to provide *some* patients with immediate relief, the most intriguing aspect of Chenevix's demonstration was the way in which he 'disabled' one female patient, depriving her of the use of her limbs. 'Deception was impossible. Mr C looked round at me, and asked in French, if I was satisfied. I really felt ashamed to say no and yet could scarcely credit my senses enough to say yes.'

Elliotson was prevented from further testing the nature and efficacy of magnetism by Chenevix's sudden death in 1830.

Several years would pass before he was ready to give an unequivocal assessment of the facts of animal magnetism, and several more still before he and his contemporaries could begin to answer the vexing question that Shelley had posed on his first encounter with mesmerism: 'Does it lead to materialism or immaterialism?'

Chapter Two

Magnetic Mockeries

Though Fam'd was Mesmer, in his day
No less in ours, is Dupotet
To say nothing of all the wonders done
By that Wizard, Dr Elliotson
                Thomas Moore, 'Animal Magnetism', 1838

The instruction that Jules Dupotet de Sennevoy received in animal magnetism as a young man owed a huge debt to Joseph Deleuze, a naturalist whose public courses and textbooks fostered a revival of amateur interest in France, 'encouraging those who practised magnetism in secret to declare themselves open practitioners'. Inspired by Deleuze's teachings, Baron Dupotet proved a highly effective operator, capable of inducing the 'gentle crisis' in a high proportion of patients and volunteers. While earning a living as a lecturer and demonstrator in his home town of Montpellier – where he had considerable success with his methods of collective treatment, and a stage act whose highlight involved the production of '*chocs électriques*' – the director of the Hôtel Dieu in Paris invited the twenty-four-year-old magnetist to demonstrate his techniques. These experiments, particularly those undertaken upon a teenage hysteric, Catherine Samson, provided a platform for the raft of somnambulant powers that Puységur had unveiled, bringing Dupotet's talents to the attention of the medical world.

Elizabeth Blackwell, the pioneering woman doctor, recalled Dupotet as 'an honest, enthusiastic man, engaged with his whole soul in pursuing what seems to him the most important of all discoveries'. While these qualities would help Dupotet forge a reputation as the 'grand master, the prince of French mesmerists', he was, for all his early experience as a journeyman magnetist, quite ill prepared for the 'saintly mission' he undertook to convert the English sceptics in 1837. Lacking letters of introduction and unable to speak English, he had no clear plan for bringing Mesmer's prodigal science to the attention of the physicians, alienists and surgeons whom he hoped to win over.

In France, Dupotet had always trumpeted his presence in a new city via the local newspapers. Arriving in London in the weeks following Victoria's accession, Dupotet fell back on the same tactic, appealing to any metropolitan 'gentlemen who desired instruction in the doctrine of animal magnetism' to visit him. The days passed. There were no callers. In July 1837, at a meeting of the Royal Society, Dupotet had his first stroke of good fortune: he met Lord Philip Henry Stanhope (1781–1855), 'a real gentleman, who owned many books on magnetism, and had himself induced magnetic phenomena'. Lord Stanhope was only too keen to help. He advised Dupotet against holding private séances in his cramped rooms at Portland Square, and secured him an introduction to Drs Mayo and Wilson at the Middlesex Hospital. The few trials that Dupotet undertook failed to impress. Plan B – a prospectus for a twelve-week course by subscription – fared no better. Dupotet was beginning to give up hope when, following Mayo's and Wilson's suggestion, he made the short journey across Tottenham Court Road to University College Hospital, London's newest and most progressive hospital, where a certain Dr John Elliotson was said to be keen to make his acquaintance.

Elliotson offered Dupotet the opportunity to demonstrate the effects of animal magnetism, with one proviso: though he promised to acknowledge any 'useful results' that were achieved on the wards, he would, he insisted, be equally emphatic should the trials fail to produce definite effects. Dupotet agreed and set to work immediately. Several students, various gentlemen and Dr Elliotson himself were among the first to be submitted to trials of animal magnetism. The results were mixed – some reported sensations of drowsiness, difficulties in breathing or a heaviness about the forehead; others, including Elliotson himself, experienced 'a tingling or some strange sensation in the arms, legs or face, frequently with twitchings'; and a small number appeared immune to Dupotet's 'passes'. The most spectacular of the early trials was on Elliotson's parrot, which fell from its perch on being subjected to Dupotet's deft manipulations.

The first of the hospital patients that Dupotet was permitted to treat suffered from epilepsy and hysteria, nervous afflictions as common among charity patients as they were difficult to treat. All patients proved in some degree susceptible. Yet while the only male patient became increasingly averse and hostile towards Dupotet, Elizabeth Okey, 'a sixteen-year-old housemaid of diminutive confirmation' who had joined her sister

Jane on Ward 3 in April 1837, was 'mortified whenever she was not subjected to it with others'.

Elliotson subscribed to the prevailing medical wisdom in finding epilepsy 'to be produced by various causes on the body', usually from some form of inflammation to the head. Though rarely able to achieve an outright cure, he claimed to have controlled the frequency of violent convulsions in the vast majority of epileptic patients by confining patients to a spare diet, by lessening the circulation through cupping and bleeding, and administering sulphate of copper, ammoniated copper or nitrate of silver. After two months of this regime, Jane Okey's fits had all but disappeared. When her older sister Elizabeth was admitted on to the wards she was ready to be discharged.

According to the hospital casebooks, Elizabeth was suffering from weekly seizures, which were followed by a 'restless, fidgety state' in which her head throbbed and her thinking was wandering and confused. Her mesmeric treatment began at the end of July, shortly after she menstruated for the first time. At this point she had already begun to fall into spontaneous trances – in which she was apt to say 'all sorts of ridiculous, witty and spiteful things' – and it was during these periods of 'ecstatic delirium' that Elliotson and Dupotet attempted to magnetise her. Within a few weeks, Elliotson found that he could quite easily induce sleep, bring Elizabeth back to her senses or produce the delirium artificially – often by simply staring. After being magnetised throughout July and August, Elizabeth's fits quickly subsided, but they were, much to Elliotson's surprise, replaced with regular 'fits of somnambulism' of which she would retain no recollection. 'All at once she would become insensible to the effect of light; pulling her hair produced no effect on her. Her sense of hearing was lost to all ordinary sound. Though her eyes were open yet she was perfectly blind.'

Meanwhile, back home in St Pancras, Jane Okey's local physician, Dr Thornton, was also endeavouring to employ magnetism to rouse her from attacks of insensibility that she had been subject to since the age of thirteen. Significantly, Thornton's treatment had no discernible effect. It was only on rejoining her sister that Jane would be 'suddenly snatched away' by the slow wafting passes to which patients were daily submitted. Within a few weeks, Jane's susceptibility almost matched that of her sister: 'By a single wave of the hand with only one or two fingers extended she is rendered insensible, striasmus is produced and the arms and legs remain exactly in their same position they occupied when the pass was made ... if the hand is waved before her with all fingers extended she drops into a profound sleep – the same movement produce the same effect when extended behind her, but not so readily – she goes to sleep if she waves her own hand before her face.'

Elizabeth's fits of 'ecstatic delirium' were, however, altogether more intriguing to Elliotson. Abandoning her natural diffidence and temerity, Elizabeth would talk constantly – 'very sensibly and wittily too' – and entertain the staff and patients by dancing, singing and displaying 'a great spirit of mimicry'. As one visitor on the wards observed:

Under the influence of magnetism all her good sense appears lost, but her good feelings remain in full force, and she evinces deep sympathy with some of the pupils ... out of the preliminary minute of slumber, she seems to enjoy at once a revival of her previous magnetic-dreaming existence, inquires affectionately for Dr Elliotson or some friends who has [sic] been lost to her mind's eye during her ordinary waking intervals, and then begins to chatter away in her 'gypsy *patois*', free from headache, untroubled by prudential considerations, unconscious of any operations, however painful, which may be performed on her – tells comical stories, mimics the crooked-mouthed family who could not blow out the little farthing rushlight, and whistles very prettily telling comical tales. Her senses meanwhile appear but half awake – her fingers at times lose their perception and her eyes the power of adjusting their axes ... This state of magnetic semi-existence will continue – we know not how long; she has continued in it for twelve days at a time, and when awakened to real life, forgets all that has occurred in the magnetic one! Can this be deception? We have conversed with the poor child in her ordinary state, as she sat by the fire in the ward, suffering from the headache, which persecutes her almost continually when not under the soothing influence of magnetic operation, and we confess we never beheld anybody less likely to prove an impostor.

The transformation in Elizabeth Okey's character came as no surprise to Dupotet. In a letter to the *Lancet*, Dupotet observed that: 'The individual obedient to magnetism, the man who experiences the effects of this power, ceases, for an instant, to be the same person. Everything is modified in his organization. All his perceptions are quickened, they become more comprehensive, and he is rendered capable of executing things which he could not accomplish before, and of which he had not thought in his habitual state.' These gifts were, according to the French magnetist, testament to the 'spiritual ascendancy of man', a mystical preview of 'a future state of being' in which the soul would become free of the body. Dupotet told Elliotson that he had induced many magnetic subjects to see through walls, to hear and see with their bellies, fingers and toes, to report on events occurring at a distance, and relay the life histories of complete strangers. Some magnetic patients could speak languages they had never previously heard, display scientific knowledge they had never acquired, and make anatomical observations of their own frames, and those of others. Elliotson was incredulous. This was all 'too wonderful for belief'.

When Elliotson left to holiday in Switzerland at the end of August, Dupotet was allowed to continue with his magnetic treatment of Elizabeth Okey and three other female patients. For Dupotet this was, at long last, a chance to 'invite all the world to become auditors' of his beloved science. Losing no time, he was swept into a frenzy of self-promotion, attempting to secure use of the lecture theatre, while issuing an open invitation to local charity patients to apply for magnetic treatment at the hospital. Naturally enough, the medical committee frowned on this breach of protocol. On learning of Dupotet's intention to use the hospital as his personal clinic, they immediately suspended the French magnetist. Retaining the faint hope that Elliotson would be able to reinstate him on his return, Dupotet began to treat patients and give private exhibitions at new lodgings in Orchard Street.

Elliotson was in no position to back Dupotet. During his absence, *The Times* had reported 'exhibitions of the revolting imposture, which is known as animal magnetism' in the so-called 'cockney college', complaining that 'parents have sent their sons to learn the science of medicine, not to be taught to practise the arts of the charlatans'. Concurring with the decision of the medical committee, Elliotson took charge of Elizabeth Okey and her fellow magnetic patients. Deploying the techniques he had learned from Dupotet, he was determined to give the mysteries of animal magnetism a fair test. Having established himself as the capital's most able physician and medical innovator, Elliotson would soon be remembered for the 'gipsy-like credulity' that had led him to wander into 'paths of darkness'.

Born in October 1791, John Elliotson was the eldest son of a Southwark 'chymist and druggist' who had hung his golden key at 106 Borough High Street in south-east London. At the age of fourteen, after receiving a robust grounding in the classics from the rector of nearby St Saviours, Elliotson was sent to Edinburgh University. Not yet five foot tall, the dark-eyed apothecary's son was thrown into the *vita scholastica*. Immersing himself in physic, surgery and material medica (and taking tickets for metaphysics and moral philosophy) Elliotson graduated from the medical faculty in 1810 and went directly to Jesus College, Cambridge, where he began to dedicate himself to a translation of Johann Blumenbach's *Institutions of Physiology*, the very book that would prompt Coleridge to reassess his scepticism towards animal magnetism.

Elliotson's translation of Blumenbach appeared in 1817, a crucial juncture in the history of the life sciences. Only a few months prior to its publications William Lawrence, professor of anatomy and surgery at the Royal College of Surgeons, had attacked philosophers and physicians for supposing 'the structures of the body contain an invisible matter or principle, by which it is put in motion'. Lawrence's call for a purely material physiology of the body, for a science free from ethical or theological constraints, was a direct rebuttal of his teacher, John Abernethy, who had tried to breach the schism that was beginning to divide religious orthodoxy and scientific materialism by proposing that living matter was charged with an invisible substance that was 'analogous to electricity'. Lawrence ridiculed Abernethy's compromise, arguing that the scientific inquiry into human origins required no concession to scripture. Rebuffing these 'noxious opinions', Abernethy and his fellow vitalists suggested that Lawrence (and the 'no less terrible' French physiologists that he had championed) were quite literally demoralising mankind.

Abernethy's brand of vitalism found an unlikely ally in Mary Shelley, whose 1819 novel *Frankenstein* had been partially inspired by long conversations between Byron and Shelley on the possibility of discovering 'the principle of life', and of manufacturing a creature that might be endowed with 'vital warmth'. But Elliotson's commentary to the 1820 edition of Blumenbach's *Institutions of Physiology* revealed him to be little disposed to the 'French doctrine to which Mr Lawrence is a proselyte'. Far from providing early signs of the 'flamboyant materialism' with which he would soon be associated, the young Elliotson fully endorsed Blumenbach's commitment to Bible-black truths. 'If I have written a word that can be proved contrary to scripture, or to the Articles of the Church of England,' Elliotson intoned, 'I acknowledge it false and declare it unsaid.'

Elliotson's 'open avowal of materialism', his transformation into a free-thinking secularist, occurred after his appointment as assistant physician at St Thomas's Hospital, in around 1821, when he and his brother Thomas began to take a serious interest in phrenology, the first science of the mind to gain a popular following in nineteenth-century Europe.

Based on the work of Franz Josef Gall (1758–1828), a German-born physician who attempted to achieve a 'perfect knowledge of human nature' by studying the connections between the shape of the head and the intellectual faculties and moral sentiments, phrenology was a science of hands-on observation. Gall's search for a cerebral map of the mind had begun in the hospitals and asylums of Vienna, where he was first struck by the 'external signs' of mental aberration. After dissecting hundreds of animal and human brains with his pupil Johann Spurzheim, Gall was able to confirm the precise location of twenty-seven organs, from firmness and veneration, on the crown of the head, to acquisitiveness and combativeness in the low rear. The size and formation of each organ was directly responsible for the power of each respective faculty. The physiology of the brain underpinned 'the diversity of moral and intellectual character of individuals', explaining the 'differences in the two sexes and in different nations', and indicating 'the source of their customs, their mode of judging of what is virtuous and what is vicious or criminal, of their religion, of their barbarism or their civilization'.

While Gall tried to resist metaphysical speculation, generally restricting himself to evidence drawn from dissection and anatomical research, Spurzheim laid more emphasis on the application of phrenology to other fields – such as the treatment of the insane and the development of secular education – increasing the tally of faculties to thirty-five. Breaking with Gall, Spurzheim, a tireless self-publicist, arrived in Britain in 1814. His first English apostle was George Combe, a thirty-year-old Edinburgh lawyer and journalist whose large head, with its 'beautifully developed frontal and coronal regions', appeared to suggest formidable powers of reflection. Combe's writings and lectures championed the fledgling science as a master key for unlocking the secrets of human nature. Phrenology was, Combe claimed, the necessary backbone for the 'improvement of the human race', the only science capable of establishing rules for 'wise and virtuous conduct'.

Rebuking Christianity's failure to deliver a worldly

philosophy, Combe brought phrenology and the promise of self-knowledge to the masses. While his *System of Phrenology* (1825) established itself as the most comprehensive of the nineteenth-century guides (mushrooming to over a thousand pages in later editions), his most famous work, *The Constitution of Man* (1828), created 'a sensation unparalleled by any philosophical work ever published in the language'.

After a long correspondence with Elliotson, Combe decided that he was 'the only man in London worth a farthing to the science' of phrenology. A daring innovator and experimentalist, Elliotson had an enviable reputation as a teacher and diagnostician. The first of his profession to champion the use of the stethoscope, Elliotson had proved that glanders was communicable to humans, established the environmental causes of hay fever, and experimented with acupuncture and other new therapies in the treatment of rheumatism, chorea and tetanus. Having long abandoned the physician's unofficial uniform of stockings and knee breeches, the short and swarthy bachelor would, Combe thought, prove an able lieutenant.

For all his efforts, Elliotson never managed to win over a respectable following for phrenology. Failure to provide meaningful evidence for an organic science of human nature ensured that phrenology was, by the mid 1830s, becoming a forlorn creed. With the London Phrenological Society amounting to little more than 'a Tea-and-coffee coterie', Elliotson, now a professor of the Principles and Practices of Medicine at the newly founded University of London, began to turn his attention to the field of therapeutics. Recalling the 'extraordinary facts' that Chenevix had once opened his eyes to, Baron Dupotet proved a welcome visitor.

To establish the scientific validity of animal magnetism,

Elliotson realised that he would need to exclude the possibility of collusion or imposture, the eternal refrain of the magnetic sceptic. Aware of the lengths to which hysterical patients such as Elizabeth Okey might go to 'excite attention or simply deceive', Elliotson took the precaution of magnetising Elizabeth and other patients when their backs were turned. On 15 October he took only ten minutes to recover Elizabeth from the delirium that had overtaken her by making secret passes. In the following days Elliotson found that he was able to rouse her from her delirium simply by stretching his hand – if her eyes were closed or bandaged, or if her back was turned, it took only a few minutes. Trials conducted on other patients appeared to confirm what Elliotson had suspected. First, the physical and psychological phenomena that he had induced could not be ascribed to imagination, collusion or deception. Second, the true effects of magnetism were no more than occurred in health or disease:

> To yawn and fall asleep . . . is nothing wonderful. To become more or less insensible to all around . . . and have one or more of the intellectual faculties or external senses highly exalted beyond their usual pitch in the individual, to have not only trains of thought and inclinations, but to speak and sing, and walk, write, &., in the midst of extreme sensibility, and afterwards to forget what has occurred, or even to remember it when the same state returns, and only then, is no more than what we occasionally see in patients.

After two months of experimentation, Elliotson was ready to accept that all these effects 'must be ascribed to a peculiar power . . . to a power acting, I have no doubt, constantly in all living things, vegetable and animal'. Since the precise nature of

Magnetic Mockeries

this agent was not yet known, Elliotson rejected the term 'animal magnetism'. From now on he would adopt the word 'mesmerism', readily acknowledging that Mesmer was (despite his wayward motto: one health, one disease, *one remedy*) 'the great restorer and modern establisher' of the same universal agent that had been previously described by the natural philosophers. 'Mere touch does wonders, not by imagination but mesmerically,' Elliotson wrote. 'A boy at Salamanca is mentioned who cured numberless persons by touching with his hands . . . the efficacy of the royal touch has been known from the time of Vespian [the Roman emperor Vespasian], who performed two miracles ascertained to be mesmeric.'

While Elliotson continued to mesmerise Elizabeth Okey and several other hysterical and epileptic patients, Dupotet turned to the *grand seigneur* who had, after providing his first introduction to Middlesex Hospital, been present at many of his demonstrations. Dupotet's patron, Lord Philip Henry Stanhope (1781–1855), was a freethinking 'ultra-Tory' who opposed the Poor Law Amendment and Catholic Emancipation and championed parliamentary reform. Stanhope's father, the third earl, was an accomplished scholar, electrical experimenter, inventor of the first hand-operated printing press and an outspoken supporter of mesmerism, Rousseau and the French Revolution. Before disinheriting all his children, the irascible 'Citizen Stanhope' insisted that each should acquire a trade. Philip, the first 'brick-maker' to have entered the Lords, succeeded to the title and family seat at Chevening in 1816. By this time he had spent much time in Germany, where he acted as agent for various biblical and missionary societies, and became embroiled in the *demi-monde* of political espionage. And, like his stepsister, the celebrated traveller and 'Queen of the Desert' Lady Hester Stanhope, he had become a student of astrology, crystal gazing, the cabbala and other Masonic pursuits.

Lord Stanhope's presence at Dupotet's magnetic demonstrations at University College Hospital had been sourly noted at meetings of the medical committee. 'There is a Count Stanhope who has come here to see it – a Count Stanhope!' exclaimed the anatomist Richard Quain, warning that if animal magnetism did not bring the hospital into public disrepute, its followers certainly would. One reason many physicians shared Quain's dislike of Stanhope was that, as president of the Medico-Botanical Society, he had used his platform to inveigh against the medical establishment for neglecting Nature's healing dispensary and for conspiring to deprive the sick of the means of self-help. But Stanhope's advocacy of herb baths and vegetable medicine was of less concern than his adoption of Kaspar Hauser, the Nuremberg foundling who was rumoured to have been the son of Grand Duke Karl of Baden, in 1831. This curious episode had cast a lingering shadow over his Lordship's public reputation.

Unable to recollect his former life, Hauser had been in Nuremberg for three years when Stanhope began to ingratiate himself with municipal officials, making a series of extravagant overtures to Hauser. Stanhope was granted full guardianship of the boy, whose true identity was the talk of European salons. Yet having promised to take his newly adopted son to Chevening, Stanhope instead arranged for him to be sent to Ansbach, where he was to become the hapless beneficiary of Johann Georg Meyer's relentless pedagogy. In his *Tracts relating to Caspar Hauser*, Stanhope sought to defend his involvement with the celebrated

Magnetic Mockeries

foundling, arguing that Hauser had in fact been encouraged to act out the role of despoiled heir.

Dupotet knew nothing of Stanhope's chequered past as emissary to the House of Baden, or his occult predilection for employing young children as seers. The only question that preoccupied the French magnetist was how, with his Lordship's assistance, he might discover a new audience for his scientific endeavours. Stanhope secured Dupotet a number of useful contacts, advising him to continue holding private demonstrations at his home in Orchard Street. Soon enough, a *Times* journalist conceded that there was 'something sufficiently curious in the torpor of his pupil patients' and Dupotet found himself in constant demand. Aside from the visitors that packed the daily séances ('2s.6d, every afternoon except Sunday'), Dupotet was sought out by physicians, surgeons, politicians and literary gentlemen. Over the next year or so, Dupotet séances would introduce the wonders of animal magnetism to around two thousand or so 'highly distinguished visitors'. His moment had arrived.

Dupotet's afternoon séances typically began with a demonstration on one of a handful of patients whom Dupotet had continued to treat since leaving University College Hospital. The best-known of these, Lucy Clarke, had been referred to him by George Denton, a Tottenham surgeon who had successfully magnetised her in July 1837. Lucy had, while magnetised, already prescribed her own treatment and proclaimed the date on which she would finally be cured, and Dupotet added another dimension to her *délire prophétique*, prompting Lucy to discourse on French and English politics with great ease, elocution and insight. The other patients and medical students that Dupotet recruited were, to begin with, rather less attuned to his magnetic passes. One visitor, who attended a busy October séance, observed that in three cases 'nothing occurred'.

Relocating to a larger and more comfortable suite of rooms in Wigmore Street, near Cavendish Square, the Frenchman sensed that he was fast becoming a '*véritable célébrité*'. Playing host to well-heeled visitors such as Lord Grey, 'Radical Jack' Lambton and Richard Monckton Milnes, Dupotet did not, however, succeed in making many public converts. Dupotet's illustrious 'friends' often left Wigmore Street under the impression that, though able to induce definite physiological effects on his own patients, the Frenchman was rather less adept at demonstrating clairvoyance and other 'higher phenomena'. Thomas Trollope (Anthony's older brother), a guest at an evening séance on 17 August 1838, was not alone in finding that 'the general impression left by the Baron was not a favourable one':

The phenomena I have witnessed are certainly most extraordinary and unaccountable. That one young woman was thrown into a convulsive state, is entirely undeniable. Her muscles, which we felt, were hard, rigid, and in a state of tension, and so remained for a longer time than it is possible for any person to voluntarily keep them so ... A little girl became to all appearance somnambulous. This, however, might more possibly be imposture. When this little girl and the young woman were placed near each other, the effect on both was increased, and the girl instead of being merely somnambulous became convulsive. The little girl, *as far as the CLOSE observation of the onlookers could detect*, saw the colours of objects, &c., with her eyes closed. This, however, is evidence of a nature easily deceptive. When waked from her magnetic trance, she forgot, or professed to have forgotten, all that she had said or done when in it. But when again put into a state of trance or somnambulism, she again remembered and spoke of what had occurred . . . After these patients were disposed of, two young men of the spectators offered themselves as subjects to the magnetiser. He said they were not good subjects for it . . . He then tried me, and after a short space of time, I think not more than half a minute, he said that I was *very* sensitive to magnetic influence, and that in two or three sittings he could produce '*des effets extraordinaire*' on me; but that he was tired, and that '*rien ne coule plus*' from his fingers.

Unlike Thomas Trollope, who was still to be convinced of the reality of artificial somnambulism, London's occult fraternity found that the *séance magnétique* afforded clear proof of 'the immateriality of the mind'. A number of 'ladies and gentlemen' who 'claimed alchemy, medieval Rosicrucianism and modern Freemasonry were offshoots of the original Cabala' were certain that Dupotet had mastered the missing link between spirit and matter, the subtle fluid which had been pursued through all branches of ancient magic. Lieutenant Richard Morrison, a Christian astrologer and prominent member of the shadowy 'Orphic Circle', was one of the first occult experimenters to record the insights achieved through this higher state of 'lucid vision'. On putting questions to an entranced seventeen-year-old girl whom he had previously employed as a crystal scryer, Morrison discovered the planetary whereabouts of various famous figures, including Voltaire and Henry VIII. He received an extemporised introduction to the cosmography of the Other World, learned that the tides were actually produced by electricity and that some thirty years would pass before the next millennium.

The secrecy that surrounded these occult rites – members of the Orphic Circle were sworn never to reveal the identity of the society they belonged to, or their fellow initiates – helped fan rumours that mesmerism was being used by 'persons of noble rank' to exploit and abuse young somnambules during mystic ceremonies. Emma Hardinge, a one-time child somnambule who went on to become a leading spiritualist propagandist, made vague references to abuses she endured at the hands of London's 'vicious aristocracy'. Once he had returned to France, Dupotet himself acknowledged that many of his illustrious visitors appeared to take perverse pleasure in testing the insensibility of his patients.

Whatever horrors Hardinge and other somnambules were subjected to in the name of medicine, magic or entertainment, one thing is clear: few people of social standing attended a public or private demonstration of magnetism in the hope of being mesmerised, let alone healed. Invalids, domestics and orphans, almost always female, were destined to remain the swooning servants of the magnetic séance.

In the spring of 1838 the London dailies began to turn their attention away from Dupotet's séances and back to University College Hospital, where Elliotson and his clinical clerk Mr Wood were busy conducting their own trials of magnetism. Over the previous six months, Elliotson had personally magnetised around twenty patients. Still convinced that a material agent was responsible for all the physical and psychological modifications he had witnessed, he was puzzled by the variability of effect. Temperament and intelligence seemed unreliable indicators to a patient's susceptibility. Having 'tried for weeks without sensible effects upon some persons who were very feeble and thin and trembled from head to foot at any sudden noise', he thought that poor health was also, generally speaking, no guarantee of a patient's susceptibility to magnetism. The only class of patients that seemed to be consistently attuned to magnetic influence were those, like Elizabeth Okey, who were naturally subject to 'sleep-walking and other forms of hysteria'.

Elliotson was now able to recover the teenage housemaid from her regular relapses into delirium by simply extending his hand towards her face, or looking at her intently for several minutes. The procedure was effortless, requiring none of the effort of will that de Mainauduc and other magnetists held to be the true secret of animal magnetism. Satisfied that Mesmer's 'imponderable fluid' remained the only viable explanation for the trance phenomena, he insisted that his trials were being conducted 'in the same way as chemists investigated the properties of organic matter'.

In reality, Elliotson's inferences were too often deductive. His material hypothesis led him to fasten on some facts and ignore others. Numerous failures to induce trance in Elizabeth were attributed to her being distracted by conversation on the ward. Instances of 'spontaneous mesmerisation' were put down to the simple fact of physical proximity. Clearly, Elliotson was becoming something other than the humble empiricist he imagined.

Encouraged by the *Lancet*'s decision to refrain from carrying any 'speculative or philosophical' criticism of animal magnetism, Elliotson continued to invite friends and acquaintances to observe the transformations that Elizabeth and other patients were subject to under animal magnetism. On 4 January 1838 Charles Dickens and the illustrator George Cruikshank made their second visit to University College Hospital, joining the swelling ranks of visitors who were now regularly huddled at the bedside of the Okey girl. Dickens was fascinated to see Elliotson produce delirium in a few passes. When Dr Elliotson raised a digit and asked how many she saw, she said two. When he showed two fingers, she said there were 'such a many'. Further questions provoked other strange turns of expression, such as 'I such a Much', 'It is such a big', and 'When it was just now'. The most perplexing aspect of her trance state, Dickens thought, was her inability to recall her pre-hospital life. Asked where her home was, she explained that she had 'always lived here' with her family: her six mothers (the house surgeons), her father (Dr Elliotson) and her brothers (the students).

Elliotson's use of animal magnetism to produce artificial delirium in Elizabeth Okey coincided with another equally significant shift in protocol. From around the end of January certain patients were permitted to magnetise each other. The first patient Elizabeth operated on was Hannah Hunter, a 'delicate looking girl of twelve' who was, on admittance in early February, diagnosed as suffering from 'Hysteria Multiform'. This provided welcome relief to the clinical clerks who had already complained of the long hours that they were required to spend 'pawing' at patients, but the hospital board was, once again, dismayed by reports of the mayhem and quackery that had overtaken the Women's Ward. Worse still, the 'magnetic madness' was attracting increasing press notice. While *The Athenaeum* and the *Quarterly Review* greeted Elliotson's trials of animal magnetism as the return of a debased and idiotic superstition, and *The Times* continued to rail against north London's 'seminary for mountebankery', *Blackwood's* and the *Comic Annual* were beginning to lampoon the 'universal physic' in a series of long-running drolleries.

The *Lancet*'s unqualified support for Elliotson's trials did little to mollify the chorus of doubters. It was only when the professor announced that a committee composed of members of the Royal Society would be investigating magnetic phenomena that publications once vehemently opposed to animal magnetism were coaxed into declaring themselves open-minded. When a reporter from the *Morning Post* spotted Michael Faraday on the wards of University College Hospital, 'exerting his acute and sagacious powers' in an attempt to detect imposture on the part of magnetised patients, it was clear that the subject might, after all, deserve serious scrutiny.

Faraday called on Elliotson on at least two occasions in February 1838. After studiously watching Elizabeth Okey magnetise Hannah Hunter, during his first visit, he attempted to 'elicit some blush of mental confusion by his *naïve* and startling remarks'. When vigorous rubbing of thumbs on her brow failed to wake Hannah, Faraday, suspecting that the child was dissembling, loudly suggested that she might be bled and cauterised. His scare tactic provoked no response from the impassive child. Faraday was subsequently shown how to restore patients to ordinary consciousness by drawing his thumbs two or three times across their eyebrows. Unable to detect any obvious signs of imposture he returned again, only to declare that 'the matter was beyond his philosophy to unravel'.

Elliotson was disappointed that Faraday was unable to give any more of his time to his investigations. Still, other distinguished experts were ready to lend a hand. Herbert Mayo, having overcome his initial disbelief, was already undertaking physiological observations at Middlesex Hospital. The well-known writer and lecturer Dionysus Lardner was keen to test the magnetic powers of the Okeys. And Charles Wheatstone, the stuttering co-inventor of the electric telegraph, was ready to help in devising practical experiments.

Far from assuaging complaints from within the medical faculty, the apparatus that Elliotson and his fellow experimenters deployed in March and April provoked further consternation. Mirrors were placed at angles to test the reflectivity of magnetic effluvia. Pasteboards and screens of various materials were set up to examine the limits of magnetic induction. Leyden jars and galvanic batteries were brought in to test the patients' apparent insensibility to electric charges. For Richard Quain, Robert Liston and William Sharpey – faculty members who had neglected to attend any of the trials that Elliotson had overseen – this was science of the lowest order. 'From what I have heard of these exhibitions,' Sharpey later wrote to Elliotson, 'I am inclined to think, however different be your intentions, they are calculated to minister to the popular love of the marvellous rather than afford . . . opportunity of testing the alleged efficacy of Mesmerism.' Sharpey testily suggested that Elliotson might want to conduct further trials in his own home.

Adamant that no *liberal* institution would require its professors to undertake experimental treatments 'behind closed doors', Elliotson insisted that the efficacy of animal magnetism was already proven. The first patient to be actually cured on the wards, Charlotte Cook – an eighteen-year-old 'servant of all work, ruddy and of a full habit' – had been admitted in the first week of April suffering from 'brain fever'. About three weeks previously, Charlotte had fallen into a listless state, appearing to be unconscious of what was happening around her. After bleeding and purging failed to relieve her symptoms, Elliotson 'determined at once to trust the case entirely to mesmerism', instructing his clinical clerk Mr Wood to mesmerise daily using vertical passes only. On the first occasion Charlotte ('too lost and stupid to know what mesmerism meant, what its effects were, or to feign them') fell asleep for a few minutes, with no other effects being produced. After three further 'mesmerisations', she began to abandon some of her delusions and to recover her voice. Over the next few weeks she showed regular improvement. Six weeks later she was well enough to be discharged.

Elliotson's *Human Physiology* (1840), one of the most popular medical textbooks of the day, claimed that many other patients had greatly benefited from relatively short courses of mesmerism:

> A severe case of periodic insanity, which had resisted all other treatment, was remarkably relieved by the operation of magnetism, and in a fortnight the patient was well. A child who had laboured under paraplegia and incontinence of urine during nine months, was perfectly cured by this agent. In a case of epilepsy in which a fit had occurred every day for nine months, the performance of magnetism at once arrested the fits, not one occurring during a month after its first application, and the patient went home well. In a case of delirium in a young woman who was subject to hysteria, which lasted during five days . . . the patient, on the second time that she was magnetised, became tranquil, and afterwards went home well. In a case of St Vitus's dance, in which no other remedy was tried, magnetism effected a cure.

Elliotson's findings were echoed by other magnetic experimenters. A former pupil, Thomas Chandler, claimed immediate success upon his wife and a patient suffering from violent attacks of rheumatism. Dr Macreight, a physician from nearby Middlesex Hospital, reported a more novel application for mesmerism at a meeting of the Royal Medico-Botanical Society. Macreight had mesmerised a hysterical patient at his home in Queen Anne Street. On being asked what might afford her some relief, the patient replied, 'There is only one medicine that will be of service to me. It is contained in a bottle on the third shelf of your private chest – the second bottle from the right.' The bottle in question contained ammoniated tincture of iron, which was used to treat the patient successfully. Lord Stanhope, who was chairing the meeting, gave a knowing nod. Having travelled extensively in Germany, the prophetic powers of entranced patients came as no surprise to him. Magnetism's ability to empower patients to prescribe for themselves and others had, he believed, been well established, particularly by Karl Wolfart at Berlin's Mesmeric Hospital.

Most experimenters remained rather more doubtful. During trials of magnetism carried out at the workhouse of St Martin-in-the Fields, the parish surgeon, Richard Bainbridge, induced a young epileptic girl to replicate the phenomena that he had seen Elizabeth Okey perform at University College Hospital. After lulling her into a mesmeric coma, and allowing her hair to be pulled, and arms to be pricked, without any signs of sensation, Bainbridge directed her 'into the somnambulic or delirious state, when she began to converse freely with persons around her, but more especially her magnetiser. She would sing if required, even dance in obedience to his command, and pretended to see him although her eyes were constantly blindfolded.' Finding that the girl would succumb to his influence even when passes were not made, Bainbridge's experiments convinced him that 'imagination only, and not the mesmeric fluid, was the great agent by which these phenomena could be produced in persons of strong faith and weak bodies'.

To demonstrate that the action of animal magnetism was due to a material agent whose properties might be inferred from its repeated action, Elliotson modified his procedure for induction, altering the distance between operator and subject, changing the direction and sweep of the passes, and 'conducting' simultaneously with the ever-present Mr Wood. Early in May 1838, after some weeks of experimentation with Elizabeth Okey, Elliotson reported a breakthrough. The 'first law of magnetic induction' was, he rashly claimed, '... that the influence was greater in an experiment in proportion to the surface employed'. A pass made with one finger on Elizabeth produced light stupefaction. Two fingers led to protracted torpor. Three produced stupor, four immediate sleep. Buoyed by this new insight into the 'fixed principles' of animal magnetism, Elliotson responded to faculty complaints with arch derision. Look at the history of scientific progress, study the reception that the most momentous breakthroughs had received. Had William Harvey been applauded for discovering the circulation of the blood? What did the savants say when Cuvier uncovered the principles of modern chemistry? And Luigi Galvani, had he not been pilloried as the frog's dancing master?

The surgeon Robert Liston was fast losing patience with Elliotson's magnetic fulminations – and the sheepish expediency of the hospital board. Having already threatened never to set foot in University College Hospital while Elliotson was conducting his trials, Liston spearheaded the faculty backlash, pressuring Sharpey finally to impose some form of restriction on Elliotson's 'Gallic mummeries'. But Elliotson had been instrumental in the foundation of the medical school and hospital. He had helped lay out its liberal vision 'of offering education and the honours of industry and talent to the youth of all creeds', securing a much-lauded reputation among 'the Godless students of Gower Street'. Aside from Thomas Wakley's *Lancet*, Elliotson had the support of Lord Brougham,

President of the Council of the University of London, and the ear of influential donors and patrons, many of whom had observed his trials on the wards. He was, in short, too powerful to be reined in by the usual faculty ultimatums.

On 10 May Lord Brougham joined Sir Charles Paget, the Earl of Burlington, the Marquess of Anglesea, Dr Faraday, Dickens, Cruikshank, several MPs, and around two hundred medical gentlemen on the bench seats of the hospital theatre. With Elizabeth Okey seated at his side, Elliotson informed the audience that he was fully aware of the risks to which he had exposed himself in prosecuting his mesmeric inquiries, but having found mesmerism to be a powerful remedial agent, he would not be deterred from promulgating 'new facts' to the medical profession or 'men of education who might take an interest'. England's first public exhibition of mesmerism began with Elliotson making a few swift passes on Okey. Immediately, her dull countenance was transformed into 'one of mingled archness and simplicity'. Rising to her feet, looking towards the sea of spectacles and opera glasses, Okey approached the Marquess of Anglesea and addressed him with easy familiarity: 'Oh! How do ye? White trousers. Dear! You do look so tidy. What nice things. You *are* a nice man.' As she turned to take Sir Charles Paget's hand, Elliotson, standing directly behind Okey, made a downwards pass and sent her tottering backwards into the arms of Mr Wood.

After demonstrating 'the effect of mass or surface in producing sleep', Elliotson next instructed Okey to mesmerise herself by bringing her hand towards her face. After six passes her head dropped, and she whistled 'The Green Hills of Tyrol' and sang two psalms. Finishing with a verse from 'Jim Crow', 'her ripe faculty of music had been amply exhibited'. To the disappointment of the audience the entranced housemaid was not permitted 'to wheel about, and turn about' as she wished. Confining her to a chair, Elliotson rubbed his thumbs transversely across her brow, attempting to restore her to natural wakefulness. The procedure was repeated several times to no effect. Eventually, Mr Wood bent down and asked Okey when she would wake. 'In five minutes,' she answered. 'By rubbing the back of my neck.' George Mills, the *Lancet*'s subeditor, watched closely as Wood returned her to her natural state:

> No two manners could exhibit a greater contrast than did her deportment now and that which she presented during the 'delirium'. Her manner was downcast and reserved, and indicative of fatigue. On asking her where she had been, and how she felt, she only replied that her head ached . . . On proceeding to leave, as the throng of persons opened to let her pass by, many gentlemen, won by her apparent amiability, shook hands with her, which compliment she engagingly acknowledged by a slight curtsey, seemingly greatly wearied, depressed and much abashed at her situation.

Back with her needlepoint on Ward 3, Elizabeth Okey retained no memory of the scientific pantomime in which she had starred. Two days later, when the *Lancet* sent an artist to sketch Elizabeth in her magnetic delirium, she had, however, begun to extend her repertoire. Beyond the 'peculiar manners' that overcame her when mesmerised – her garbled and vulgar speech, her tendency to sing and dance, her gushing affection for Dr Elliotson and Mr Wood – Elizabeth now began to consult a spirit guide, the 'Negro', to whom she silently mouthed all questions during her trance state.

Towards the beginning of the 10 May demonstration Elliotson had announced that 'a body of members of the Physiological Committee of the Royal Society had considered the subject [of magnetism] to be one of so much importance that they had attended to witness its effects, and test its truth'. Among these were Professor Grant, Dr Arnott, Dr Roget, Mr Mayo, Mr Kiernan, Dr Bostock, Professor Wheatstone and Professor Sylvester. 'If the science of mesmerism was a folly, these gentlemen would not fail to prove its claims to that title.' Facing increasing criticism from rival journals, and rising complaints from the *Lancet*'s own readership, its editor, Thomas Wakley, was greatly relieved to learn of the committee's activities. He urged Elliotson to deliver the committee's finding as soon as possible, and instructed George Mills to give prominent coverage to future lectures and exhibitions.

A second public exhibition of mesmerism was given in the hospital theatre on 2 June. On this occasion the Bishop of Norwich had to stand throughout, while the poet Thomas Moore found a shelf from which he later emerged covered in whitening from the walls. After introducing some patients who had been greatly relieved by mesmerism, Elizabeth and Jane Okey were brought into the theatre. Elliotson explained that Elizabeth was now subject to three different mesmeric states. The first was 'a state of harmless delirium, in which vivacity, kindness and familiarity of manner are very conspicuous'. The second was a state of mental absence in which her eyes squinted under drooping lids. If subjected to further manipulations, Elizabeth would finally pass into the third stage – deep sleep.

On being mesmerised by Mr Wood, Elizabeth began to count the 'white people' in the audience. 'Why, where the devil did you all come from,' she enquired, provoking roars of laughter in the audience. A few minutes later, she began to skip and sing:

> I went into a tailor's shop
> To buy a suit of clothes
> But where the money came from
> God Almighty Knows

To subdue this 'excessive merriment', Elliotson went on to stupefy Elizabeth on several occasions throughout the course of the exhibition. After demonstrating all the 'peculiar manners' for which she was now well known, he undertook a new experiment. Some cast-iron weights were tied together with a rope, which Elizabeth, in her natural state, was requested to lift. Initially objecting to the 'dirty things', she attempted and failed to lift the eighty-four- and fifty-six-pound weights. Then, after a few more passes, her hand and arm were bound to a splint and heavily bandaged. She was now asked how much she would be able to lift. Taking a moment to consult with her 'Negro', she replied eighty and proceeded to lift the heavier weight three or four inches above the ground, leaving the most sceptical members of the audience genuinely perplexed.

At the end of the lecture a select group of gentlemen were taken to an antechamber, where Elliotson and Herbert Mayo began an experiment designed to demonstrate Elizabeth's newly heightened powers of perception. Placed behind a large screen of brown paper, Elizabeth began to imitate the actions of her unseen experimenters. That Elizabeth had her eyes partially open throughout suggested that this was possibly not evidence of thought reading or unconscious mental rapport. As George Mills later noted in his *Lancet* report, 'she *could* have seen what was before her, by the usual exercise of vision, and therefore the proceeding should not be received as a magnetic phenomenon of the least value.' Mills returned the following day to witness another series of experiments on Jane Okey, whose reflection was mesmerised in a looking-glass. Mills accurately reported what he saw, but it was clear that this curious science left him more puzzled than ever.

As Elliotson commenced further trials to investigate the 'excessive magnetic sensibility of the mucous surfaces of the eyes, lips, and the mouth', the Okeys continued to take advantage of the new licences they were granted. Regularly mesmerising other patients – and soliciting confessions of imposture from those who vied for Elliotson's attention – the sisters would, with the assistance of Elizabeth's 'Negro', foretell the onset of their seizures and prescribe the means by which they would be relieved. A new patient called Anne Ross also discovered her own spirit guide, 'a being with the face of an angel, with wings like a dove and clothed in a long white robe'. Anne Ross's angel informed her that she would be well again in three months as long as two decayed teeth were removed within twenty-four hours. Willing to believe that 'a sleepwalker may prophesy morbid changes in himself with accuracy', Elliotson allowed the operation to proceed before a large group of visitors. Both teeth were removed without any outward sign of pain or discomfort.

The *Lancet* soon reported two important new discoveries – Elizabeth Okey's ability to employ '*her hand* as an *organ of vision*', and the transmission of 'soporific fluid' via gold and silver – but Wakley was beginning to wonder whether the Royal Society had really sanctioned an *official* committee to report on Elliotson's experiments. At the end of July, when the medical committee barred Elliotson from undertaking further public exhibitions, Wakley realised that he had been misled. Within a matter of weeks, the *Lancet* announced that 'the effects which were said to arise from what had been denominated "animal magnetism", constituted 'one of the completest delusions that the human mind ever entertained'.

Thomas Wakley was a fire-bellied radical who tackled 'the satanic system of quackery' with the same vigour that he had once defended the Tolpuddle Martyrs. Trained as a surgeon, the Devonshire yeoman's son gave up private practice for a career as a coroner and medical journalist. The *Lancet*, the sixpenny medical weekly that he established in 1823, took aim at the untrained empirics who hawked their nostrums across the country, and at the pomp and excesses of elite physicians, providing its fast-growing readership with eyewitness accounts of surgical operations and verbatim reports of hospital lectures.

Though Wakley's journalistic forte was a brand of scurrilous, hard-boiled polemic that often landed him with sizeable claims for libel, the *Lancet* was also a great enhancer of reputations, providing younger, reform-minded physicians with a valuable profile. By publishing Elliotson's weekly lectures at St Thomas's and applauding his appointment to the chair of medicine at the newly-formed University of London, the *Lancet* was instrumental in the young professor being recognised as the 'best clinical teacher of his generation'. For Elliotson the financial rewards of this publicity were considerable. Within three years his income from his private practice had increased eight-fold, affording him tenancy of one of London's most prestigious addresses, 37 Conduit Street, the one-time home of George Canning, the brief-serving Tory Prime Minister.

Ten years on, Wakley was beginning to nurse grave concerns about Elliotson's magnetic experiments. With disgruntled complaints from nineteen out of every twenty *Lancet* readers who pestered him with letters on the subject, it was time to act.

On 16 August 1838 Wakley invited Elliotson to bring the

Okey girls to his Bedford Square home, so that the professor could demonstrate the 'startling mesmeric effects' that nickel was apparently able to produce. Wakley chose three of his closest physician friends to act as invigilators during the drawing-room trial. Elliotson brought Baron Dupotet, Dr Richardson and John Fernandez Clarke, a one-time pupil who was now a *Lancet* journalist.

There was no time for pleasantries. The first experiment commenced with Elizabeth Okey being mesmerised and placed behind a thick pasteboard. Once Wakley's party was satisfied that the board was completely opaque, Elliotson charged a small piece of nickel with 'mesmeric fluid' by rubbing it in his hands. Meanwhile Wakley ensured that a piece of lead (which Elliotson believed to be an ineffective conductor) was similarly manipulated, so that Okey would be unable to distinguish the temperature of the two metals that were to be tested. Both metals failed initially to have any effect. When the nickel was passed before her again, Clarke observed that Elizabeth's face 'became violently flushed, the eyes convulsed into a full squint, she fell back into the chair, her breathing was hurried, her limbs were rigid, and her back and abdomen assumed the position which is assumed in an attack of opisthotonos'. Okey remained fixed in this position for almost fifteen minutes, oblivious to the dispute that had broken out between Elliotson and Wakley, who was not at all convinced that the attack was precipitated by nickel.

A second comparison of the metals was agreed upon. Without Elliotson's knowledge, Wakley now passed the nickel to Clarke, who slipped it into his waistcoat pocket before stationing himself at the far side of the drawing room. As Wakley rubbed a fisted hand against Elizabeth Okey's hands, one of his invited friends whispered loudly, 'Take care, do not apply the nickel too strongly' and Okey, who had only just recovered from her first paroxysm, was thrown into yet more violent convulsions. These effects, Elliotson remarked, were only produced by nickel.

Wakley shook his head, called Mr Clarke forward and asked him to show Elliotson the piece of nickel. Elliotson was genuinely puzzled. Glancing back at Elizabeth, he informed Wakley that he was presently unable to account for this anomaly. Convinced that he had uncovered deliberate fraud, Wakley suggested that Elliotson might think about asking Elizabeth Okey a few blunt questions.

Elliotson later recalled that he was 'obliged to leave the poor little girl in an intense coma . . . little imagining that any further experiments would be attempted in my absence, by a person ignorant of the subject and altogether incapable of making experiments'. Within a few weeks he had, however, contrived an explanation for the awry happenings at Bedford Square. Wakley and Company had been negligent in their trials: the surface of the lead had probably been 'nickelised' or 'aurified' by contact between the two metals. Through 'want of information and philosophic power', these observers had failed to grasp that frequently repeated experiments could 'derange the susceptibility to mesmerism'.

Wakley had in fact conducted twenty-nine further experiments, mainly testing the effects of mesmerised water and gold. Satisfied that the science of mesmerism was nothing more than trickery and imposture, the *Lancet*'s editor seemed certain that Elizabeth Okey was a charlatan, and that her sister, Jane, was merely 'a tame imitation'. 'Careful investigation and a consideration of the experiments', Wakley announced in September 1838, 'have convinced us that the phenomena are not real.' Preferring not to draw attention to Elliotson's personal failings, Wakley directed the brunt of his rancour towards Baron Dupotet (for seducing the men of science) and Herbert Mayo (for judging mesmerism a physical agent that caused the mind to be 'in part dislocated and displaced from her corporeal tenement'). Although the Okeys had probably been 'unwittingly *tempted* into a course of deception', they had clouded Elliotson's judgement, beguiling him with performances that any stage actress would have been hard pressed to match:

> JANE O'KEY [*sic*] appears, on a cursory examination to be but a tame copy of her sister. ELIZABETH is a genius in her line. This is betrayed by her dark, piercing eye, her wonderful performances, and power which she exercises over all who come into contact with her. One of her performances, it is said, was assayed at the chapel of the mad and Rev. Edward Irving: O'KEY arose during the service, prophesied and spoke the 'unknown tongues' so clamorously that the deacons were induced to lead her out of the midst of their congregation. Her improvisations at the mesmeric sittings, the sarcasms, the snatches of song, which she spouted so prodigiously were, not infrequently, worthy of the licensed folly of the old comedy . . . The talent which she possesses in greatest perfection is imitation; the talent possessed by few of representing feelings and states of mind so vividly, so as to impress the spectators with their reality . . . The coaxing, flattering strain in which she addressed Dr Elliotson, and her other favourites, displayed tact, consciousness of power in dealing with other minds, and a full knowledge of the advantages of her position.

The 'fantastic tricks' that the Okeys performed had, Wakley concluded, been carefully investigated and shown to be 'infinitely improbable'. Confident that mesmerism was now thoroughly discredited, the *Lancet* predicted a dismal future: it would 'carry on a precarious existence wherever there are clever girls, philosophical bohemians, weak women, and weaker men, but it can no longer affront the common sense of the medical profession'.

Wakley's profile of the Okeys contained nothing new on either sister. In fact, rumours that Elizabeth had prophesied and spoken in 'unknown tongues' at the orations of Edward Irving, a fact previously reported in the *Christian Observer*, were almost certainly unfounded. Irving's Regent Square congregations received the gifts of tongues and prophecy in late 1831, shortly after a church deputation was sent to observe an outbreak of tongue speaking in Rhu in the West Highlands. Initially sceptical, Irving was soon convinced that the Holy Ghost had descended upon his services and prayer meetings, and that the spoken exhortations — a mix of Latinate gibberish and pious augury — were true testimony to the Second Coming. By December 1832, Irving's evangelical cult was beginning to gather an army of troubled and wayward souls. The 'Irvingites' were soon ousted from Regent Square, but Irving continued to preach to large crowds at Newman Street and Islington Green, and it was here that Elizabeth Okey was said to have developed her dramatic gifts.

Wakley and the anti-mesmerists had good reasons for conflating Elliotson's experiments with London's most recent episode of 'impious fanaticism'. Like Irving, Elliotson had, they believed, conceded authority to the semi-literate ravings of charity patients. Abandoning his Hippocratic duties, Elliotson had become lost within a maze of speculative enquiry. Seduced by their respective infatuations, refusing to follow the protocols of their professions, preacher and physician were kindred souls:

men of excess, victims of wayward *enthusiasm*. Rejecting the claim that Elizabeth Okey owed a debt of apprenticeship to the Irvingites, Elliotson insisted that her physiological constitution rendered her inordinately sensitive to the 'mesmeric fluid'.

Wakley's sceptical assessment of the Okeys was nevertheless echoed by a number of important physicians, including Thomas Laycock, another of Elliotson's former pupils. An expert on hysteria and hypochondriasis, Laycock believed that everything he had seen of mesmerism illustrated the power of the will over the nervous system: 'After an individual has been mesmerized repeatedly, certain movements (passes) are no longer necessary to the excitement of sensorial volition, it has become a habit, and it is produced by an insignificant circumstance . . . It is thus that disinterested observers have been imposed upon; and thus hysterical girls can bring on convulsions, and any ideas, sensations, and mental emotions, with more or less facility.'

John Fernandez Clarke, the journalist who had played a minor role in Wakley's exposure of the Okeys, was not quite so sure. Reflecting on the trials he had participated in, Clarke could not help but think that 'the experiments of Mr Wakley, whilst they proved some things, failed to prove others; and, in fact, left the subject under discussion still more mysterious'. Like the previous French commissions, Wakley had merely shown that notion of a mesmeric fluid or charge was a misnomer. He had not, Clarke pointed out, ventured to explain the true nature of the physical or mental manifestations, or made enquiries into the more general remedial properties of magnetism.

The physical and psychological phenomena that Elizabeth Okey exhibited during her trance were certainly not unique to mesmerism. All the signs and symptoms of epilepsy, hysteria and somnambulism could, as Elliotson had observed towards the beginning of Dupotet's trials, be artificially stimulated by mesmeric fluid. Elliotson's *Human Physiology* cited numerous examples of nervous disease characterised by the same kind of 'double consciousnesses' he had induced in the Okeys. There was the cataleptic patient of Dr Petetit in Lyon, who was found able to taste, read and smell through her stomach. An uneducated young woman from the Hospital della Vita da Bologna, who spoke Latin, diagnosed the ailments of people not known to her, and described the geography of cities that she had never visited, while in a coma. And a case of 'double personality', reported to the Royal Society of Edinburgh in 1822, was uncannily redolent of Elizabeth Okey. The sixteen-year-old servant also suffered from regular bouts of somnambulism 'attended with some advantageous manifestations of the intellectual powers'. During these sleeping fits the young girl sang musical airs (sacred and profane), extemporised prayers, danced, arranged and tidied, recalled the day's events and mispronounced words. Throughout the drowsy seizures that overcame her on an evening, the girl's eyes remained half shut and squinting, and she retained no memory of her actions. As with Elizabeth Okey, the onset of this double consciousness coincided exactly with the onset of puberty.

While most observers agreed that even the most accomplished actress would be unable to feign Elizabeth Okey's insensibility and delirium, some did suspect that *an element* of collusion or acting might have played a part in her magnetic transformation. After visiting the Okeys in March 1838, the great Shakespearean actor William Macready, a close friend of Elliotson and Dickens, concluded that the sisters were 'partially under a morbid influence and partly lend themselves to a delusion'. Macready was close to understanding the psychological drama that had taken place. Neither outright impostors nor mesmeric automatons, the afflicted housemaids had stumbled into a scientific drama that had allowed them to postpone returning to the relentless drudgery that awaited them.

The life the Okeys had sought to escape was increasingly typical for girls of their age and background. Nearly two hundred thousand domestic servants were employed in British households by the end of the 1830s, and a sizeable proportion of these were, like the Okeys, the daughters of labouring men who were recruited to wash, cook, scrub, shop, dust, polish, fetch and skivvy in middle-class homes. It was unending work – tiring, monotonous and lonely – and the health and welfare of young domestics was not a question their masters and mistresses lost any sleep over. Though early-Victorian manuals gave explicit guidance and instruction to maids on how best to tend to their mistress's maladies – 'whether her illness be real or imaginary' – the sufferings of domestic servants were casually swept aside. 'The health of servants is really better on the whole than that of their ladies. It is better . . . than that of any class of people in society. They have none of the hardships of poor people and few or none of the cares which drag down the health of the rich.' Young and robust maids were apparently not prone to the bouts of insanity or nervous disorder that affected middle-class valetudinarians.

London's hospitals and asylums told a different story, of course. On visiting St Luke's Hospital for the Insane, Dickens would find 'that female servants were more frequently affected by lunacy than any other class of patients'. At Hanwell Asylum a third of all female inmates were servants, a large proportion of these being unmarried domestic servants whose symptoms were attributed to 'moral' factors, such as domestic unhappiness, fright, grief, disappointed affection and religious enthusiasm. If anxieties of this kind were behind the Okeys' original illnesses, then it is quite easy to imagine why they would have elected to delay their return to service by becoming 'prima donnas of the magnetic stage'.

Elliotson never seriously considered the possibility that Elizabeth and Jane Okey were buying time, or that he was unwittingly directing them. Believing that the Okeys were highly susceptible to magnetic influence, he continued to investigate the 'new condition of existence' that they so easily succumbed to. Ignoring the mounting opposition from Wakley and the medical school, Elliotson allowed Elizabeth to accompany him on a late-night vigil through the wards in November 1838. On passing one patient's bedside, Elizabeth shuddered, observing that 'Great Jack, the angel of death' was by the man's side. Before leaving the ward, Elizabeth gave a slight shiver and pointed to 'Little Jackey', whom she saw seated by another bed. When the first patient failed to survive the night and the other 'escaped scarcely with his life', Elliotson decided that she was able to give 'correct indications of the fate of the patients'. The following morning, as news of Elizabeth's prophecies spread through the hospital, Elliotson was besieged by students and patients. Making his way to the lecture theatre, he explained that there was a simple olfactory explanation for Okey's singular insights. A person nearing death exudes a peculiar 'effluvium' that is ordinarily undetectable. A mesmerised subject, with all her senses preternaturally heightened, could quite easily, even at some distance, become aware of this effluvium.

Wakley was outraged to learn that Elliotson was still being allowed to practise 'the mighty magic of mesmerism' on the hospital wards. Petitioning the Council of University College, he obtained authorisation for the medical committee to issue a request to discharge Elizabeth Okey. Elliotson, acting with characteristic impetuosity, wrote to the secretary of the council:

> I have just received information that the Council, *without any interview or communication with me*, has ordered my patient Elizabeth Okey, to be instantly discharged, and forbidden me to cure my patients with mesmerism. I *only* am the proper person to judge when my patients are in a fit state to be discharged, and what treatment is proper for their cases.
>
> As a gentleman in the first place, and as a physician in the next, I feel myself compelled to resign my office of Professor of the Principles and Practice of Medicine, and of Clinical Medicine in the College, and of Physician to the Hospital; and hereby resign them all, and will *never enter either building* again.

Several days later Elliotson's students convened in the anatomical theatre and moved to 'entreat the council to adopt such measures as shall ensure the return of our esteemed professor'. The council chose not to revoke its decision, leaving ex-Professor Elliotson to ponder the future of mesmerism and to find a new home for his sleeping housemaids.

Chapter Three

London Trance

What do you think of my setting up in the magnetic line with a large brass plate.
'Terms, twenty-five guineas per nap.'
                    Charles Dickens, letter to John Foster, 1845

As the medical journals and learned societies followed the *Lancet*'s lead in closing ranks against mesmerism, Elliotson was roundly condemned by his peers: 'all at once considered destitute of my previous knowledge and skill, incapable of observation and investigation, and unwanting of any practice'. Equally hurtful were the oblique suggestions of sexual impropriety in his treatment of the Okeys, who were now living with Elliotson and his two sisters. The ensuing decline of his lucrative private practice caused some concern, but rumours that Elliotson had abandoned mesmerism were unfounded. With Dupotet having left London shortly after attending Wakley's experiments with the Okeys, Elliotson decided that he would assume sole responsibility for carrying knowledge of mesmerism *beyond* the medical profession.

Contrary to George McKay's *Extraordinary Popular Delusions* (1841) mesmerism did not immediately skulk into obscurity, 'affronting no longer the common sense of the age' after Wakley's investigations. The *Lancet*'s exposure of mesmerism was of little consequence to many of the ladies and gentlemen who had witnessed public exhibitions of the Okeys, and even less so to the well-heeled sensation seekers who had attended Dupotet's séances at Portman Square. With the exception of Thomas Carlyle – who was characteristically brusque in rejecting all mesmeric bona fides – most mid-Victorian intellectuals and socialites were intrigued by the outpouring of books, journals, lectures and demonstrations that ensured the wider diffusion of mesmerism after 1838. Diaries and correspondence from the period confirm that mesmerism proved of enduring interest to an extended coterie of writers, actors and artists, many of whom were active champions of this 'holy science'.

Viewed through the eyes of the mid-century's men and women of letters, Elliotson was more than a pugnacious champion of 'emblematically unorthodox causes', or an embittered 'enemy of legitimate medicine' with a 'suicidal disregard of opinion'. Recent accounts of Elliotson's career have tended to underline only the enmity he provoked among influential physicians such as Benjamin Brodie (who disliked turning his horses in the direction of Russell Square, fearing that people might think he was going to witness the humbug that Elliotson had brought to University College) and within the corridors of the Royal Society (whose fellows were sorely angered by his brazen attempts to pin the society's badge on his private mesmeric committee). Yet for the unending trail of friends and visitors who descended on Conduit Street after Elliotson's resignation, the protagonist of the latest 'Gower Street scandal' remained a brilliant innovator as well as a 'delightful fellow'. Aside from a visiting Maori chief who asked Elliotson to turn out his pockets, suspecting that he was hiding some magical device that placed his patients under a spell, London society regarded Elliotson as a highly credible advocate for a new science of the mind.

Thomas Trollope was one of the first of the London literati to become immersed in mesmerism. He and his mother, the prolific novelist Fanny Trollope, made Elliotson's acquaintance at a dinner party in February 1839 and accepted the doctor's invitation to see mesmerism performed on one of his patients the following day. Joining Elliotson on a visit to Red Lion Street, mother and son watched as he 'put the little boy to sleep very shortly, then drew him by magnetic passes out of his chair, and caused him while evidently all the time asleep, to imitate him [Dr E] in all his attitudes and movements'. A subsequent visit to another patient, Emma Melhuish, provided them with even more emphatic proof of the reality of mesmerism. Emma, the sixteen-year-old daughter of a glazier, was being treated for cataleptic fits. The effect of Elliotson's passes was to imbue the girl with a 'truly wonderful spiritual beauty', throwing her into 'attitudes of adoration' which made a lasting impression on Thomas. Some fifty years later, in his memoirs, *What I Remember*, he recalled:

> [H]er face and features, eyes especially, assumed a rapt and ecstatic expressiveness which no Saint Theresa could have equalled. It was a conception of Fra Angelico spiritualised by the presence of the breath of life. Never shall I forget the look of the girl as I saw her in that condition! I can see her now! And can

remember, as I felt it then, the painfulness of the suggestion that such an apparent outlook of the soul was in truth nothing more than the result of certain purely material conditions of the body. But was it such?

Though Thomas Trollope would never subscribe to Elliotson's materialist theory of mesmerism, he was quickly won over. In sharp contrast to Dupotet, he thought Elliotson 'a gentleman, a highly educated and accomplished man, and so genuinely in earnest ... that he was ready to spend and be spent in his efforts to establish the therapeutic usefulness of its pretensions'. Over the spring and summer of 1839, he and his mother had ample opportunity to observe the Okeys in their trance states, witnessing the powers of prophecy that Elizabeth continued to demonstrate. After personally mesmerising both sisters on more than one occasion, Thomas was convinced that no element of imposture was involved in their performances, yet confessed to having 'no shadow of a theory to offer in explanation'.

This was essentially the same conclusion that another eminent visitor to Conduit Street reached after spending two afternoons with Elliotson. Robert Chambers, co-conductor of the *Edinburgh Journal* and the future author of *Vestiges of Creation*, happened to meet 'the celebrated Dr Elliotson' in the summer of 1839. His first impressions were positive. 'The good humour of the professor, the vivacity of his manner, and the truthful force of his observations when they bore upon philosophical subjects' led Chambers to think that the professional animosity he had incurred was ill deserved. As Chambers steered the conversation round to the subject of mesmerism, he found that Elliotson had 'no distinct code or law or precise theory regarding mesmerism'. The doctor was

assured of the existence in nature of an 'unseen agent or agency
... which flowed from one living animal to another like a
stream of electricity', but he 'did not pretend to account for or
to understand the nature of that agency'. All he insisted upon
was that the agent was, as a truth of nature, worthy of being
recorded and examined.

At four o'clock on the following day, Chambers called on
Elliotson and was introduced to the Okeys, who were now said
to be cured of their epilepsy. Chambers found the giggling
sisters overcome with 'extreme silliness'. The Okeys could
understand what was said to them, and respond sensibly on
occasion, but otherwise they were in a state of 'absolute idiocy'
with no recollection of themselves. Less impressed with the
diminutive housemaids than previous visitors, Chambers
proceeded to observe how Elliotson was able to stupefy the
sisters with a single wave of the hand, or by applying
mesmerised gold, silver and nickel. To recover them, Elliotson
only had to blow on their faces, apply his thumbs to their
palms, or press his fingers to their faces. Once again, Elizabeth
appeared to be the more alluring of the sisters. Thrown into a
state of 'perfect somnambulism' by Elliotson, this 'beautiful girl
of dark complexion' predicted accurately that she would
remain in her current state for ten more minutes.

Chambers was bewildered. The effects of mesmerism were,
he told Elliotson, manifestly 'extraordinary', 'almost magical'.
Returning the next day, he joined a group of thirty or forty
ladies and gentleman at a public exhibition and watched Jane
Okey lift an eighty-six-pound weight. In his account of his
'Visits to Dr Elliotson's', published anonymously in the
Edinburgh Journal on 31 August 1838, Chambers did not furnish
any opinion on the phenomena he had witnessed, except to say
that no deception was involved on Elliotson's part. Chambers

did, however, put one rather pointed question to him: if he was able to restore the Okeys to reason by way of mesmerism, why not allow them to remain in that condition and restore them to society? Their infantile condition was, Elliotson replied, most conducive to a strengthening of the physical frame and the cure of their nervous irritability. It was 'an act of humanity' to allow them to remain under his magnetic regime.

Fanny Trollope was more forceful in expressing her doubts as to benefits of maintaining the Okeys in this puerile state. Though she shared her son's respect for Elliotson, she appears to have been the only one of Elliotson's new converts to be genuinely preoccupied by the long-term effects of mesmerism on the Okeys. When Mary Mitford wrote to Elizabeth Barrett Browning, informing her that 'Mrs Trollope is a thorough-going mesmerite, constantly at Dr Elliotson's and believing through thick and thin', neither seems to have been aware that Fanny Trollope was instrumental in securing the Okeys time away from their 'keeper' and in eventually returning them to their family. The reunion, which occurred early in 1840, was more difficult than Mrs Trollope had anticipated:

> Memory seemed only gradually, and at first, very partially, to return to them. The mother was a respectable, but poor and very uneducated woman, and of course, wholly different in intelligence and manners from all the surroundings to which the girls had become habituated. And the expression of repulsion and dismay, with which they at first absolutely refused to believe the statements that we made to them, or to accept their mother as such, while she, poor woman, was weeping at what appeared to her this newly developed absence of all natural affection was painful in the extreme.

In his private practice Elliotson continued to employ mesmerism principally in treating nervous maladies 'to which young ladies are so liable'. Ongoing experiments on these 'fitty' patients soon led him to modify and extend his understanding of the trance state. For the first time he acknowledged that the mental will of the mesmeriser was a possible factor in the induction of the mesmeric trance. And mesmeric phenomena could, he conceded, be triggered merely by the expectation that they would occur. Given these concessions to the power of expectation and suggestion, it would certainly not be fair to suggest that Elliotson 'never passed beyond Mesmer's own doctrines'. As entrenched as he was in the materialist theory, Elliotson was clearly attuned to the emotional alchemy of mesmerism. After having mesmerised on hundreds of occasions, it became clear to him that deep, psychological forces were also at work:

> The attachment of the patient to the mesmeriser has various degrees – from a mere satisfaction with the company and proximity of the mesmeriser, to such intensity of affection that will not allow him to move an inch away, perhaps not to withdraw from actual contact . . . I had one patient whose attachment in the mesmeric state was so violent and exclusive, that she always insisted on holding my hand; was displeased, when even apparently in a very deep sleep, if I spoke to others . . . I have invariably observed, without a single exception, in all my mesmeric experience, from the time of the Okeys to this very day – that the mesmeric state has, even if characterised by affection, and the most intense affection too, apparently nothing sexual in it; but it is of the purest kind, simple friendship, and indeed exactly like the love of a young child to its mother.

Four years after his first experiments with the Okeys, Elliotson was still reluctant to acknowledge that mesmerism could stimulate any 'higher powers' beyond the lowest degrees of clairvoyance. It was only after meeting Reverend Chauncey Hare Townshend, a wealthy and ebullient aesthete who had scoured the Continent in search of talented somnambules, that his scepticism began to waver slightly.

Chauncey Hare Townshend was a man whose enthusiasm for mesmerism was of a very different bent to that of the free-thinking professor. A scholar, poet and collector of precious stones, Townshend had abandoned plans to pursue a clerical career shortly after taking holy orders. Making his home at the splendid villa Mon Lorici in Lausanne, Townshend indulged his appetite for the exotic. In the winter of 1836, while residing in Antwerp, the handsome dilettante was introduced to 'an agreeable and well-informed person' who had been taught to mesmerise by a German physician. When Townshend asked this 'Mr K' for an exhibition of mesmerism, he suggested that the truth of mesmerism would best be demonstrated upon someone who was a complete stranger to him. The subject chosen by Townshend, Anna M, had previously waited on his family. Keen to know what the sensation of being mesmerised entailed (and apparently knowing 'absolutely nothing' of the phenomena associated with it) Anna was happy to attend her first *séance magnétique*. With Anna occupying an armchair opposite him, Mr K took each of Anna's hands in his, and maintained constant contact with his knees and feet:

> In this position he remained for some time motionless, attentively regarding her with eyes as unwinking as the lidless orbs that Coleridge has attributed to the Genius of Destruction.

London Trance

> We had been told previously to keep utter silence, and none of our circle – composed of five or six persons – felt inclined to transgress the order. . . . As soon as the first symptom of drowsiness was manifested, the mesmeriser had withdrawn his hands from those of Mademoiselle M— and had commenced what are called the 'mesmeric passes', conducting his fingers slowly downwards, without contact, along the arms of the patients.

The operation took seven minutes, sending Anna into a deep sleep. When Mr K awakened her by wafting air into her face with his handkerchief, she had no recollection of her sensations, except for the heaviness that had overcome her. During a second trial Townshend observed two unusual phenomena. First, Anna's rapport with Mr K enabled her to taste the things he drank and ate as he stood directly behind her. Second, she seemed to acquire a new mode of vision, apprehending objects and people without opening her eyes.

Throwing himself into 'experiments on as extensive a scale as possible', Townshend set out to determine 'how far individuals of different ages, status and temperaments were capable of mesmeric sleepwalking'. During a visit to Cambridge in 1837 he carried out a number of séances, with undergraduates of Trinity College as his subjects. Convinced that he was witness to 'a state of man which is peculiar and distinctive', he turned to Anna M and a small number of gifted somnambulists, recording further instances of physical and mental rapport, thought reading, clairvoyance and mesmerisation at a distance. Bringing precious stones into contact with these mesmerised subjects, he also noted something that previous mesmerists had missed: that diamonds provoked highly agreeable sensations, that opals had a 'soothing effect' and sapphires gave rise to 'a positively painful sensation'.

These 'unbiased personal observations' formed the basis of Townshend's *Facts in Mesmerism* (1840), which paid lip-service to the subtle agent hypothesis that Elliotson had committed himself to (Townshend had observed that several of his entranced subjects had actually perceived the imponderable medium in the form of a fine vapour or electric light), while presenting the new science as a means of accelerating 'moral and intellectual advancement', and unveiling 'a new mode of spiritual existence'. In fact, not one of the séances that Townshend had overseen produced instances of coma or delirium, as routinely induced by Elliotson. The 'facts' that he observed led him to believe that mesmerism offered uniquely profound insights into the twin worlds of spirit and matter:

> [T]he philosopher, who desires to have large views of man and creation in general, cannot take his stand on a better vantage-ground than one which the inquirer into mesmerism is compelled to occupy. Thus expanded, his mind can scarcely fail to be cured of that dogmatism which cries out 'impossible' to all that is not within the narrow round of its own experience. The first time of witnessing a successful experiment in mesmerism must be an era in the life of every thinking being; while the student in this science, who at length arrives at the knowledge of the ethereal medium, connected with all animate beings, and with thought in particular, beholds a flood of light illuminating mysteries which have probably long weighed on his heart and brain.

Townshend returned to England in May 1841 with Alexis, a young German somnambule, whom he was eager to demonstrate before Dickens and the city's growing circle of mesmeric cognoscenti. During his first visit to Conduit Street, Townshend regaled Elliotson (to whom he dedicated his book) with further tales of the wondrous feats undertaken by his entranced somnambulists, offering to perform 'mesmeric revolutions' on the head of Mr Dickens. Dickens declined but harboured no doubts relative to the flamboyant Townshend or 'the statements contained in his book'. Indeed, he was very interested to learn more from this 'gentleman of very high and varied attainments'.

After several exhibitions at Dr Elliotson's, Townshend took Alexis to perform for Countess Blessington at Gore House, and to the home of the actress Frances Kemble, who would later recall Alexis as 'the first of the long train of mesmerists, magnetizers, spiritualists, charlatans, cheats and humbugs who subsequently appealed to the credulity of London society':

Mr Townsend [sic] had almost insisted upon our receiving this visit, and we accordingly assembled in the drawing-room, to witness the powers of Alexis. We were all of us sceptical, one of our party so incurably so, that after each exhibition of clairvoyance given by Alexis, and each exclamation of Mr Townsend's: 'There now, you see that?' he merely replied with the most imperturbable phlegm, 'Yes, I see it, but I don't believe it.' The clairvoyant power of the young man consisted principally in reading passages from books presented to him while under the influence of mesmeric sleep, into which he had been thrown by Mr Townsend, and with which he was previously unacquainted. The results were certainly sufficiently curious, though probably neither marvellous nor unaccountable. To make sure that his eyes were really effectually closed, cotton-wool was laid over them; during another trial the hands of our chief sceptic were placed upon his eyelids ... in spite of which he undoubtedly read out of a book held up before him above his eyes.

Despite Mrs Kemble's misgivings, Alexis was an immediate sensation. While Richard Monckton Milnes observed that 'Alexis & his Mesmerism/ Have thrown fair ladies into fits/And made a formidable schism/ Philosophers and Wits', both Elliotson and Dickens were evidently persuaded that Alexis's powers were genuine. Writing to Lady Blessington, Dickens recommended that 'the magnetic boy' was best viewed before a crowd of no more than eight people, adding that he often 'fails in a crowd and is marvellous before a few'. Elliotson concurred. When Elizabeth Okey had very briefly exhibited occult powers of perception – imitating the movements, grimaces and attitudes of people behind her – she too, he recalled, had been very easily distracted or made anxious by the interference of bystanders.

Prior to embarking on his reading tour of America in January 1842, Dickens's experience of mesmerism was limited to his observation of the Okeys and Alexis, and to a few brief stints as operator to Elliotson's patients. He had never written on the subject, never made his support for Elliotson public. But within weeks of his arrival in America, the East Coast press announced that 'Mr Dickens is a believer', paying tribute to the 'manliness and courage' with which he risked 'detracting a little from his well-earned popularity' by publishing the following statement:

With regard to my opinion on the subject of mesmerism, I have no hesitation in saying that I have closely watched Dr Elliotson's experiments from the first – that I have the utmost reliance in his honour, character and ability, and would trust my life in his hands at any time – and that after what I have seen with my own eyes, and observed with my own senses, I should be untrue to myself if I shrunk for a moment from saying that I am a believer, and that I have become so against all my preconceived opinions and impressions.

Dickens returned from his tour of America with an untrammelled faith in the science of mesmerism. In Pittsburgh, after 'holding forth upon the subject rather luminously' before a group of steamboat companions, he had undertaken his first magnetic operation on his wife, Catherine, employing the same steady manipulations that he had seen Elliotson deploy on numerous occasions. Catherine became hysterical after six minutes. Two minutes later she fell into a sound sleep. By making transverse passes with his thumbs, and blowing on Catherine's face, he was able to recover her. Alarmed by his success, believing himself prodigiously endowed with 'the influence', he gave a repeat performance on the following evening.

Looking forward to demonstrating his newfound powers to friends such as Macready and Elliotson, Dickens arrived back in England in the spring of 1842. Elliotson was in buoyant mood. Towards the end of January, only a few days after Dickens had boarded the steamship *Britannia*, he had received some extraordinary news. Two American physicians, Dr Collyer and Dr Buchanan, had been jointly credited with discovering that distinct cerebral organs could be acted on by mesmerism, a fact they had separately demonstrated in public in Boston and Kentucky. Mesmerism had proved phrenology true. As reports of the American fusion of mesmerism and phrenology were being circulated, William

Engledue, a young Southampton physician who was even more trenchant in his materialism than Elliotson, and a number of English phrenologists, including a certain Henry Atkinson, undertook similar experiments. At last it seemed that decisive proof of the materiality of the human mind had been found.

Elliotson initially refrained from exciting the cerebellum in any of his patients, being anxious 'to abstain from any course which might at all be considered incorrect in reference to them'. But shortly after reporting 'the grandest phenomenon ever brought to light by man' at a lecture to the London Phrenological Society, he found that he was able to arouse the faculties in subjects who were '*totally ignorant* of phrenology'. In a letter to Engledue, Elliotson described the amazing results he had achieved with one young lady of excellent cerebral developments:

> On placing the point of a finger on the right organ of attachment, she strongly squeezed my fingers on the other hand, placed in her right hand, and fancied I was her favourite sister; on removing it to the organ of self-esteem, she let go my fingers which were in her right hand, repelled my hand, mistook me for a person she disliked, and talked in the haughtiest manner . . . I removed my finger to destructiveness, and she let go my fingers again, repelled my hand, mistook me for some one she disliked, and fell into a passion. The finger upon benevolence silenced her instantly; and made her amiable, though not attached. I could thus alter her mood, and her conception of my person at pleasure, and play upon her head as upon a piano . . . These experiments I have repeated twenty times. But a fact more wonderful is this. The state of the organ on one side gives evidence of itself on only half the system. For instance, if I place

my fingers in her right hand, and mesmerize attachment in the *right* side, she squeezes them and mistakes me for a dear friend; if I then mesmerize self-esteem, on the *left* side, she still speaks to me kindly, and squeezes my fingers with her right hand as much as ever. But if I place my fingers in her left hand, she repels them, and speaks scornfully to me . . . These simultaneous, and especially the opposite, influences on the two sides, are the most astonishing and beautiful that all physiology affords; and the sight of them enraptures every person . . . Oh, that Gall could have lived to see this day – these astounding proofs of the truth of phrenology.

Courtesy of these experiments, Elliotson claimed to have converted more people to the truth of phrenology in a single month than he had in all his previous years. Phreno-mesmerism would, he thought, throw new light on diseases whose character and nature continued to elude alienists. By subjecting distinct parts of the brain to the influence of mesmerism, Elliotson thought that it might also be possible to effect a cure of monomania and other nervous diseases.

This momentous proof of the materiality of the human mind was not well received by most phrenologists. At a June meeting of the London Phrenological Association, Engledue's paper on 'Cerebral Physiology and Materialism' caused a commotion. His emphatic advocacy of the materialist doctrine was considered irreligious and dangerous to the phrenological cause, causing many to resign. To make matters worse, many Edinburgh phrenologists flatly refused to entertain any talk of mesmerism. The ensuing rift with Combe's Phrenological Association provided the impetus for the *Zoist*, a quarterly journal which Elliotson and Engledue established in 1843 as a vehicle for promoting the twin sciences of mesmerism and 'cerebral physiology' – the term they adopted in preference to phrenology.

The marriage of mesmerism and cerebral physiology proved brief and less fruitful than Elliotson had anticipated, soon prompting the *Zoist* to expand its remit, becoming a clearing house of medical wonders and scientific oddities – or, as one sceptical reader put it, an 'amusing record of pretended miracles'. With Elliotson as its chief contributor, the journal would carry articles from the likes of Herbert Spencer (on the organs of amativeness and benevolence), Frederic Hockley (on clairvoyance and crystal scrying), J. J. Garth Wilkinson (on Swedenborg's trances), the Duke of Marlborough (on the mesmerisation of dogs) and Lieutenant Richard Burton (on mesmerism in the East). But while the pages of the *Zoist* provided a vital forum for lay mesmerists like Townshend, who reported cures, experiments and painless operations, mesmerism continued to be a science that was principally conducted behind closed doors, an intimate subject best kept for diaries and private conversation. And Dickens, like most Victorian mesmerists, was not willing to advertise the results he had achieved with his own patients.

The case of Augusta de la Rue, the 'sad invalid' on whom Dickens had lavished his magnetic attentions during an Italian sabbatical, was of too sensitive a nature to be conveyed to Elliotson's *Zoist*. Madame Augusta de la Rue, the English wife of a Swiss banker, was afflicted by spasmodic muscular contractions of the face and limbs, and convulsive seizures – ailments that Dickens knew to be particularly responsive to mesmerism. Shortly after becoming friendly with the de la Rues in October 1844, Dickens resolved to 'derive great happiness from being the fortunate instrument of her relief'. For the best part of a month Dickens placed himself at Madame de la Rue's constant disposal, sometimes ministering to her in the early hours, often when her husband was not present. Playing the role of 'anxious physician' with aplomb, he induced her to explore the landscapes through which she was invariably transported under mesmerism. Where are you? How many persons are present? What are they doing? Agitated by the scenes that unfolded before her, Madame de la Rue solemnly described her trance visions. There were 'unseen people' who sent stones down the hillside. There was a lost brother, 'Charles', whose sadness moved her to tears. And, most disturbingly of all, a dark phantom that stalked her.

Dickens, uncertain as to the true nature of this 'bad spirit', sensed that it might prove crucial to her recovery: 'I cannot yet quite make up my mind', he confided to Monsieur de la Rue, 'whether the Phantom originates in shattered nerves and a system broken by pain; or whether it is the greater representative of some great nerve or set of nerves on which her disease has preyed – and begins to loose its hold now, because the disease of those nerves is itself attacked by the inexplicable agony of magnetism.' After three weeks of acting as 'humble servant and physician' to Augusta de la Rue, Dickens left Genoa, dragging his family and an expectant Catherine on a tour of the cities. His thoughts, however, remained very much with Madame de la Rue. Every morning at eleven o'clock he concentrated on his patient for one full hour. During one of these morning clinics he found unexpected confirmation of his powers. As Dickens sat in his carriage en route to La Scala, secretly ministering to distant Madame de la Rue, Catherine, who was sitting on top, fell into a trance. Hearing her muff fall, Dickens looked up to find 'her eye-lids quivering in a convulsive manner'. When she awoke, she said that 'she had been magnetised'. For Dickens, this was 'really quite a fearful thing, and the strangest instance of the strange mysteries that are hidden within this power, that I have ever seen or heard of'.

Separated from his patient, Dickens began to worry that the Phantom might renew its hold over Madame de la Rue. His anxieties were exacerbated by a dream or vision of his own, in which he saw the spirit of his sister-in-law, Mary Hogarth, and beseeched her for 'some token that you have really visited me'. The spirit world seemed to be creeping ever closer, suffusing him with a sense of inchoate dread. He thought about his patient constantly, feeling the menace of the Phantom which haunted Augusta de la Rue more keenly than ever. Was it possible, he wondered, that the Phantom might choose to take revenge on him? Reunited with the de la Rues in Rome, Dickens found that Madame de la Rue's condition had indeed deteriorated. He set to work immediately.

Leaving Catherine and the children to their own devices, Dickens spent the spring months as Augusta's personal mesmerist, attending to her on an almost daily basis. Sure enough, the convulsions abated, her health improved, and Madame de la Rue became 'perfectly acquainted with the nature and origins of the phantoms by which she was haunted'. As for Dickens, he confessed to nursing 'the perfect conviction that I could magnetize a frying pan'.

Far from becoming a 'mighty engine for man's regeneration', or an agent for 'man's emancipation from the incubus of error', mesmerism was failing to win over that large body of Victorians who were, in the words of Thomas Carlyle, 'destitute of faith and terrified of scepticism'. Failing to flourish as a viable scientific faith, mesmerism suffered from the lack of an effective network of local societies, from antipathy towards its materialist rhetoric, from competition from other heterodoxies and popular sciences, and from the increasing employment of mesmerism and clairvoyance as 'an entertainment for the people' – all these factors played their part in impeding its progress among the middle classes. Yet, as far as Elliotson was concerned, a single enemy had denied the science of mesmerism its glorious destiny: the 'anti-mesmeric fabrications' of orthodox physicians.

In 1842, when Elliotson had begun to alert the medical community to painless operations that had been undertaken during mesmeric sleep, the Royal Medical and Chirurgical Society refused to endorse the claim that mesmerism could render patients unconscious of surgical intervention. The *Zoist*'s report on the case of James Wombell, a Nottinghamshire labourer whose diseased leg had been amputated after being mesmerised by William Topham, a barrister and amateur operator, provoked strenuous opposition. According to Topham, the patient 'lay like a statue' for twenty minutes as the bone was sawed and the arteries secured. On gradually waking, Wombell reported hearing a kind of crunching noise but claimed to have 'never felt any pain at all'. Several surgeons responded to the paper, all agreeing that Wombell was an impostor who had 'disciplined himself to bear pain without expressing feelings'. At a subsequent meeting the society resolved formally to withdraw the paper. 'The fact was unworthy of consideration,' claimed Dr Copland, a long-standing critic of mesmerism, because 'pain is a wise provision of nature, and patients ought to suffer while their surgeon is operating'.

When the *Lancet* commissioned Charles Radclyffe from the London College of Physicians to undertake a comprehensive review of the reputed effects of mesmerism in the spring of 1845, the journal made two very significant concessions to the science it had previously deemed an affront to the common sense of the medical profession. First, the 'quieting and composing effect' of mesmerism was recognised as having remedial benefit on patients of a dyspeptic, bilious or hypochondriacal disposition. Second, the mesmeric passes were now acknowledged as the 'probable' cause of many of the phenomena that Elliotson had induced during his demonstration of the Okeys, such as muscular rigidity, convulsions, heightened sensibility and double consciousness. Yet 'insensitivity for pain for a given length of time', as reported in Elliotson's *Numerous Cases of Surgical Operations without Pain in the Mesmeric State*, was still deemed highly improbable. According to Wakley, Liston and other commentators, the principal effects of mesmerism, including imbecility of the nervous system and abandonment of will, still relied on the cunning and vanity of patients of an 'inferior type'.

This blinkered attitude towards the reality of mesmeric analgesia showed signs of abating after the *Zoist* published a report on numerous mesmeric operations undertaken at the Hooghly Charity Hospital, Bengal. The author of the report, a young Scottish surgeon called James Esdaile, had paid close attention to the progress of mesmerism in England, France and Germany during the early 1840s. Struck by the uniformity of mesmeric phenomena described by different authorities, and impressed with 'the conviction that some new general law of nature had been discovered', Esdaile undertook his first post-surgical trial on a local hog dealer. Never having seen mesmerism practised, Esdaile straddled his patient, placing his knees between his own, and passed his hands slowly over his face and stomach. After forty-five minutes the patient opened his eyes and reported seeing smoke in the room. Esdaile continued with the passes, while breathing on his head, and after half an hour the patient's countenance suggested perfect repose:

> I now pinched him, without disturbing him, and then asking for a pin in English, I desired my assistant to watch him narrowly, and drove it into the small of his back; it produced no effect whatever ... Being now satisfied that we had got something extraordinary, I went over to the Kutcherry and begged Mr Russell, the judge, and Mr Money, the collector, to come and see ... Fire was then applied to his knee, without his shrinking in the least, and liquor ammoniae, that brought tears into our eyes, was inhaled for some minutes without causing an eyelid to quiver. This seemed to have revived him a little, as he moved his head shortly afterwards, and I asked him if he wanted to drink; he only gaped in reply, and I took the opportunity to give, slowly, a mixture of ammonia so strong that I could not bear to taste it; this he drank like milk, and gaped for more. As the 'experimentum crucis', I lifted his head, and placed his face, which was directed to the ceiling all this time, in front of a full light; [he] opened his eyes, one after the other but without producing any effect upon the iris; his eyes were exactly an amaurotic person's, and all noticed their lack-lustre appearance. We were all now convinced that total insensibility of the senses existed.

A year on, when Esdaile was introduced to Elliotson in London, he was able to provide reports of more than seventy painless mesmeric operations – including amputations of the limbs, mastectomies and the extraction of eighty-pound scrotal tumours – many of which had been undertaken in the presence of European observers. Attributing his extraordinary success with mesmerism to the 'natural debility' of the Bengalis, and to their unthinking submission to this 'Medicine of Nature', Esdaile speculated that a virtual transfusion of some vital agent from one body to another was the basis of the healing arts among all the savage races: 'the Mumbo Jumbo men of Africa, the medicine men of America, and the charmers of this country [India]' were, to his mind, truly mesmerists who had artfully concealed their actual powers with their incantations and fumigations, or had, perhaps, come to believe in the efficacy of these 'sundry mummeries'.

Esdaile's surgical achievements were duly recognised by the governor-general of India, who secured him the post of presidency surgeon, enabling him to use public funding to promote the use of mesmerism in Bengali hospitals. But despite receiving wide coverage in the medical press, the surgical use of mesmerism was almost immediately overshadowed by widespread experimentation with chemical anaesthetics. Following the pioneer demonstration of ether's anaesthetic properties at Massachusetts General Hospital, Boston, in 1846, James Simpson, Professor of Midwifery at the University of Edinburgh, found that inhalation of the sickly-sweet gas could effectively alleviate the pain of childbirth. This led Simpson to experiment with gases that were easier to administer and longer lasting. His first trials of chloroform were undertaken with colleagues who, after a period of exhilaration and lively conversation, fell into profound stupor. When Simpson first used chloroform in childbirth, in 1847, the only problem he encountered was convincing the mother that the child she was presented with was her 'own living baby'.

As the growing use of chloroform and other anaesthetic gases – in childbirth, surgical operations and dentistry – provoked rabid objections from clerics who decried the gases as 'a decoy of Satan', Elliotson and his fellow mesmerists engaged in their own protest, closely monitoring anaesthetic fatalities. In 1850 Elliotson opened the London Mesmeric Infirmary, 'for the alleviation and cure of diseases, and for the relief and prevention of pain, by means of mesmerism'. With a board of governors that included Bishop Whatley, Earl Stanhope and the Reverend Chauncey Hare Townshend, the Weymouth Street hospital deployed a small number of full-time staff and volunteers who collectively treated around three hundred outpatients a year. From the very beginning the infirmary was beset with problems (many due to disgruntled neighbours who could not, in Elliotson's words, 'afford to suffer the degradation of having one of its houses devoted to silent deeds of sympathy and the removal of suffering') and in 1854 Elliotson was forced to relocate to smaller West End premises, where the infirmary had continuing success in treating rheumatic and neuralgic complaints.

Dwindling donations and continued opposition from the medical establishment eventually led Elliotson to close the Mesmeric Infirmary, but one practitioner who remained emphatic in his resistance to anaesthesia was Theodosius Purland, a Mortimer Street dentist who had performed countless operations on mesmerised patients. Long after the infirmary closed its doors, Purland continued to bemoan the widespread use of anaesthetic gases. When the celebrated naturalist Alfred Russel Wallace requested that Purland have a doctor administer nitrous oxide during the extraction of three or four molars, Purland became 'totally enraged'. In 'a most violent letter', Purland explained that he could not maintain a friendship with 'a man who could ask him to do such a thing' – and that was his last word on the matter.

Chapter Four

'Lecture Mania'

My brethren, there are men who, whether designedly or not, are in league with the fallen spirits – wizards and necromancers, using enchantment and divination, and producing diverse effects beyond the power of man . . . I have no hesitation in reckoning this mesmerism, which is now performing its real effects – real, supernatural, but diabolical.
The Reverend Hugh M'Neile, 'Satanic Agency and Mesmerism', 1842

Prior to the publication of Reverend Townshend's *Facts in Mesmerism* in 1840, aspiring students of magnetism had relatively few resources available to them. Baron Dupotet's account of his 'saintly mission' contained little to whet the appetite of would-be experimenters. The only practical guides were Colquhoun's *Hints on Animal Magnetism* and *A Short Sketch on Animal Magnetism*, which cautioned all would-be investigators 'to determine with precision whether the wonders which appear to be presented are feigned or real'.

When the first edition of the *Zoist* rolled off the Soho presses in March 1843 the situation had altered considerably. Mesmerism was on the up. While Baillière's bookshop on Regent Street stocked around a dozen of the more 'philosophical' titles on the subject of mesmerism, including works by Deleuze and Bertrand, London's standing street patterers hawked tuppenny chapbooks that promised to divulge the terrible secrets behind the 'newly-discovered and most wonderful power'. And affordable practical guides and monthly journals, such as the *Mesmerist* and the *Phreno-Magnet*, were now inviting the literate working classes to embrace the science.

Most mid-Victorian tradesmen, artisans and factory workers did not, however, acquire their knowledge of mesmerism from printed sources. For the most part, initiation into mesmerism took place at mechanics institutes, assembly rooms and temperance halls, where public lectures and demonstrations from itinerant mesmerists could be attended for the price of a flimsy chapbook. According to one estimate, up to three hundred lecturers on mesmerism and phreno-mesmerism were touring Britain in 1843. For the literary and philosophical mesmerists who were inclined to regard mesmerism as a kind of secular covenant, these public exhibitions were nothing short of a calamity. As Jane Carlyle sourly noted, men who could not sound their 'h's were preaching that mesmerism 'consisted in moral and intellectual superiority'.

While the 'strange practices' and 'secret experiments' that Dr Elliotson continued to undertake at his Conduit Street mansion remained a staple subject of popular chapbooks in the early 1840s, the self-styled 'professors' of mesmerism were openly accused of being mercenary quacks and unscrupulous infidels – or, as Liverpool's Reverend Hugh M'Neile informed his parishioners, 'wizards' and 'necromancers'. Public fear of mesmerism was exacerbated by several broadsheet reports of trance mishaps and misadventures. The case of James Cook, 'the sleeping boy of Deptford', had a particularly damaging effect. Cook was mesmerised by a novice mesmerist who had recently attended an experimental lecture. On falling into a prolonged trance, Cook's predicament was reported to the police and newspapers. Though he woke after three days, *The Times* and *Examiner* led many to believe 'that persons sometimes never awake from the mesmeric state'. Elliotson thought that these ill-informed reports 'prevented thousands from being mesmerised who might have been cured or benefited beyond measure', adding to the growing fears of the dreadful abuses that might stem from the magnetiser's extraordinary moral ascendancy over the magnetised.

The first pulpit diatribes against the unholy science of mesmerism were occasioned by the Liverpool lectures of Charles Lafontaine, an itinerant Swiss mesmerist whose demonstrations were responsible for 'awake[ning] curiosity and wonder in high degree' throughout the industrial North. Filling the vacancy created by Dupotet's return to Paris, Lafontaine's highly theatrical demonstrations first attracted considerable attention in London in the summer of 1841. Powerfully built, with a long black beard and dark eyes, Lafontaine was an alluring showman who induced trance without recourse to the passes that his predecessor had relied on. Holding the thumbs of Eugène and Mary, the two young somnambules who accompanied him, Lafontaine would simply fix them with his unblinking gaze. Members of the audience would be invited to ply them with snuff, to prick them with needles and apply lighted candles to their lips and noses. Once physical insensibility had been established to the satisfaction of the platform, Lafontaine would invite volunteers to be 'put to sleep'.

Having captivated respectable London audiences, Lafontaine embarked on a breakneck tour of the major cities. Though his *Memoires d'un Magnétiseur* (1866) certainly exaggerated his success (Lafontaine claimed to have earned 30,000 francs from his Manchester séances alone) his influence was undeniable. By the time he reached Edinburgh, a legion of copycat lecturers were trailing in his wake. According to one interested observer, it was entirely due to Lafontaine that there was 'now no community of the slightest importance in the north which does not contain a numerous body of believers in the truths of mesmerism'.

Lafontaine's first convert of note was Spencer Hall, a young schoolmaster who quickly established himself as a highly popular lecturer in mesmerism. Born on the edge of Sherwood Forest to Quaker parents, Hall was apprenticed to a local stocking maker at seven years of age. After an 'early awakening' to the 'sublimity of simple and common nature', he read a life of Benjamin Franklin and ran away from home to find employment as a printer's apprentice in Nottingham, where he became friendly with William Howitt, a well-known Quaker journalist. After taking charge of a large printing establishment in York, and publishing a second volume of poetry, Hall was appointed as master to Hollis Hospital. It was during his tenure there that Hall returned to Sheffield to attend a lecture by Lafontaine, whose experiments he went on to emulate with considerable success.

Howitt was dismayed to learn that Hall had begun to lecture on mesmerism. Still to be converted to the new science, the older man thought it 'all folly' and advised Hall to 'let that unpopular thing alone' if he valued his post. Hall was beyond dissuasion. The experiments he had conducted (with David Goyder, editor of the *Phrenological Almanac*) had provided him with striking evidence of the phrenological faculties. Ignoring Howitt's advice, Hall launched himself into his new career, giving lectures and *conversazioni* on an almost daily basis. Before founding the *Phreno-Magnet*, a short-lived monthly journal, which aimed to encourage 'common people' to experiment and form their own societies, he was also able to divest Howitt of his lingering scepticism. Howitt recalled:

> We invited him [Hall] to Clapton, and he came with a boy of about twelve years of age, the son of a shoemaker of Leicester. The boy was said to be a very remarkable mesmeric sensitive. We had plenty of opportunity for witnessing and testing the phenomena produced by mesmeric action upon him, and these were truly amazing. The lad was simple and artless, and during the month that he remained in our house had lessons with our sons . . . By this means we ascertained that he knew no foreign tongue, ancient or modern. Yet, when he was thrown into the mesmeric trance, and his organ of imitation was touched, he would immediately pronounce, with the most perfect accuracy, any words of any language which were spoken before him. A very plain-featured boy he was. Yet when in trance, certain phrenological organs in his head being touched, he would, through the transfigured expression which suddenly lit up his face, acquire the countenance, as it were, of an angel.

Seeking to promote phrenology and mesmerism as agents of physical and moral regeneration, the *Phreno-Magnet* ostensibly shared the same objectives as the *Zoist*. But while Elliotson envisaged that ordinary working people would be the principal *beneficiaries* of the new mental science, he could not bring himself to countenance the democratisation that Hall and other lecturers were intent on. Not having the benefit of a proper 'scientific education' Hall was, according to Elliotson, simply 'follow[ing] the promptings of an unimaginative brain, rather than the calm, persevering, philosophical course essential to the cultivation of inductive science'. Hall's London lectures and *conversazioni* brought him to the attention of Lord Morpeth, Robert Chambers and George Combe, but his social status seemed always to preclude his acceptance as an expert – the higher echelons of Victorian society were generally only interested in Hall as a practical demonstrator.

Significantly, the only eminent man of science whom Hall succeeded in converting to the wonders of phreno-mesmerism hailed from a background very similar to his own. In 1844, while working as a schoolmaster in Leicester, Alfred Russel Wallace took a few of his older boys to attend one of Hall's lectures. The ever-curious Wallace was 'greatly impressed and astonished at the phenomena exhibited', and quite taken with Hall's manner of presentation, which was entirely free of showmanship or artifice. 'At the end of the lecture . . . he assured us that most persons possessed in some degree the power of mesmerising others, and that by trying with a few of our younger friends and acquaintances, and by doing what we had seen him do, we should probably succeed. He also showed us how to distinguish between the genuine mesmeric trance, and any attempt to imitate it.'

Following Hall's recommendations, Wallace went on to mesmerise several schoolboys, being able to induce semi-torpor and catalepsy by suggestion alone. In one often-repeated experiment, Wallace would place a shilling on the table in front of a mesmerised boy, telling him, 'Now you can't touch that shilling.' The boy would invariably move his hand halfway towards the coin and find himself unable to move it further. Even when promised the shilling, all his efforts would prove futile. After acquiring a small phrenological bust and acquainting himself with the location of the organs, Wallace was also able to emulate Hall's lecture demonstrations of phreno-mesmerism. On successively touching the organs of combativeness, acquisitiveness, fear, veneration and wonder, Wallace was staggered to see many of his volunteers overcome by a change in attitude and expression 'superior to that which the most finished actor could give to a character exhibiting the same passion or emotion'. Fifty years on Wallace recalled that these experiments had taught him an invaluable lesson: 'that the antecedently incredible may be nevertheless true; and, further, that the accusations of imposture by scientific men should have no weight against the detailed observations and statements of other men'.

Around half of the mesmerists who joined Hall in touring Britain in the early 1840s were probably former phrenologists who had been active in spreading the Combeian gospel across the mechanics institutes. According to the historian Roger Cooter, this travelling legion of lecturers included 'shoemakers, shopkeepers, teachers, dentists, bank clerks, fustian cutters, exiles from Harvard, swindlers, Catholics, Methodists, Swedenborgians, freethinkers, Chartists, Owenites, men with limps, and persons inscrutable, simple-minded, and with flaming pretensions'. Typical of the demonstrations given by these motley adventurers was the evening lecture delivered to 'a small and respectable audience' at the Temperance Hall, Newport, in March 1844:

The attendant of the lecturer was placed upon the table, and after some little expression concerning collusion, which the lecturer disavowed, he was thrown into what was termed the mesmeric sleep. In that state two medical gentlemen examined the pupils of his eyes, and declared him, after some hesitancy, to be asleep, according to their opinion. His eyes being closed, he was then practised upon.

The mesmerist touched certain organs – principally organs of amativeness, destructiveness, and combativeness, and by turns he exhibited great indications of the amatory passion – regard for a particular nymph, much anger against a supposed rival, and many threats of doing him or her, personal violence. On the organ of veneration being touched, it did not appear that the previously mentioned organs were quiescent, in as much as he still uttered threats etc. against the imagined rival. On the organ of tune being touched, he struck off with a merry song.

Meanwhile a gentleman present was slyly practising upon the leg of the 'subject' with a needle, which he thrust about an inch into his limb, without his betraying an emotion. Various modes of pinching, pricking etc., were then practised upon his arms, legs and body, but he bore all without the slightest emotion. He had been in this state for about half an hour when they expressed themselves satisfied that the subject had been exhibited long enough; and he was accordingly awoken, when after rubbing his eyes and staring about him very wildly for a few moments, he described his perfect unconsciousness of all that had transpired, save that his leg, arm, hand, ear, and some other parts of his body had been most 'callously pinched up' by somebody, and should 'just like to know who done it.'

The company had certainly tested the experience of the lecturer to some considerable extent and he went through it with the boldness and bearing of a man, who believed at least, that his doctrines were based on truth.

'Lecture Mania'

Demonstrations of mesmerism and phreno-mesmerism were often delivered by itinerant lecturers who had formerly held forth on physiology, botany, chemistry, electricity and pneumatics, as well as those of a more literary or political bent. The vast majority of these glib-tongued scientific performers remain as faceless as the 'attendants', 'somnambules' and 'patients' whose talents they showcased, but their influence should not be underestimated. Besides exciting the attention of thousands of working-class autodidacts who went on to undertake experiments of their own, the self-styled 'professors' succeeded in securing the participation of medical and scientific gentlemen in their exhibitions, and in encouraging the formation of mesmeric institutes and local societies dedicated to the investigation of mesmerism.

The 'culture of psychological display' that these lecturers sustained was, as Alison Winter writes in a recent study of mesmerism in nineteenth-century Britain, probably of more relevance to the average Victorian 'than most of the elite intellectuals whose names we more quickly associate with psychology and political philosophy of this period'. John Dove, an early Scottish lecturer on mesmerism, believed that there were nine states of mind that an entranced subject might pass through, beginning with 'contemplative abstraction' and ending with 'devotional ecstasy'. Add Dove's nine-point schema to the forty-two faculties that the phreno-mesmerists were potentially able to excite and we are confronted by an uncommonly rich seam of 'unconscious' marvels.

William Vernon, the most popular of the London demonstrators, lectured on phrenology for three years before branching into mesmerism. Particularly adept at stirring controversy and adapting his performance to suit his diverse audiences, Vernon delivered one of his earliest lectures at the Greenwich Literary Institution, in January 1843, 'to a company of 1,000 persons, including a great number of county magistrates, gentry, and professional and scientific men'. Accompanied by an alternating chorus of boos and cheers, Vernon proceeded to mesmerise a young patient and demonstrate his insensibility when a certain Mr Harris jumped on stage and struck the boy with a stick, to prove that the boy was shamming – which he evidently was not. Incidents such as this were commonplace. A cool head and a flair for drama allowed Vernon to turn controversy to his advantage.

A year on, Vernon could be found touring the southern counties with a Dr Owens, giving demonstrations featuring 'Adolphe, the celebrated somnambule de Paris'. In his introduction, Owens rejected the materialist interpretation that Hall and most itinerant mesmerists touted. Forget talk of invisible agents, electrical or otherwise, mesmerism was 'an effect produced by the abstraction of the patient's mind'. For this reason, 'mesmerisers could not operate upon persons inclined to disbelieve the matter'. The operations that Vernon went on to perform on Adolphe were designed to demonstrate the peculiar powers of clairvoyance that mesmerism made possible. Though not always successful in trials to identify the contents of trinket boxes or sealed envelopes, Adolphe's talent for playing card games with his eyes securely bandaged only rarely failed to impress. As the *Cheltenham Examiner* observed of one of his performances, 'the patient played several games of écarté with a gentleman present, in the whole of which he was successful, shuffling the cards with great rapidity, or reading them the reverse way, and playing altogether as he understood his business.' The patient that Owens usually exhibited was a twelve-year-old girl named Jane Knowles. Weighing only forty-seven pounds, she was said to be capable of lifting a fourteen-stone man.

The 'deep converse and high discussion' that mesmeric lecturers generated among their audiences did not preclude mutterings of disapproval and lingering allegations of collusion. In April 1845 the *Leamington Spa Courier* reported that four boys, demonstrated at a lecture by Cornelius Donovan, had, on examination by the town surgeon, confessed to 'pretending to be put into the mesmeric trance' and displaying a great number of phreno-mesmeric 'manifestations'. Part of the appeal of the mesmeric lecture was the promise of confrontation between the advocates of the new science and the sceptical experts who were called on to the platform to invigilate. With audiences often divided over the reality of the phenomena exhibited, lecturers could rarely expect a quiet or sympathetic hearing. Questions from the audience and interruptions from the platform were commonplace. Members of the audience might scramble on stage, striking subjects who were thought to be faking. Lecturers who proved unable to mesmerise volunteers met with cries of derision. Worse still, ticket fees might have to be returned to pacify threatening crowds. This was the fate that befell one John Brown, a carpenter's apprentice from Ipswich who decided to turn his hand to mesmerism in November 1843. After failing to mesmerise four local volunteers during his very first public demonstration, Brown was confronted by an angry crowd who, after demanding their money back, passed a resolution that exposed him as a fraud.

Contrary to popular rumour, the only mid-Victorian somnambule to have transferred a talent for mesmeric fakery to the mainstream theatre was Ellen Monroe, the fictional heroine of George Reynolds's hugely popular penny magazine, *The Mysteries of London*. After receiving several days' tutelage from an unnamed foreign professor – a man 'of about fifty, of prepossessing exterior, elegant manner and intelligent mind' – Ellen gives her first private exhibition, feigning magnetic sleep and demonstrating 'the power of describing places that she has never visited, and homes whose interiors she has never seen'. Miss Monroe goes on to repeat her winning performance in private *conversazioni* and public lectures, but one evening, while describing the interior of a library of a gentleman, 'her eyes opened... the clairvoyance was forgotten... the catalepsy disappeared – and the patient became un-mesmerised in a moment, in total defiance of all the prescribed rules and regulations of Animal Magnetism'. The audience is overcome with laughter. The professor's friends and followers look on each 'with suspicion depicted on their countenance', and in the ensuing confusion Miss Monroe flees into the night – returning, in the next number, to embark on a new career as a *figurante* in the grand theatre.

Widespread suspicion of mesmerism helped briefly sustain the careers of a small number of lecturers who sought to disprove and deny the phenomena exhibited at public lectures. The first of these 'anti-mesmerists', J. Q. Rumball, made a brief living by shadowing better-known lecturers such as Vernon and promising to explode 'The Fallacies of Mesmerism'. His showmanship could not, however, match that of his more illustrious rivals. On one occasion, while lecturing in Ipswich, Rumball was confronted by a formidable lecturer called Henry Brooks and accused of dissemblance. With the audience demanding 'experiments', a volunteer was brought on stage and a red-faced Rumball made a sharp exit.

The Scottish surgeon James Braid was a very different kind of 'anti-mesmerist'. Born in Fifeshire in 1795, Braid received his medical training at the University of Edinburgh and gained his first appointment as surgeon to the miners in Hopetown works in Lanarkshire. After transferring to Manchester the plain-speaking Scotsman began to specialise in operating on club feet and spinal contortions. Having followed the *Lancet*'s reporting of Elliotson's experiments at University College Hospital, Braid considered 'the whole as a system of collusion or illusion, sympathy or imitation'. Like Spencer Hall, his first opportunity to witness the effects of mesmerism at first hand came at a lecture given by the theatrically inclined Charles Lafontaine. Motivated by 'an anxiety to discover the source of the fallacy in certain phenomena I had heard were exhibited at M. Lafontaine's *conversazioni*', Braid found his attention arrested by an entranced patient who was unable to open his eyelids.

The private experiments that Braid went on to prosecute at his home in Peter's Square confirmed that the trance state was most easily induced 'by insisting on the eyes being fixed in the most favourable position, and the mind thus riveted to one idea'. One of Braid's very first trials was on a servant – who, he assumed, 'knew nothing of mesmerism' – whom he called up to watch the preparation of some medicine. After two minutes the servant, who was given no instruction except to observe the process that was under way, closed his eyes and, with a deep sigh, fell into profound sleep. With further experiments confirming that contact with the patient was not necessary for the induction of trance, Braid thought that he had discovered the secret of mesmeric sleep:

> The mode by which I produce my phenomena, I feel convinced, does not depend on any peculiar influence of the operator upon the patient, in the way the Animal Magnetist presumes their patients are affected . . . [S]ome peculiar impression is made on

the nervous system, which induces a state of somnolency, and a capability of being acted on in a manner so extraordinary that no one could credit who did not witness the phenomena, and even many who do witness them cannot credit their genuineness.

The greatest difference I have ascertained between my mode of operating and that of the Animal Magnetists is this – that they seem only to succeed with a few individuals, who are of a highly susceptible temperament, whereas I seldom fail with any one.

Contrary to the fluidic theory of trance championed by Elliotson, Braid contended that the phenomena induced by most platform mesmerists could be explained by their 'monotonous movements' fixing the patient's attention '*entirely through the imagination*'. Around the beginning of 1842, Braid began to give public demonstrations of his methods to 'mixed audiences' in Manchester, Rochdale and Stockport, hurriedly publishing accounts of further trials and cures in the *Medical Times*. Braid reported particular success in the treatment of paralysis, deafness and tic douloureux, also claiming to have employed his technique in rectifying 'an incorrect musical ear' in a patient who previously had been unable to sing in tune. Beguiled by the elegant postures and 'taste for dance displayed by most patients', he speculated that 'nervous sleep' might explain the attitudes represented in Greek sculpture as well as the wonderful feats of the Hindu fakirs, but did not believe in clairvoyance or any of the 'higher powers' that were ascribed to mesmerised subjects.

Braid gave his first London lectures at the Hanover Rooms (where Lafontaine had previously exhibited) and the London Tavern. These *conversazioni*, delivered in March 1842, brought him his first notable London convert, the physiologist Herbert Mayo, who found himself very quickly overcome by a feeling of stupor when compelled to stare at the top of a bottle. Buoyed by Mayo's support, Braid attempted to present his new theory to the medical section of the British Association for the Advancement of Science, which was due to meet in Manchester. Braid's paper was rejected, but many of the association's members went on to witness Braid's experiments at a private lecture, which he convened towards the end of June. In *Neurohypnology, or the Rationale of Nervous Sleep* (1843), Braid documented the treatments he had thus far undertaken, pressing his claims for originality with a new lexicon of entrancement:

HYPNOTIC: The state or condition of *nervous* sleep
HYPNOTIZE: To induce *nervous* sleep
HYPNOTIZED: One who had been put into the state of *nervous* sleep
HYPNOTISM: *Nervous* sleep
DEHYPNOTIZE: To restore from the state or condition of *nervous* sleep
DEHYPNOTIZED: Restored from the state or condition of *nervous* sleep
HYPNOTIST: One who practises Neuro-Hypnotism

Although Braid is today remembered as the father of hypnotism, his fixed-attention theory was by no means as novel as most historians of psychology have suggested. A rival claimant whose work was fairly widely reported in the North was the Manchester lecturer Joseph Catlow. As early as 1839, two years before Braid turned his attention to the subject of mesmerism, Catlow had claimed that mesmeric phenomena could be induced by 'undue continuance or repetition of the same sensible impression' on any of the senses. In order to prove this hypothesis Catlow employed a 'soporific machine' in lectures in Nottingham and Manchester. The vigour with which Braid attacked the 'unlearned Catlow', while respectfully acknowledging Professor Elliotson's experiments, is quite revealing. Upbraiding Catlow for not having exhibited the phenomena on 'a number of patients taken indiscriminately from a mixed audience', and for failing to have employed his procedure in a therapeutic context, Braid was clearly sensitive to his rival's claim for priority.

A technique parallel to those employed by Catlow and Braid was eventually responsible for generating 'The Mesmeric Mania of 1851'. Heralded as a new mode 'of illustrating a very familiar fact – that the imaginative faculties, the nervous sensations and muscular motions, are not always under the control of the will', electrobiology was brought to Scotland and England by a quartet of American performers – Darling, Lewis, Stone and Fiske. Working separately, these star-spangled performers gave rise to scenes that are almost identical to those orchestrated by modern stage and TV hypnotists. Standing before a row of seated subjects, these electrobiologists would invite their volunteers to stare at zinc-coated copper coins, usually held cupped in their left hands. After ten or fifteen minutes those who appeared most susceptible – to electric forces deemed capable of circumventing their ordinary sense of volition – would be made to obey various commands. Dr Darling's demonstrations began with his subjects being deprived of the use of a hand or arm, or rendered insensible to acute pain. Darling would then impose 'involuntary dumbness', induce volunteers to forget their own name and draw the most suggestive to enter into fictitious proceedings:

[Dr Darling] bade the lady look at her husband, who, to our

apprehension, sat smiling at her. He told her that her lord and master had taken a great dislike to her. She seemed arrested with a sudden sorrow, gazed painfully at her husband, and then we saw her eyes slowly fill with tears. This deception was quickly undone, but only to be followed by one not much less distressing to the patient. She was told that the company were enjoying themselves at her expense: they were all laughing at her. She assumed a proud expression, rose up majestically, and looked round and round the room with an air of contemptuous defiance. On this feeling being banished from her mind, she sat down again. The lecturer, pointing to the floor, said, 'You are fond of flowers – here is a fine flower-garden before you . . .' The lady looked and gradually began to assume a pleased expression, such as she would have manifested if led into the precincts of a Chatsworth or a Kew.

Drawing ladies away from the pianoforte, rendering students unable to attend classes, and leading schoolchildren to 'forsake marbles to play tricks with the nervous systems of their companions', electrobiology' provoked a moral panic in Scotland. Spreading southwards, it claimed at least one teenage victim, George Walker, who was rendered temporarily insane after being operated upon in a Northamptonshire lecture hall. Not having been properly released from the state that he had been lulled into, 'the boy became violent, had no rest by night or day, kept on incessantly shouting, leaping, running to and fro and creating the greatest noise and confusion'. After ten days of febrile excitement, the boy's father appealed to the curate and Dr Elliotson's advice was sought. By being mesmerised twice daily George Walker was restored to sanity.

While respectable scientists lamented that electrobiology had revived belief in 'the old and exploded doctrines of electro-nervous currents and animal magnetism' among the educated classes, Braid's complaints were more proprietorial. The discs employed by electrobiologists were 'merely visible and tangible objects for aiding the patients in fixing their attention, and inducing that state of mental abstraction which is the real origin and essence of all that follows'. His own experiments had, he insisted, already demonstrated the extent to which trance subjects could be induced to receive mental and physical impressions. Electrobiology did not, however, detain its critics or aficionados for long. Within a year or so, the flamboyant purveyors of electrobiology had either dispensed with their electrical contrivances, or gone on to discover new scientific prodigies.

Relatively little is known of the lives and careers of most of the itinerant lecturers in mesmerism and electrobiology from the 1840s and 1850s, but the 'private mesmerists' who made a living solely from healing remain even more elusive. One of the few lay practitioners to receive press coverage of any description in this period is Thomas Capern, brother of 'Postman Poet' Edward Capern. Introduced to the 'wondrous power of mesmerism' by the lectures of William Davey (whom he saw demonstrating upon a 'Miss Henly, the deaf and dumb daughter of the late Capt Abb' in 1846), Capern began to dedicate much of his time to relieving pain in 'persons of all ages'. By employing the same passes as he had seen Davey use – holding the balls of the patients' thumbs in the left hand, his right would make passes over the forehead and chest – his operations confirmed the remedial value of mesmerism, particularly when applied to weak, enervated agricultural workers. Capern was subjected to abuse and insults from his neighbours. 'Finding it difficult to satisfy the public mind and promulgate that such a power existed, I invited the whole of the clergy, the dissenting ministers, the gentry of the parish and neighbourhood and especially the medical profession to attend and investigate.' From then on, Capern found his services in constant demand.

After ministering to a number of patients who had been discharged as incurable from Exeter Hospital, Capern began to assist his local physician, Dr Richard Harrison, and became very quickly known as a 'humble operator' who was 'gifted with a power similar to that which the Almighty bestowed on Mr Valentine Greatrakes'. Dedicated to mitigating suffering in his fellow men, Capern would regularly approach strangers he saw 'limping or labouring', taking them to a public house or barber shop to be mesmerised. In contrast to Spencer Hall, whose scientific ambitions led him to court the attention of London press and luminaries, Capern was happy with his lot. Championed by Elliotson and his fellow mesmerists, he was eventually able to ply his trade at the London Mesmeric Hospital, where he continued to garner glowing testimonials. As late as 1862 Capern could be found tramping the lanes around Lamport Hall, the Northamptonshire estate of Sir Charles Isham, providing his eccentric host with daily demonstrations in the art of 'healing by hand and will'.

None of the 'attendants', 'patients' and 'somnambules' that accompanied mesmeric lecturers around British towns and cities attracted the degree of attention that the Okeys had received at University College Hospital. Anne Vials, an invalid from St Albans, was probably typical of many who appeared on the platform. Compelled to give up work to look after her ailing mother, Anne was deprived of the use of a painful and diseased left arm. The arm was amputated in March 1841, but within three months of returning to St Albans she was overcome by violent fits. Two 'benevolent friends' arranged for Anne to undergo treatment by an amateur mesmerist by the name of Henry Atkinson. After a five-day trial, Atkinson succeeded in curing all her symptoms and in introducing the 'ignorant factory girl' to the most ethereal of occupations: 'Not only did she become a somnambulist, i.e. not only were the common results of the sleep-waking state produced, but an ecstasy – a spirituality – a rapt devotional feeling, such as appeared to draw a veil over the sense of this lower world, regularly came on. . . . The effect was truly sublime. It approached the character of what we may conceive of the devotional rapture of the seraph.'

In January 1844 Anne was rediscovered by George Sandby, the vicar of Flixton, who was among the first to have seen her demonstrated at the home of Henry Atkinson: 'What a contrast met our eyes! We found her in a miserable lodging in a back lane, with all the usual accompaniments of poverty.' Sandby decided to see if mesmerism might alleviate the pains that had now transferred to her right arm. Anne responded positively and was duly taken back to Flixton. Once Sandby's circle had completed their inquiries into this 'curious case', Anne was once again returned to St Albans. Thanks to the assistance of Atkinson and the benevolent friends who had introduced her to mesmerism, she was able to delay her reception into the workhouse.

For most somnambules the workhouse remained a more likely destination than the theatre. Only the most resourceful of them would go on to employ their talents independent of their professorial keepers, assisting physicians or offering private consultations for the locating of lost and stolen items. Mesmerism offered somnambules such as Anne Vials refuge from illness, drudgery and invalidism. The séance was for them a liminal zone, a place where alternative roles and identities could be explored with impunity. The possibilities were tantalising. Where else was it possible for a twelve-year-old girl to lift a man three times her weight, for a factory girl to adopt the demeanour of a priestess, and for a deaf and dumb girl to convince thousands that there was indeed a truth 'opposed to the Philosophy of Ages'?

Chapter Five

The Infidel in Petticoats

There is no God, and Harriet Martineau is his prophet.
Douglas Jerrold, 1852

One of the more surprising chores that young Jane Arrowsmith was asked to undertake while serving at her aunt's boarding house at 57 Front Street, Tynemouth, on the north-east coast, was to repeat the motions that a visiting mesmerist had performed on the previous day upon their long-standing lodger, Miss Harriet Martineau. As usual, it was a task she carried out with the 'greatest alacrity'. Within one minute the celebrated writer and long-suffering invalid was assailed by shimmering spectral lights – the very lights she had previously witnessed when attended to by Mr Hall. The relief was immediate. All her pain and distress seemed to ooze away:

> During that hour, and almost the whole evening, I could no more help exclaiming with pleasure than a person in torture

crying out with pain. I became hungry, and ate with relish, for the first time for five years. There was no heat, oppression, or sickness during the *séance*, nor any disorder afterwards. During the whole evening, instead of the lazy hot ease of opiates, under which pain is felt to lie in wait, I experienced something of the indescribable sensation of health, which I had quite lost and forgotten. I walked about my rooms and was gay and talkative. Something of this relief remained till the next morning; and then there was no reaction. I was no worse than usual; and perhaps rather better.

Like most Victorian maids, Jane Arrowsmith had considerable experience of ministering to the sick. In the years she had spent at Front Street she had prepared poultices, applied leeches and dressed blisters; Jane's aunt maintained that 'she had been as well nursed as any lady in England by this girl'. Yet mesmerism had very rarely been practised by domestic servants. As one French physician observed, it is 'always landlords who operate upon their subalterns never the latter upon their superiors, magnetism always works downwards, never upwards'. This tradition was preserved in mid-Victorian Britain. The most effective mesmerists were physicians, church ministers, army officers and aristocrats such as Earl Stanhope and Lord Morpeth – figures whose social and intellectual authority appeared to amplify their subjects' susceptibility to mesmerism.

Desperate to seek relief from an ovarian illness (and the opium dependency it had led her into) Harriet Martineau was initially happy to break this unwritten rule, falling back on the services of an untrained servant to whom she had grown much attached. Yet after six weeks of almost daily treatment, with the prospect of recovery apparently looming, Martineau had a change of heart. The patience and purpose required in the treatment of an intractable illness could, she now decided, 'only be looked for in an educated person'. Servants might be usefully employed in the treatment of minor ailments or sudden pain, but for her nervous system truly to benefit from an infusion of the 'vital force' Martineau thought that it was probably unwise to promote a lowly housemaid to the office of mesmerist.

Mrs Wynward, a more genteel lady's companion with considerable experience of mesmerism, duly replaced her 'little maid Jane'. A few days after her arrival, Martineau took her first steps under open skies in four and a half years. There was 'no faintness, exhaustion or nervousness of any kind'. With all her symptoms fast attenuating, Martineau had Mrs Wynward hide the opiates that she had come to depend on. Fortified by daily sessions of mesmerism, the nights became bearable, her daylight hours transfigured. During one of her first long walks, Mrs Wynward placed a hand to her forehead and 'the phosphoric lights appeared, glorifying every rock and headland, the horizon and all the vessels in sight . . . if I had been a pious and ignorant Catholic, I could not have escaped the persuasion that I had seen heavenly visions'.

Born into a family of middle-class Norwich dissenters, Harriet Martineau (1802–77) was one of the first Victorian women to earn a living from her pen. An anxious and sickly child – 'constantly longing for heaven, and seriously and very frequently planning suicide in order to get there' – Martineau's first writings, published in the *Monthly Repository*, were aimed at a Unitarian readership, but her attempts to 'grasp a conviction' soon led her to the utilitarian credo ('the greatest happiness of the greatest number') of Bentham and Mill.

Driven by the death of her father to pursue a literary career, Martineau hit upon the idea of 'exhibiting the great natural laws of society by a series of pictures of selected social action'. The success of *Illustrations of Political Economy* (1832–4), a didactic guide to the vagaries of taxes, tariffs and the national budget, allowed the newly dubbed 'economist in petticoats' to transfer to London, where she came to the immediate attention of Robert Owen, Thomas Malthus and Ralph Waldo Emerson. Thomas Carlyle's first impression of this 'notable Literary woman' was that she was 'very intelligent-looking, really of pleasant countenance . . . full of talk, tho' unhappily deaf almost as a post'.

Martineau had already established a reputation as a prolific journalist and 'mannish' champion of abolitionism, women's rights and free trade when, while escorting her cousin to the Continent in the summer of 1839, she was struck down by an 'internal disease'. The breakdown was, she believed, caused by nervous excitement and overwork. Deciding that 'solitude and silence, free from responsibility and domestic care was a blessed change from the life I had led', Martineau transferred to Tynemouth, to be near her brother-in-law and medical adviser Thomas Greenhow. Her flight into invalidism was, as with so many nineteenth-century writers, surprisingly productive. Freed from the responsibility of caring for her mother, Martineau passed the first years of her 'depressing malady' shuffling between bed and bureau. When too exhausted to write, she trained her telescope on the seashore and the steam tugs that had yet to acquire their other-worldly allure.

Invalidism bore early fruit with the anonymously published *Life in the Sick-Room* (1844), which described the spiritual and intellectual consolations of illness and dispensed advice on a range of more commonplace matters, such as the management of visitors. Though *Life in the Sick-Room* was in many ways an unacknowledged ode to opium, it was well received, garnering a myriad of accolades for its wise and sensitive reflections on the inner life of the invalid. Martineau would, however, soon find reason to deplore the morbid flights of introspection that underscored the retreat into her Tynemouth 'sanctuary'.

The first of her friends to suggest that she might benefit from a dose of mesmerism was Edward Bulwer-Lytton, who recommended a visit to a Parisian somnambule in order to identify the precise nature and best treatment for her disease. Martineau replied that she had 'long been entirely convinced of the truth of somnambules' but that, problems of travel aside, she remained constrained by 'the prejudice of a certain part of my family against mesmerism'. Two years on, three more letters advising mesmerism arrived in the space of a fortnight:

> My youngest sister wrote to me about a curious case which had accidentally come under notice first, and then the management, of her husband – a surgeon – a case which showed that insensibility to pain under an operation could be produced, and that epilepsy of the severest kind had given way under mesmerism, when all other treatment had long been useless. Mr and Mrs Basil Montagu wrote to entreat me to try mesmerism, and related the story of their own conversion to it by seeing the case of Anne Vials treated by their 'dear, young friend, Henry Atkinson' – of whom I had never heard. The third was from a wholly different quarter, but contained the same counsel, on very similar grounds.

Still fearful of the response from certain members of her family, particularly her younger brother James, Martineau equivocated. Her final decision was given impetus by Thomas

Greenhow, who, after seeing Spencer Hall lecture in Newcastle, suggested that she might undergo a trial of mesmerism to assist with her withdrawal from opium. Disregarding friends and relatives who considered mesmerism either 'delusion or imposture', Martineau went ahead. On the afternoon of 22 June 1844, Hall and Greenhow arrived to find Martineau 'between the expiration of one opiate and another':

> Various passes were tried by Mr Hall; the first that appeared effectual and the most so for some time after, were passes over the head, made from behind . . . A very short time after these were tried, and twenty minutes from the beginning of the *séance*, I became sensible of an extraordinary appearance, most unexpected, and wholly unlike I had ever conceived of. Something seemed to diffuse the atmosphere . . . like a clear twilight, closing in from the windows and down from the ceiling, and in which one object after another melted away, till scarcely anything was visible before my wide-open eyes. First, the outlines of all objects were blurred; then a bust, standing on a pedestal in a strong light, melted quite away; then the table with its gay cover; then the floor, and ceiling . . . I cried out, 'O! deepen it! deepen it' supposing this the precursor of sleep.

En route to a lecture in Newcastle, Hall could only permit Miss Martineau another twenty minutes of his time. The sleep that she expected never came but the feelings of 'lightness and relief' produced by Hall's passes persisted into the evening.

During a subsequent séance Martineau felt her spirits lifted but remained uncertain as to whether her levity should be attributed to mesmerism or her customary medicine. The issue was resolved on the following day. With Hall unable to pay a third visit, Martineau decided to forgo her opium and requested that her housemaid attempt to repeat the passes that Mr Hall had performed the day before. Following instructions from Miss Martineau, Jane Arrowsmith was soon able to bring about a 'radical amendment' to her mistress's condition. Over the following weeks, Martineau felt 'more firm in nerve, more calm and steady than at any time of my life before'. Her opium intake was gradually reduced and the distressing pains returned only on the occasional days that the presence of visitors prevented her from being mesmerised.

A few days after Mrs Wynward's arrival in Tynemouth, Martineau was able to walk outdoors without an inkling of nervousness or faintness. After less than two months of treatment a five-mile circular presented no difficulty. With every symptom of her 'incurable disease' in remission, Martineau instantly withdrew from her opiates, confident that her new mesmerist would be more than able to obviate 'the accumulation of miseries under which the unaided sufferer is apt to sink'. When the diarist Henry Crabb Robinson visited in January 1845 he found that 'Miss M's appearance at least is such as I never saw before – Her complexion is become beautiful – and her whole air is that of happiness.'

Martineau was not only cured – she was converted. In November and December of 1844 the *Athenaeum* published a series of six letters that avowed her belief in mesmerism as an agent capable of effecting 'practical changes in the mutual relations of human beings' and of raising the highest faculties to new heights. Dismissing the common objections that had been raised against mesmerism, Martineau railed against the philosophers, physiologists and medical men who refused to confront the facts of the mesmeric trance, and turned on the itinerant lecturers who had debased her new covenant through public exhibitions. Here, she argued, was 'a power sacred to higher purposes'. True believers in mesmerism (approaching its mysteries with 'unclouded reason' and an 'ingenuous heart') would be blessed with inestimable insights into human nature.

Martineau's *Letters on Mesmerism* were far from the straightforward 'narrative of recovery' that had been promised *Athenaeum*'s editor, Charles Wentworth Dilke. Martineau's description of the mesmeric treatment she had received, especially in relation to her withdrawal from opium, was cursory. The claims she made for mesmerism and its power to transform the 'scope and destiny of the human being on earth' were calculated to offend readers who retained a 'childlike dependence upon the Creator'. But perhaps the most perplexing and controversial aspect of the letters was Martineau's account of the séances that Mrs Wynward had conducted with nineteen-year-old Jane Arrowsmith. After very quickly developing the power to discern the true nature of disease, the entranced housemaid had apparently delivered unexpected discourses on the nature of the soul, mind and body, revealing insight into other people's silent thoughts and demonstrating powers of travelling clairvoyance.

The moral backlash to Martineau's letters was led by Charlotte Elizabeth Tonna, editor of the *Christian Lady*. Tonna took issue with the 'supernatural manifestations' ascribed to 'J' in the *Athenaeum* letters, warning Martineau that she was tampering with an agency that was 'assuredly diabolical'. The objections raised were by now all too commonplace. Across the country, pastors and ministers were cautioning their parishioners that mesmerism would lead to spiritual contamination. Tonna echoed these churchly fears:

> When your somnambules describe events occurring at a distance; when they reveal the seat, and the nature, and probable

termination of diseases impenetrable by mortal skill; when the uneducated and uninformed express themselves with elegance and perspicuity, in terms the signification of which they are still ignorant of in their natural waking state; and, above all, when they prove, as they invariably do, that mind and memory present a perfect blank with regard to the transactions of their entranced hours; then, Madam, I tell you, without hesitation, that the body, which you have thrown into such torpor, becomes the helpless, passive, unconscious, polluted receptacle of an evil spirit, who uses the organs of speech and motion in that wretched individual for the manifestation of his own craft, and subtlety, and superhuman powers.

The derision and disbelief which so many readers expressed on reading the *Athenaeum* letters was privately shared by some of Martineau's most intimate and respected friends. The poet William Wordsworth, Martineau's teenage idol, retained an open mind as to the subject of mesmerism, but thought it dangerous 'for anyone's wits to be possessed in the manner this extraordinary person is'. Crabb Robinson observed that 'everybody joins in ridiculing her. And I am hard put, not to join in with the multitude – She may have confidence in the Somnambulism of her Servant, but she can't properly communicate her faith to others.' And on reading Martineau's 'outpourings', Jane Carlyle noted that 'a vast deal of what one hears is humbug – this girl of Harriet's seems half diseased – half makebelieving – I think it is a horrible blasphemy they are perpetuating in *exploiting* that poor girl for their idle purposes of curiosity!' With the exception of Elizabeth Barrett Browning (who wondered whether Martineau's 'apocalyptic housemaid' could establish if her dog Flush had a soul) the literary response to Martineau's letters was unequivocal. It was left to Elliotson's

Zoist to defend Martineau for encouraging ladies in a similarly wretched state to seek relief through mesmerism.

The most stinging response came from Thomas Greenhow, who felt that his professional reputation had been tarnished by association with mesmerism. Insisting that Martineau's recovery was 'the natural sequel of progressive improvement', Greenhow furnished (without the permission of his famous patient) a short but detailed account of her condition, treatment and recovery in his *Medical Report of the Case of H—— M——*. Though Martineau was justifiably aggrieved to find her intimate gynaecological details laid out in a shilling pamphlet, Greenhow's report did contain some interesting insights into her much-publicised recovery. Greenhow's case notes indicated that many of the symptoms of his patient's uterine condition had begun to abate more than six months before she commenced her mesmeric treatment with Spencer Hall: 'How far the relief from the systematic nervous distress, attendant on this case, is to be attributed to the direct agency of mesmerism – whether it has acted by a power *sui generis*, or by supplying a well-timed stimulus to the mind ... is a question which everyone must be left to answer for himself.' Greenhow had, he claimed, always believed that Miss Martineau would eventually be released from her long confinement, despite the strange satisfaction that she derived from believing 'that she must ever remain a secluded invalid'. In his opinion, mesmerism had provided her with a powerful psychological stimulus, enabling her to shake off a morbid attachment to invalidism.

Suspecting Greenhow's 'evil influence' of having induced other members of her family to regard her 'experience and recovery as unpardonable offence', Martineau made immediate plans to leave Tynemouth for the Lake District. Contrary to newspaper reports that claimed she was as 'ill as ever', Martineau continued to enjoy good health. In the spring of 1845 she was finally able to meet Henry George Atkinson, whom many considered the true source of the irreligious views that she now espoused. Atkinson, the son of a wealthy London architect, was an amateur geologist and a prominent member of the London Phrenological Society. While his private demonstrations of various somnambules, including Anne Vials, earned him a reputation as one of the most patient and able of operators, Atkinson was best known as the first of the English mesmerists to excite 'individual cerebral organs in the mesmeric state with his fingers'. This co-discovery of the truths of phreno-mesmerism, given due recognition in the pages of the *Zoist*, transformed him into a secular naturalist who insisted that the mind was no more than a function of the brain.

Making no concessions to the 'First Creator' invoked by his fellow mesmerists, Atkinson joined with Elliotson in looking forward to the day when mesmeric science would be 'employed in teaching man to know himself, morally, intellectually, and physically; to know what is the constitution of his nature; the duties of life, and the best interests of men'. Martineau claimed that she had known nothing of Atkinson's 'philosophical opinions' until after the publication of the letters. It was, she recalled in her *Autobiography* (1876), only after her first meeting him in Nottingham in May 1845 that she too began to reject the 'old superstitions' of Christianity and move towards Atkinson's more 'effectual philosophy':

> [Mr Atkinson] astonished and somewhat confounded me by saying how great he thought the mistake of thinking so much and so artificially as people are for ever striving to do about death and about living again. . . . I was however struck in a

certain degree by the nobleness of his larger view, and the good sense of the doctrine that our present health of mind is all the personal concern that we have with our state and destiny; that our duties lie before our eyes and close to our hands; and that our business is with what we know, and have in our charge to do, and not at all with a future which is, of its own nature, impenetrable.

She soon realised that Atkinson's 'outspoken doctrine' was not only consonant with the 'necessarian' philosophy that she held: it was its natural apotheosis. 'Yes, it *is* faith, is it not?' she insisted in a letter to Atkinson, 'and not infidelity, as ninety nine hundredths of the world would call it.'

Prior to making a permanent home in Ambleside, a mile and a half down the road from Wordsworth, Martineau found lodgings at Waterhead and set about methodically exploring the lakes and mountains that she had first visited as a child. She had not been settled long when a number of sick neighbours made appeals to her landlady, asking if they might derive benefit from mesmerism. Not feeling able to refuse, Martineau opened her sitting room to the impoverished locals. The first of the 'wondrous cures' she performed was upon a poor youth who was about to lose both arms to a scrofulous disease. After being attended to twice a day over a period of ten weeks, the young man was relieved of all his consumptive symptoms. The case that Martineau took most pride in, however, was the complete cure of a young nursemaid who was sent to her suffering from debilitating headaches. Within a few days, Martineau found that she could mesmerise the young woman almost immediately, sending her on unconscious errands around the house. When the girl's parents travelled many miles to thank Miss Martineau, 'their reluctant and hesitating request was that

I would not mesmerise her in the presence of any body who would tell the clergy'.

Martineau's response to the passes that she continued to benefit from was now beginning to alter. Throughout her mesmeric treatment at Tynemouth she had remained conscious, never slipping into the somnambulism that so easily overcame Jane Arrowsmith. Now that she had recovered her health, she was easily lulled into mesmeric sleep by Mrs Wynward. During a visit from William Gregory, an Edinburgh chemist who had been experimenting with mesmerism for a number of years, Martineau was 'double mesmerised' by the professor and his wife, while a shorthand writer took note of her 'preachments'. The recorded fragments of speech were 'wholly unlike anything I had ever said under any other circumstances'. During further experiments with Professor Gregory, Martineau entered an intermediate state between sleep and wakefulness, in which her highly detailed impressions assumed a prophetic or clairvoyant character. It was thanks to the 'cool judgement' of Professor Gregory that she was able to perceive these supernatural dreams as nothing more than the ghosts of her own thoughts.

Martineau finally arranged for Jane Arrowsmith to be transferred to Ambleside in the spring of 1846. The housemaid had suffered considerably since Martineau's departure: she had gone temporarily blind, been refused recourse to mesmerism by her aunt, and been harassed by journalists and physicians intent on exposing her imposture. Within ten days of treatment by her new mistress, Jane recovered her sight and began to treat the sick child of a nearby cottager. Now that up to seven patients could be found asleep at any one time in Martineau's sitting room, rumours regarding the Ambleside 'lady who does it through the Old 'Un' were rife around Windermere. Though many of the locals expressed disapproval towards her lay healing, she remained immune to the ill feeling aroused by her mesmerism and made Ambleside her permanent home. The speed at which The Knoll emerged from its woodland plot led one neighbour to speculate that she must have mesmerised her workmen.

Returning from a tour of the holy lands in June 1847, Martineau began an 'intimate correspondence' with Atkinson, with a view to securing his opinion on 'how you have us set about the study of the powers of man in order to understand his nature, and his place and his business in the universe'. Atkinson's advocacy of inductive science to detect the laws of human nature was instrumental in her final emancipation from Unitarianism, edging her towards the secularism espoused by Robert Owen, George Holyoake and the growing legions of atheists. Atkinson's and Martineau's *Letters on the Laws of Man's Social Nature*, published in 1851, proclaimed the need to look beyond the 'unfathomable mystery' of creation and attend to the rational and scientific basis of the natural world. In this respect its central tenets were consonant with George Combe's *The Constitution of Man* (1828) and with Robert Chambers's *Vestiges* (1844), an enormously popular account of biological evolution based on observation of the animal world. But while Combe was less than explicit about his unbelief and Chambers chose to publish anonymously, Martineau was prepared for the onslaught that her materialist heresy would provoke. Though she did not deny a 'First Cause', Martineau's rejection of popular theology marked her out as an inveterate atheist.

Martineau's new faith was science. Mesmerism had revealed to her 'that the one essential requisite of human welfare in all ways is scientific knowledge of human nature'. The critical reception of *Letters on the Laws of Man's Social Nature* was as

The Infidel in Petticoats

hostile as she had anticipated. Charlotte Brontë, a recent visitor, feared that the book would provoke 'a popular outcry'. George Eliot thought it 'the boldest book I have seen in the English language' and considered it 'studiously offensive'. The only positive notices that the book received came from the circle of progressive freethinkers who were in the habit of meeting at the home of John Chapman, the book's publisher. George Lewes, writing in the *Leader*, commended Martineau and Atkinson for their 'honest, independent thinking', but stopped short of endorsing the claims made for mesmerism. James Anthony Froude expressed similar reservations towards phreno-mesmerism but thought the letters were 'the first flame of a smouldering feeling now gaining the air'.

Martineau's Ambleside neighbours were predictably shocked. Although Edward Quillinan, Wordsworth's son-in-law, was not alone in proclaiming himself unable to enjoy the author's society after the publication of 'such a book', Martineau believed that *Letters on the Laws of Man's Social Nature* had been an 'inestimable blessing' to her, 'dissolving all false relations, and confirming all true ones'. One response did, however, cause her more anguish and remorse than she cared to admit: that of her younger brother James, who took it upon himself to launch an unflinching attack on the letters, and on Atkinson in particular. James was dismayed that his sister had *submitted* herself to the 'hierophant of the new atheism'. Taking exception to their secular manifesto, his ill-tempered review caused a permanent breach in their relationship.

The journey from mesmerism to scientific secularism that Martineau undertook was daring and scandalous. While many lay mesmerists privately endorsed Atkinson's belief that mesmerism and phrenology provided new methods of studying man 'as a creature endowed with definite properties, capable of being observed and classified like other phenomena', most stopped some way short of rejecting Christianity as an impediment to rational progress. Martineau remained uncompromising in her irreligiosity. After reading Darwin's *Origin of Species* in 1859, she wrote an enthusiastic note to George Holyoake, praising the book for its opposition to 'revealed Religion on one hand, & Natural (as far as Final Causes and Design are concerned) on the other'. Her only regret was that Darwin had made two or three concessions to 'The Creator', a 'needless mischief', which neither she nor Atkinson would ever again indulge in.

A post-mortem examination undertaken on the seventy-four-year-old infidel in June 1876 discovered a 'vast tumour', which had dragged the uterus down into the lower pelvis, and 'so produced the retroversion observed when Miss Martineau was at Tynemouth'. When the findings were conveyed to Thomas Greenhow, he was pleased to confirm that '*no cure* was affected [by mesmerism], but temporary suspension of suffering took place from natural causes connected with local disease'. The 'peculiarities of character' that the eminent lady demonstrated through her remarkable career might, he speculated, be partially explained by the progress of the disease.

Chapter Six

News from Nowhere

WANTED – One Event, Occurrence, or Fact, of a public nature, which has turned out to verify an assertion of a Clairvoyante.

Punch, 1853

When Baron Dupotet commenced the first trials of magnetism at University College Hospital in the summer of 1837, the French Academy of Medicine had just circulated its final report on animal magnetism, declaring no evidence for clairvoyance or any of the reputed séance phenomena. On 12 September a number of commissioners who recognised the need for further investigation formed a body to investigate any somnambulist who agreed to demonstrate eyeless vision in a public trial. A prize of 3,000 francs was offered to anyone who could, under strict controls, demonstrate the ability to read *'sans le secours des yeux et de la lumière'*. Mesmerists from across the country contacted the new commission but only one somnambule,

Léonide Pigeaire, the eleven-year-old daughter of a Montpellier physician, made the journey to Paris. Before the trial was about to take place, Léonide's father tried to persuade the commissioners to allow his daughter's eyes to be bandaged (rather than employ the black silk screen they had prepared), arguing that her clairvoyance was probably the function of facial nerves. The commission agreed, on the condition that any book she read from was held directly in front of her eyes and not in her lap. Finding these terms unacceptable, Monsieur Pigeaire decided to withdraw his daughter from the trial.

Extending the prize for another year, the committee did eventually investigate one somnambule who, on the authority of Alphonse Teste, a well-known Parisian mesmerist, was said to be an expert in reading writing enclosed in wooden boxes. On this occasion the commission's trial was terminated after an hour, with only two of the words in Leprevost's *La Guerre de Jugurtha* correctly identified. Having found no evidence of clairvoyance, the committee concluded that the subject of animal magnetism was best ignored.

John Elliotson had not initially been inclined to take Dupotet's claims for mesmeric clairvoyance too seriously. Nothing that he witnessed during Dupotet's séances, or in his own demonstrations of the Okeys, suggested that somnambules were able to perceive without recourse to the external organs of vision. It was not until 1841 that Elliotson observed 'the occurrence of vision with eyes firmly closed' in Townshend's 'magnetic boy', and a further three years passed before he finally witnessed 'that highest degree of clairvoyance, in which a person knows, as by vision, what is going on at a great distance, or can tell what has taken place or will take place in matters relating . . . to various events in the lives of others'.

The nameless patient who convinced him of the reality of

clairvoyance in its highest degree was, he assured the readership of the *Zoist*, 'the perfection of integrity and every other moral excellence'. In her first demonstration this exemplary lady travelled fifty miles to her father's house, reporting on who was present in each room and what they were occupied with. At Elliotson's request, the patient showed that she was equally adept at locating and describing strangers when supplied with 'a few particulars'. When exerting this power, Elliotson observed that she would knit her brow and wrinkle her forehead, giving the impression that she was able to perceive from a point somewhere above her nose. As a confirmed phrenologist, it came as no surprise to Elliotson that this was 'exactly at the spot called by some cerebral physiologists the organ of Eventuality'. A more 'remarkable peculiarity' was that by holding the patient's hands, her power of telling past and future events was greatly increased.

Though writers such as Townshend and Colquhoun had written at length on clairvoyance, cataloguing reports of its occurrence in both natural and magnetic somnambules, few of the early British mesmerists had practical experience of the magical feats that Continental somnambules were famed for, such as the ability to discern the internal state of the body, or to perceive, while blindfolded, the contents of books and packages. As for trance visions of faraway scenes and distant persons – which the mystically minded mesmerists seized upon as evidence of the soul's ability to exist independently of the body – the reality of such reports was almost impossible to verify.

Elliotson's discovery of 'exquisite clairvoyance of the highest kind' anticipated the London debut of Paris's most celebrated clairvoyant, Alexis Didier. Having been successfully consulted by a number of English gentlemen, Alexis's reputation preceded him. The story of how Alexis had assisted Colonel John Gurwood, Wellington's private secretary, in finding proof of the part he had played in the siege of Ciudad Rodrigo in 1812 was common knowledge. Elliotson read the notes of Gurwood's interview and declared himself 'astounded and satisfied' by the manner in which Alexis had located the one French prisoner who was able to corroborate the colonel's claims. Elliotson's only disappointment was that Gurwood, shy of the publicity that he had already received, declined to furnish *P Zoist* with a full personal account of his interview with Alexis. 'I find an excuse for some medical men who have families dependent for bread upon their professional success, and conceal their belief in mesmerism; but when mere bantering and jeering can be the utmost mischief, I think every person is bound to come forward to declare the truth.'

Alexis was working as a clerk in the office of a Parisian transport contractor when he attended his first exhibition of animal magnetism. Asked to climb on to the platform as a volunteer, he proved highly susceptible to the magnetic passes, prompting his office manager, Monsieur Marcillet, to repeat the trials. Emulating the demonstrations of 'higher phenomena' given by travelling lecturers such as J. J. Ricard and August Lassaigne, Marcillet embarked on a second career as a magnetist, specialising in demonstrations of eyeless vision and travelling clairvoyance. Arriving in London with Marcillet in June of 1844, Alexis made an immediate impact. The first of his five-guinea private séances, at Elliotson's Conduit Street home, was attended by 'a large number of ladies, and scientific and distinguished persons', including the physician Edmund Symes, who submitted the following report to the *Zoist*:

M. Alexis, probably 18 or 19 years of age, was placed in a

reclining chair, and his mesmeriser, M. Marcillet, stood at a distance of a yard from him, and gazed intently at his eyes. In about a minute the patient began to exhibit twitchings of the whole body and slight convulsive movements of the face, and then gradually fell off into the mesmeric state, which was deepened by the operator making a few longitudinal passes from the head downwards over the body. Before the state of clairvoyance came on – for this appears to come on gradually, and to increase in power the longer it continues – M. Marcillet produced a stiffening of the different extremities, and removed it at pleasure. So powerful was this, that as the youth sat in his chair with his legs extended horizontally, a gentleman present stood upon his unsupported thighs apparently without inconveniencing him. After a very few minutes, the operator having declared his patient to be in a state of clairvoyance, two of the visitors proceeded to bandage his eyes; first placing a quantity of wadding over each eye, they tied a handkerchief tightly round his head, two other handkerchiefs were then tied diagonally one over each eye, and different visitors satisfied themselves that vision in the ordinary was impossible, it was proposed that he should play a game of écarté. Dr Elliotson having sent out for a new pack of cards, the youth opened them and began discarding the small cards; this he did as quickly as if his eyes had been uncovered. I observed that he discarded two *sevens*, but these were his only mistakes. Captain Danniell was his opponent, and he played a game with perfect correctness. I next sat down myself and played a game with him, but by this time his powers seemed to have increased, for he frequently played without turning his cards, merely spreading them before him on the table with their backs upwards . . . Some books having been brought up out of the Doctor's library, a volume of Montaigne was placed in Alexis's hand, which he opened at random, after holding it a few seconds before his face, placed the book in the hands of a bystander, and read correctly a line which he pointed at. A large book of plates, &c., was then opened before him. Alexis described correctly one of the plates . . . M. Marcillet next proposed that he should describe some plates at the *back* of his head, but these experiments were only partially successful, as was afterwards the case when he attempted to point out the situation of the hands of watches by turning only the backs of them towards his eyes.

Alexis appeared to make a series of even more wayward observations when taking the hand of MP Edmund Phipps and imagining himself in his Park Lane home. Opposite the fireplace in the drawing room, the young clairvoyant observed a picture of a battle scene, with a crowned figure holding a truncheon. The description made no impression on Phipps. Alexis insisted that the picture was there, exactly as described, and that Phipps should examine it on returning home. On inspecting the picture with Henry Atkinson, it transpired that Alexis's description had been perfectly correct. His clairvoyance was, they both agreed, 'of too striking and curious a nature to be the effects of a lucky guess'. A sceptical *Times* reporter who had attended the same séance was also swayed: 'Without admitting that we have become believers in the possibility of producing such a condition as that known by the name of clairvoyance, we must nevertheless honestly confess that we have been staggered by what we saw.'

At subsequent séances at the homes of Lord Adare, Lady Blessington and the medical publisher Henri Baillière, and in numerous public demonstrations at a concert hall on Mortimer Street, Alexis's wondrous powers seemed to waver. While Marcillet invariably attributed these failures to the rudeness and impertinence of spectators, Elliotson's circle began to express some doubts as to the integrity of mesmerist and somnambule. Alexis's tendency to touch his bandage while playing écarté, and his 'unfortunate habit' of thinking aloud when travelling clairvoyantly or attempting to read sealed letters, did not go unnoticed. These suspicions did not, however, prompt Elliotson and his fellow mesmerists to apply more stringent test controls. The only misgiving that the *Zoist* ventured to level was directed at Marcillet, who was accused of overworking Alexis.

One physician who harboured more serious doubts as to the veracity of Alexis's clairvoyant powers was John Forbes (1787–1861), physician to the Queen's household and editor of the *British and Foreign Medical Review*. An astute and open-minded critic of various heterodoxies, from phrenology to homeopathy, Forbes had, like Elliotson, done much to promote use of the stethoscope and other Continental methods of diagnosis and treatment. His first impression of mesmerism was that the 'minor marvels' such as catalepsy and insensibility to pain were quite genuine; the higher phenomena almost certainly fraudulent or contrived. Forbes first saw Alexis, 'the pet, pride, and glory of all professed mesmerists', in action at a Mortimer Street matinée on 11 July 1844. Forbes and his companion, the physiologist William Carpenter, were less than impressed: 'The conduct of Alexis throughout was altogether that of a man who was playing a deceptive part, and looking in all directions for help in his efforts to succeed in what was given him to do.'

Before playing écarté moderately well, Forbes noticed that Alexis repeatedly touched and shifted his bandages, pressing a knuckle into the hollow of each eye. Once the bandages were removed, so that he might read *through* the books that members of the audience presented him with, Alexis was seen casually turning over the leaves, allowing himself a sideways sight of the words. In subsequent experiments designed to demonstrate Alexis's ability to read slips of folded paper and words contained in sealed packages, 'he and his friends made unconceded attempts to wheedle the party who gave the word, into conceding something as to help him in solving the problem'. Yet even with the clues provided by the willing colluders, Forbes noted that Alexis's blunders and failures outnumbered his slight successes. Failing to perceive 'one single unequivocal example' of his reputed powers, Alexis's exhibition suggested that the growing belief in clairvoyance and other mesmeric wonders was a result of spectators who were either 'totally unacquainted with the laws of evidence, or too enthusiastic in temperament to be guided by them'. According to Forbes, the spectators 'admitted, as positive facts, what appeared to calm unprejudiced observers, not only not facts, but the merest assumptions, unsupported by a tittle of the kind of evidence required in scientific investigation. It was also evident that there was, among such persons, an endeavour to *help* the exhibitor to get at the results proposed, and an eagerness to believe everything without question.'

The kinds of collusion, 'fishing' and diversion on which Alexis's clairvoyance relied became more evident at a private séance given at Forbes's Westminster home. Having noted Marcillet's habit of attributing Alexis's failures to the 'impolite' or 'hostile' interference of spectators, Forbes maintained a stony silence throughout. Once again, Alexis struggled to find his focus. In what Forbes considered the 'experimentum crucis', Alexis was given five envelopes, some folded and some sealed, each containing a word that was known to no one besides himself. After long deliberation, and much pressing of the envelopes, Alexis intimated that the first might contain a written, not printed, word of perhaps three letters. With Forbes steadfastly ignoring all conjecture, Marcillet stood up to denounce the spirit in which proceedings were undertaken. But Forbes remained tight-lipped, prompting Alexis to throw down the envelopes and refuse to undertake further trials. After consoling his crestfallen protégé, Marcillet began to berate Forbes for allowing one of his friends to take notes of the proceedings.

Almost all the printed and oral accounts of mesmeric clairvoyance were, Forbes contended, 'utterly valueless, from being defective in exact and minute details'. Recognising that a truly scientific study of séance phenomena would require precise recording of the actions and words of all parties, Forbes thought that the widespread belief in clairvoyance could be ascribed to 'a proneness of faith' – a faith which led observers to marvel at apparently successful demonstrations while ignoring numerous failures. Alexis's performance was stage magic masquerading as scientific curiosity. Capitalising on the readiness with which mesmerists like Elliotson greeted new trance phenomena, Marcillet had pioneered a new form of psychological illusion.

Hailed as '*Wakley secundus*' by Elliotson's supporters, Forbes's investigations were denounced as 'unscientific', 'dishonest' and 'disgraceful'. Insisting that he had failed to detect any proof of fraud in Alexis's exhibitions, the *Zoist* mounted an energetic defence of Alexis, arguing that ill health had caused his powers to diminish. But Forbes continued to expose the trickery and self-delusion behind the ongoing reports of clairvoyance and, on reading Harriet Martineau's *Letters on Mesmerism*, he was struck by the author's description of her housemaid's transformation into a clairvoyante and 'true somnambule'.

Martinauu claimed that the teenage domestic had, during a

series of séances led by Mrs Wynward, foretold the exact time that she would awake with unerring accuracy, grasped the nature of disease, diagnosed appropriate remedies, understood foreign languages, reported what others were silently thinking, held her own extemporising on the distinction between the mind and the soul, and accessed news that could not be obtained by 'ordinary means'. Jane's powers of clairvoyance were revealed after her aunt, Mrs Arrowsmith, received news that the ship her son was sailing on had been wrecked near Hull. With Mrs Arrowsmith away in Shields attempting to secure news from the ship's owner, Mrs Wynward quickly mesmerised Jane and asked her what she knew of the wreck. Jane explained that the boat was 'all to pieces' and that a 'queer boat' had saved all aboard except for a boy who had fallen from mast to rigging.

After being woken and sent over to her aunt's, Jane returned to confirm that all the crew were saved – except one boy who was killed after falling through the rigging. Two days on, 'J[ane] was asked, when in sleep, whether she knew what she related to us by seeing her aunt telling people below, "No; I saw the place and people themselves – like a vision."' Satisfied that there had been no contact between Jane Arrowsmith and her aunt previous to the séance, Martineau announced that clairvoyance was the only credible explanation for her insight.

On commissioning a Tyneside physician, Dr Brown, to procure information on the 'human manner' in which the account of the shipwreck might have reached Jane Arrowsmith, Forbes found that news of the shipwreck had been conveyed to Miss Arrowsmith *before* the séance had commenced. Martineau had, he concluded, been swayed by Mrs Wynward's attempts to claim Jane's revelations as 'indubitable proof of the truths of mesmerism'. Martineau published a lame reply, reaffirming her faith in Jane Arrowsmith's integrity and insinuating that Brown might have induced Jane's relations to contradict themselves. Her failure to provide names, dates and authenticated witnesses was widely remarked upon. the *Critic*, a periodical that had recently undertaken to defend mesmerism from 'the condemnation of the ignorant', found in favour of Forbes. It called upon the observers of mesmerism to provide 'careful and anxious assurance of the facts of any case, before they publish it'.

Forbes's 'fatal explosion of mesmerism and its pretended wonders' received substantial coverage in the medical and popular press. The *Medical Gazette* suggested that Forbes had finally 'stripped off the flimsy veil of imposition, under which these mountebanks attempted to deceive the public. There never was exhibition so pitiful – never exposure so luminous – never defeat so complete.' While many periodicals that had been well disposed towards mesmerism followed suit, *Punch* imagined the practical use that such a faculty might be put to at customs houses, where mesmerically trained workers would finally be able to avoid opening parcels and spilling their contents over the floor.

The London mesmerists used the pages of the *Zoist* to conduct a two-pronged counter-attack. While gathering a catalogue of testimonies from notable witnesses to Didier's clairvoyance, they retrieved scattered evidence of the natural history of clairvoyance, including the extraordinary insights of Swedenborg and Wesley. In the meantime a stream of motley wonder workers attempted to cash in on the public fascination with clairvoyance that Didier's exhibitions had kindled. The first of these, the improbably titled San Milan Tecmen (aka Madame Tecmen de Mexico) hung up her shingle in Portman Square and enjoyed some success before moving on to

Cheltenham. Madame Tecmen was followed by Adolph Didier, brother to Alexis, who drew large audiences at exhibitions with William Vernon, by stage clairvoyants such as 'Somnambule Jane' and 'The Prophetic Lady', and by the flamboyant 'Rabbi Professor Dannemark of Hungary'. Unlike most of the travelling professors who brought mesmerism to the lecture circuit, Dannemark claimed to be naturally possessed of 'extraordinary powers of memory and sight, as well as the gift of divination'. Armed with testimonials from European nobility and a large ring that he claimed was a gift from the Pope, the rabbi had the chutzpah to insist that his audiences stood respectfully while he attempted to identify sealed words and boxed objects.

The somnambules employed by mesmeric doctors and professors were, in stark contrast to Dannemark, artless and barely literate ingénues. One of the best-known of London's clairvoyant somnambules, Ellen Dawson, was a young epileptic who went on to enjoy a moment of brief celebrity when her clairvoyant powers helped secure the return of stolen jewellery. Originally a patient of Baron Dupotet's, Dawson recommenced her 'magnetic treatment' with Dr William Hands of Grosvenor Square in 1844. After four weeks of daily passes, Hands began a series of experiments on her cerebral organs and found that her faculties could easily be excited by contact. When Ellen began to prescribe her own medicine and treatment (requesting that she should be bled and have teeth removed to prevent her fits from returning), Hands began to look out for outward signs of clairvoyance in his young somnambule:

> One day Ellen being in the sleep-waking state, I observed her take up some publication which lay on the table and read the titles of them, by which I perceived she was clairvoyant. In order

to test this faculty, I filled the tops of some pill-boxes with cotton and tied them over her eyes with a fillet of ribbon, taking care the edges of the boxes should rest upon the skin; still, she read and distinguished colours as before. I now placed her in a room from which I had shut out *every ray of light*, and then presented to her some of the plates in *Cuvier's Animal Kingdom*; she described the birds and beasts, and told accurately the colour of each, as I proved by going into the light to test her statements. She also distinguished the shades and hues of silks, as indeed did her sister, who is also clairvoyant . . . I frankly own that none of the facts in chemistry, experimental philosophy, or physiology, ever gave me such delight as I experienced on discovering that she could do so.

During subsequent trials of travelling clairvoyance, Dr Hands led Ellen to Berkeley in northern California, where she spied on Mrs Hands playing cards with an elderly gentleman and two young ladies. Travelling east to New York, Ellen made her way to the Broadway home of Hands's brother, correctly describing the black enamel ring that he wore on his forefinger. And, in the company of her sister, Ellen went on to, identify the names of several vessels in New York harbour. This American journey was, for Dr Hands, striking and beautiful proof of genuine clairvoyance: 'It may here be well to remark that these children are uneducated, and have never read of these places. Had this been the case they would not have been taken so much by surprise, nor have experienced wonder on seeing what they did.'

While lesser clairvoyantes were only thought capable of securing information by 'thought-reading' or 'mental-transfer', Ellen became renowned for obtaining information that was never known to her sitters. Championed by Lady Carolina

Courtenay Boyle, and utilised by numerous mesmerists, Ellen quickly established her credentials. In 1849, after the recovery of stolen jewellery, her clairvoyant powers were widely noticed. In an article in the women's monthly *La Belle Assemble*, a Mrs M told how Mr Barth, a well-known mesmerist from Oakley Square, had procured an interview with Ellen, confident that she would be able to identify the thief and the whereabouts of her precious brooch. After Ellen being mesmerised by Dr Hands:

> [Mr B] inquired if she would like to travel with us and talk to us; she replied in the affirmative. He asked her if she could tell what I came to see her about: in a few minutes she answered, 'about a loss – about something she has lost'. She then knelt down by my side, when I took hold of her hands and commenced telling my grievance to her. I began by saying she was right – I had lost something that I wanted her to tell me about. She first said money, to which I replied, 'No.' Then she said property, to which I assented. Mr Barth then proposed that she should go (ideally of course) to my house, to the place from where the missing article was taken, and thus discover what I had lost, and how it had disappeared. I told her then where my residence was . . . what route to take, and she soon reached the house – described the exterior, so that I knew she was right, then went into my bed-room, where she gave a very minute account of the furniture. I then directed her attention to the place from where the article had been taken, and she soon found what I had lost. She first said jewellery; and when I asked her what kind, she answered, a brooch. I inquired what it was like; to which she gave a wonderfully accurate answer; she said it looked like *amber* surrounded with white. She then said that it was some time since I had lost it, that it was very old, and had been a long time in the

family. She then told me I had been out of town, which I was during the month of September. Finding her account and description so very correct in every particular, she was now told to keep her eye upon the brooch and see what became of it. She then described, in words not to be mistaken, the person who had taken it out of its accustomed place; in fact, no artist could have painted a more perfect resemblance; and it was a servant whom I never suspected . . . She then said she saw a shop window, that the brooch was in a queer place like a cellar with lots of other property – silver spoons and other things; but a cloud came and she could see no more.

Following Ellen's instructions, Mrs M was said to have secured an interview with the suspected thief, pointing out 'the enormity of the crime and the certainty of Almighty vengeance' should the brooch not be restored to its natural owner. After long protestations of innocence, the servant apparently repented and returned a pawnbroker's duplicate for the brooch.

Another equally noted clairvoyante of the 1840s, Emma L, also became known for her ability to trace lost items and missing persons. Emma, maid of all work to a Bolton apothecary and mesmerist, Dr Joseph Haddock, first exhibited her nascent powers of clairvoyance at the local temperance hall in late 1848. Unfortunately, Emma's nervousness when presented with parcels and envelopes caused her special 'glasses' (with which she imagined herself endowed when mesmerised) to darken and obscure her vision. Haddock had a ready explanation for Emma's failure: 'in the exalted condition of mesmerism, her mind was peculiarly susceptible of impressions from the minds of surrounding persons; hence when environed by a knot of sceptics . . . their mental influence, unconsciously to themselves, would seriously impede her powers'. To make matters worse, other members of the audience supposed that Emma saw by means of common vision. Expecting her to describe promptly the contents of these packages, they were intolerant of her deliberations.

In private consultation, in the parlour of Dr Haddock's shop, Emma's clairvoyance flourished. In December 1848 she assisted a tea dealer from Bolton in recovering a stolen cash box. A year on, Messrs P. R. Arrowsmith & Co. availed themselves of Emma's services in recovering £650 that appeared to have been lost or stolen. Following several consultations with Emma, the Bradford businessmen found that notes and bills had been misplaced by a bank clerk 'just as the clairvoyante had described them'. Emma's role in the recovery of Messrs Arrowsmith's money was widely noticed in the local and national press, prompting numerous applications for assistance in locating missing items and persons.

One of the many visitors who called on Emma in the aftermath of the Arrowsmith case was Harriet Martineau. Arriving unannounced at Dr Haddock's shop in February 1849, Martineau was keen to see the girl 'whose strange powers as a somnambule had just become known by accident'. '[A] vulgar girl, anything but handsome, and extremely ignorant', Emma was very quickly mesmerised and given a tightly folded letter. Clasping the letter close to her chest, she proceeded to describe the gentleman who wrote it and clairvoyantly to follow him up and down his drawing room. On being instructed to proceed into an adjoining room, Emma described some cut stones and a collection of heads, which she recoiled from. Martineau was deeply impressed. The gentleman in question was Henry Atkinson, the cut stones were fragments of the Elgin Marbles, and the heads were 'cast from a family of idiots in Norfolk – hideous beyond expression'.

A more pressing enquiry came from a 'naval gentleman', a friend of the lost Arctic explorer Sir John Franklin. Franklin had left England on 19 May 1845, taking two ships and 129 men on an expedition to find the Northwest Passage. Attempting to navigate the dense maze of ice-locked islands past Baffin Bay, Franklin entered uncharted territory and disappeared. With the nation desperate for news of Franklin's heroic enterprise, the Admiralty dispatched forty ships on an unprecedented rescue mission, but the whereabouts and fate of HMS *Erebus* and HMS *Terror* remained a subject of endless speculation. Haddock believed that Franklin and his crew were dead, and that Emma would arrive at the same conclusion.

To Haddock's surprise, an entranced Emma 'spoke of the snow, ice, &c., of the place where the writer was; said that many with him were dead, but that he was alive, and expected to get away in about nine months'. In several subsequent sittings she followed Franklin through 'other climes', going on to describe his progress homewards. Nine months on, with Franklin almost certainly perished, Haddock began to regret the publicity that Emma's statements had received in the *Manchester Guardian*.

The many somnambules who were asked to track John Franklin's progress through the Arctic wilderness in the years following his disappearance were eventually confronted with damning news. In 1859 a final search mission sent by Lady Franklin reached King William Island, 500 miles south-west of where Franklin was last sighted. Here, they found the remains of some of the crew and a record of the early years of the expedition. The log revealed that Franklin had died in April 1848, while the survivors had perished while travelling south, by foot, to the American mainland. Given that Emma L had spotted Franklin alive and making his way home in 1849, how had her clairvoyant powers betrayed her? In Dr Haddock's mind there was only one explanation: since every action of a man's life leaves 'an indelible trace, perceptible to a sufficiently lucid clairvoyante', Emma could easily have mistaken Franklin's ghostly vestiges for his living presence.

Emma had made her first sorties to the spirit world in the spring and summer of 1848. At first, Haddock hesitated to mention Emma's 'spontaneous states of exstasis', as her revelations were opposed to his 'preconceived opinions' on the afterlife and contained much of a 'private character'. In a later edition of his book *Somnolism and Psycheism* he revealed that one of the spirits Emma conversed with in these trances was a near relative who had died ten years previously. It was to this nameless lady that Emma owed her first introduction to the whys and wherefores of the Other World:

> Man is represented as a spiritual being, rising from what she calls 'the shell' of the dead material body, immediately after death; or as soon as the connection between the soul and its material covering is completely severed, which she says, does not sometimes occur, until a day or two after what appears as death. The risen and emancipated spirit is a perfectly organised existence, preserving the human form, and having a complete *sensational perception* of his fellow spiritual beings, and of the beautiful scenery of the spiritual spheres; that is, provided he possessed during his natural life, a moral state in harmony with those spheres. The male and female sex retaining all the characteristics necessary to a spiritual state of existence, being united as to their minds. Those who have been interiorly united here, coming into a state of union hereafter; those who have not been *mentally*

united here, seek their true *mental* counterpart . . . Infants and young children who have passed from this world by death, are stated to grow to a state of adolescence, but more speedily than in the natural world. During infancy and early childhood, they are confined to the care of good female spirits, or angels, whose delight it is, to instruct them by various methods, especially by *representations of things*, which form a sort of pictorial teaching . . . The first receptacle, or common place of departed spirits, she describes as a sort of *middle state* or place. From which the good, as they become prepared, ascend gradually, to higher and more delightful places; those that are the best having higher abodes than others. All, she says, are welcomed by angelic spirits on their arrival in the spirit-world; but *the evil will not associate with the good*, and *recede of their own accord*, more or less rapidly, to darker places below this middle state . . .

Emma's philosophy of the spirit world was thoroughly Swedenborgian, echoing the mystical pronouncements of Andrew Davis Jackson, Friedericke Hauffe and the somnambules of Alphonse Cahagnet, all of whom had discovered the spirit world in mesmeric trance. Haddock was convinced that Emma could not have derived knowledge of Swedenborg's teaching through any 'ordinary means'. Her religious education had not introduced her to any nonconformist credos; she had been taught to read a little as a child, but claimed to have lost the acquirement through a fever. Believing that Emma could not tell the letters of the alphabet, Haddock held 'her statements, whether true or false, as independent as any which have been made before, and as far as I know, wholly uninfluenced, by anything I have read, or any opinions I may have entertained'.

While Haddock failed in employing Emma's 'spontaneous

trances' to solicit information on the 'most intricate points of physiology', he found that by mesmerising Emma she was able to sustain contact with the spirit world. If required to diagnose and prescribe for her sitters, Emma now made recourse to 'the lady' who invariably recommended mesmeric passes (in the case of cerebral disease) or homeopathic medicine from Mr Turner's chemist in Piccadilly. On another occasion, when Haddock was contacted by a gentleman wishing to investigate a murder, Emma apparently obtained vital information *from the deceased* relating to the time, place and perpetrator of the attack. Once Haddock had overcome a slight uneasiness about the provenance of Emma's insight into the spirit world, he was convinced that her revelations might be used in 'unlocking the mysterious narratives of the New Testament' and dispelling 'that superstitious dread, which is entertained of another life'. For Haddock, Emma's clairvoyance signalled nothing less than the beginnings of 'a new science of the soul'.

While occultists, churchmen and military men attempted to secure the experimental services of clairvoyantes like Emma, their insights were also called on by heterodox physicians such as Dr Gully of Malvern (who relied on the services of a clairvoyant girl to report on the internal changes of patients undergoing the water cure) and news-hungry socialites like Isobel Burton (who consulted a somnambule to follow Captain Burton's progress through the eastern deserts of Abyssinia and into the walled city of Harar). Though Dickens's personal experience of mesmerism in the treatment of Madame de la Rue certainly disposed him towards a belief in the higher powers, the first literary figure to affirm the wonders of mesmeric clairvoyance was Wilkie Collins. Writing in the radical weekly the *Leader* in 1852, young Collins penned six unsigned letters describing a series of séances that he had attended at Weston-super-Mare. Collins confessed that he was enormously impressed by the marvellous answers proffered by the young somnambule, Mademoiselle V.

George Lewes, never shy of upbraiding his contemporaries for their 'vulgar errors', suggested that Mademoiselle V was most probably prompted by 'leading questions, by intonations, by the hundred suggestions of voice and manner'. Responding to these criticisms, Collins maintained that the questions put to Mademoiselle V were 'studiously confined to the simplest, baldest form of interrogatory', and that he had recorded the questions and answers exactly as he heard them spoken: '[M]y friend and myself were not duped by our own imaginations – not misted by any deception of our own sense – and not unmindful of using every precaution, as well as raising every fair difficulty in selecting and prosecuting our tests of clairvoyance.'

The facts of clairvoyance, as reported by Collins and other amateur investigators, were nevertheless endorsed by William Gregory, Professor of Chemistry at the University of Edinburgh. Gregory and his half-German wife had become interested in mesmerism in around 1843, when they began to host séances at their Princes Street home. Like Collins, Gregory was confident that 'it was relatively easy to render all deceit impossible' during trials of clairvoyance. Drawing on personal experiments, and the testimony of the many mesmerists he corresponded with, Gregory's *Letters to a Candid Inquirer on Animal Magnetism* identified the many forms of clairvoyance that had been observed. The first intimations of clairvoyance were, Gregory noted, usually observed in the first stages of mesmeric sleep, when entranced subjects sometimes perceived the hands of their operator and flashes of light emanating from their fingertips. Next, a certain proportion would apprehend objects placed behind them or concealed in opaque receptacles. In the travelling stage of clairvoyance, subjects not only spontaneously developed the power of sympathising with absent or unknown persons: they were also able to see deceased relatives and historical personages (which led Gregory to speculate that many obscure historical points might be settled by lucid clairvoyants). Lastly, clairvoyants might develop the facility to perceive the structure and interior of the human frame, to detect disease and make diagnoses for themselves and others. Gregory advised all well-qualified medical men fortunate enough to meet a good clairvoyant to avail themselves of his or her assistance in diagnosis.

Before the publication of Gregory's book a number of vaguely conceived theories had been put forward to explain the facts of clairvoyance. While writers such as Colquhoun and Townshend argued that clairvoyance refuted materialism, providing proof of the immortality of the soul, a significant number of mesmerists thought that clairvoyance could in most cases be explained as an epiphenomenon of thought reading or mental transfer. Gregory himself believed that the secrets of clairvoyance and other mesmeric phenomena had a natural explanation, which had been uncovered by Baron von Reichenbach, a widely respected Viennese chemist, metallurgist and expert on meteorites. After extensive research on the influence of magnets, crystals and human hands on the spontaneous somnambules, Reichenbach gathered detailed accounts of the luminous emanations that his sensitives reported and proposed the existence of a new force: Od. Described as 'nerve-stirring resultant of the general powers of cosmical nature', Reichenbach's 'odylic' force (as it became known to native mesmerists) was greeted as the imponderable agent that had eluded all previous investigators, including

Mesmer and Elliotson. Gregory's first condensed translation of Reichenbach's *Researches on Mesmerism* (1846) did much to sustain the belief that mesmerism and all its wonders could be ascribed to action of this physical agent. Haddock was not the only mesmerist to confirm that his own somnambule Emma had also seen fluid issuing from the points of his fingers.

Research into mesmeric clairvoyance eventually led Gregory into the recondite fringes of occultism, bringing him into contact with Stanhope, Bulwer-Lytton and the circle of crystal gazers that gathered at Gore House, where the enchanting Lady Blessington played host to London's most urbane and exotic students of magic. After experimenting with various crystals, mirrors and mesmerised water, Gregory concluded that the visions that were seen were neither the fruits of imposture nor suggestion. 'It appears certain that many children and adults have seen visions in crystals . . . the visions have very often been exactly such as are seen in ordinary clairvoyance; and on the whole, it appears that there are very interesting facts, whatever be their true nature, which require and deserve the most careful investigation.'

Gregory's findings were invoked some years later, in 1863, at the Courts of the Queen's Bench at Guildhall, during Lieutenant Richard Morrison's civil action for libel against Sir Edward Belcher. Belcher, the commander of one of the early expeditions in search of John Franklin, had made a series of jibes against Morrison, revealing that he employed child seers who 'pretended by their looking into the crystal globe, to hold converse with the spirits of the Apostles – even our Saviour . . . to tell what was going on in any part of the world'. The Lord Chief Justice exempted Morrison from charges of fraud but concluded his verdict with a back-handed swipe at the clairvoyant 'delusions' that filled the plaintiff's *Almanac*. It was a pyrrhic victory for Morrison (twenty shillings, no costs) and a sharp rebuke for any respectable person who lent credence to the tell-tale visions of seers and somnambules.

Chapter Seven

Tea and Table Moving

These transatlantic ghosts are superlative idiots
William Aytoun, *Blackwood's Edinburgh Magazine*, 1853

If the discovery of chemical anaesthesia dealt the first decisive blow to mesmerism's medical ambitions, its demise as a popular science was sealed by the arrival of another American-born enchantment – spiritualism. Still in its infancy, the American spiritualist movement was born in a small timber farmhouse in the village of Hydesville, Wayne County, New York. Here, on the night of 31 March 1848, Mr and Mrs Fox, tenants of the remote and reputedly haunted house, found that their two youngest daughters, Kate and Margaret, could induce their 'invisible visitor' to answer questions. After a series of knocks indicated that the spirit was amenable to further interrogation, the Foxes invited a succession of neighbours to address the mysterious poltergeist. Knocking for *yes* and remaining silent for *no*, the spirit confirmed that he was the ghost of a murdered pedlar. The curiosity of Isaac Post, a Quaker abolitionist from neighbouring Rochester, was roused. Post was beguiled by the possibility of establishing a bridge to the Other World, and it was his idea to allow the spirits to rap their response to questions while the alphabet was slowly recited in séances with the sisters.

Eventually, Post arranged for the sisters to make their first public appearance at the Corinthian Hall. Six months on, Kate and Margaret were induced to transfer to rooms at Barnum's Hotel in New York City, where they began their careers as professional mediums in earnest. With news of spiritualism spreading 'like a prairie fire', spirit circles sprang up in every town in northern and eastern states of the Union, becoming especially prevalent among Unitarians, Universalists and Quakers. 'Spiritualism's denial of death', as Ann Braude observes, 'offered a unique kind of consolation to the bereaved. Messages frequently focused on the spirit's happiness after death and continued concern for family members . . . Spirits claimed that their estate after death was a pleasant one and did not merit mourning.'

The leading lights of this new religion-cum-parlour game were generally young women who, following the example of the Misses Fox, assumed responsibility for contacting deceased family members. But spirit communication by way of the alphabet soon gave way to more direct modes of mediumship, such as automatic writing and trance oratory, and private and public séances provided a platform where entranced women spoke with remarkable fluency on matters of religion, philosophy and politics. 'That a young lady not over eighteen years of age should speak for an hour and a quarter, in such an eloquent manner, with such logical and philosophical clearness' was widely regarded as sufficient evidence 'of a power not natural to the education of the speaker'. Emerson, like many Boston intellectuals, was particularly aggrieved by this growing swathe of 'unlearned' professional mediums. Considering the new employment opportunities that the decade had presented, it was with begrudging reluctance that he listed the medium alongside the daguerreotypist, landscape gardener and railroad man.

Maria Hayden, the first spiritualist emissary to cross the Atlantic, left Boston in October 1852, only a few months after calling on the services of a medium at her child's funeral. Accompanied by her husband, the newspaper editor and journalist William Hayden, and by William Stone, a fast-talking professor of 'electrobiology', Mrs Hayden took up residence in Portman Square and advertised her services ('Spiritual Phenomena or Manifestations' from '12 to 3 and 4 to 6') in *The Times*. With the two Williams aggressively championing Mrs Hayden's powers as a conduit to the spirit world, there was no shortage of visitors who were happy to forfeit a guinea to hear the tappings of the spiritual telegraph. Following a format favoured in American spirit circles, Mrs Hayden's séances were essentially Q & A sessions in which sitters were given printed alphabets and invited to pose questions. While slowly reciting or running their fingers over the alphabet, an audible rap or tilting of the table would indicate each letter of the message that was being spelled out. Within a few weeks of Mrs Hayden's arrival, news of these other-worldly messages was sufficient to prompt a visit from Messrs 'Brown and Thompson', who went on to pen a knockabout account of 'a sitting that was not enlivened by one happy guess' for *Household Words*, the popular weekly magazine that Dickens had begun to edit in 1850.

The press was largely united in condemning the spiritual raps as pure folly. George Lewes (fresh from uncovering the humbug that Dickens had perpetuated in submitting *Bleak House*'s Krook to death by spontaneous combustion) left the offices of the *Leader* determined to have some fun at Mrs Hayden's expense. Hesitating at the appropriate letters, Lewes induced the spirits to reveal that Mrs Hayden was an impostor, that her domestic relations were somewhat questionable and that Hamlet's father had seventeen noses. Lewes took truculent delight in exposing this patent trickery in the *Leader*, and *Blackwood's Magazine* was equally forthright in drubbing Mrs Hayden's spirit rapping as 'pointless idiocy' and 'frightful drivel'. Before the end of the year, *The Times* refused to carry further advertising for Mrs Hayden, Mrs Roberts, Professor Hardinge or any of the professional mediums who were now plying their trade in the capital.

Despite the largely negative publicity that she received in print, Mrs Hayden's questionable powers succeeded in generating serious attention in the London salons and studios. In May 1853 Dr J. J. Garth Wilkinson, a Swedenborgian physician and homeopath, wrote to his close friend Henry James Snr, describing the commotion Mrs Hayden's séances had produced:

> Nothing is talked of here but table mowings [sic] and spirit rappings. There is, as far as I know, no class of persons of importance who are not yet penetrated with this odd-looking movement. The only people who are actually contra are the stony materialists and the gassy philosophers: both of them hate this noise which the approaching spiritual world makes with its big toes. The pious Atheists too want Mrs Hayden and her coadjutor to be put in prison: she is, they say blasphemous; and degrades the mighty dead by summoning them to her table: as if

After publishing his *Mémoire sur la découverte du magnétisme animal* in 1799, Franz Anton Mesmer (1734–1815) set up clinic at the Hotel Bullion, employing two *baquets* filled with 'magnetised' water to minister to the Parisian *haut monde* – and the charitable poor (back left, huddled round a smaller *baquet*). Patients responded to the waves of magnetic fluid, which Mesmer helped direct with his iron wand, by falling into a convulsive 'crisis' which alleviated a myriad of ailments.

Founded in 1834, University College Hospital provided medical and surgical training for 'godless' students from the University of London. When clinical clerks began to dabble with mesmerism on the wards, the Gower Street hospital was branded a 'seminary for mountebankery'.

John Elliotson (1791–1868) was the first English physician of repute to endorse the use of mesmerism. After resigning his position as professor of medicine at University College Hospital, Elliotson went on to found *The Zoist*, a quarterly journal which championed mesmerism, phrenology and other left field heterodoxies. The séances which Elliotson regularly hosted at his Conduit Street home provided a stream of famous Londoners with their first introduction to the mysteries of 'artificial somnambulism'.

As editor of the *Lancet*, Thomas Wakley (1795–1862) gave robust support to therapeutic trials of mesmerism. When public opinion turned against the 'Gallic mummery' Wakley conducted experiments of his own, concluding that Elliotson's principal subjects, the Okey sisters, had been 'unwittingly *tempted* into a course of deception'.

A FULL DISCOVERY
OF THE
STRANGE PRACTICES
OF
Dr. ELLIOTSON
On the bodies of his
FEMALE PATIENTS!
AT HIS HOUSE, IN CONDUIT STREET, HANOVER SQ.
WITH ALL THE SECRET
EXPERIMENTS HE MAKES UPON THEM,
AND THE
Curious Postures they are put into while sitting or standing, when awake or asleep!

A female Patient being blindfolded, to undergo an operation.

THE WHOLE AS SEEN
BY AN EYE-WITNESS,
AND NOW FULLY DIVULGED!
&c. &c. &c.

A number of chapbooks from the early 1840s purported to reveal the sinister experiments which Elliotson was subjecting female patients to in the name of medical science. This eye-witness account (pirated from the *Edinburgh Journal*) was nowhere near as lurid as readers might have hoped for.

In this *Punch* cartoon from 1843, John Elliotson is seen performing phreno-mesmerism, exciting the cerebral organs of his entranced patient. A year earlier, at a meeting of the London Phrenological Association, Elliotson had announced that the fusion of mesmerism and phrenology was 'the grandest phenomenon ever brought to light by man', but his enthusiasm for the hybrid science quickly waned.

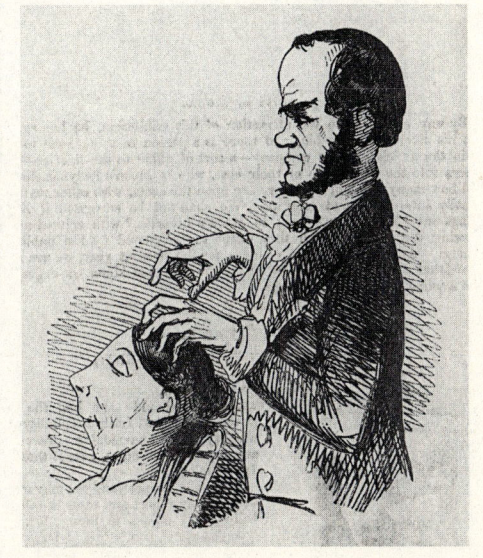

In 1852, the historian Thomas Macaulay (1800–1859) visited an unnamed expert who specialised in 'feats of phrenology and mesmerism'. After pawing at the bumps of Macaulay's head, and using a pendulum-like device to measure the vital influence emitted by his phrenological organs, the 'Dr' deduced that Macaulay was almost certainly a painter.

Alexis Didier (1826–1886), the most celebrated 'travelling clairvoyant' of the nineteenth century, specialised in reading closed books, recovering lost objects and playing blindfolded cards and billiards.

Between 1847 and 1859, when a series of expeditions was launched to locate the whereabouts of the Arctic explorer Sir John Franklin (1786–1847), a number of English clairvoyants volunteered information which suggested that Franklin and his crew were alive and well.

Victorian mesmerists claimed that the well-known Irish healer Valentine Greatrakes (1629–1683) had unwittingly harnessed the power of animal magnetism to effect his cures. Routinely accused of sorcery, Greatrakes stroked the most enfeebled parts of his patents' bodies, expelling 'morbifick matter' by vigorously rubbing the extremities.

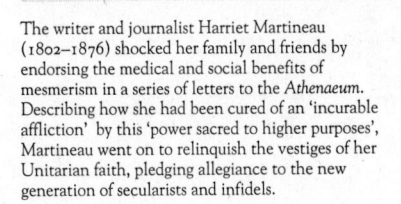

The writer and journalist Harriet Martineau (1802–1876) shocked her family and friends by endorsing the medical and social benefits of mesmerism in a series of letters to the *Athenaeum*. Describing how she had been cured of an 'incurable affliction' by this 'power sacred to higher purposes', Martineau went on to relinquish the vestiges of her Unitarian faith, pledging allegiance to the new generation of secularists and infidels.

Margaret, Kate and Leah Fox, spiritualism's first 'unwilling martyrs', embarked on lengthy careers as professional mediums after communicating with the rapping spirit of a Hydesville peddler in 1848. Forty years on, Margaret appeared at the New York Academy of Music, revealing that she had produced the rapping sounds by cracking her toe joints.

In 1853, English spiritualist circles experienced an 'epidemic' of table moving. All classes of Victorian society found that the spirits would happily communicate by tilting and rotating furniture which sitters laid their hands upon.

Daniel Dunglas Home (1833–1866) forged a towering reputation as a physical medium in the 1850s, giving séances for Italian, German and Russian royalty. Never 'paid' for his services, he was not averse to receiving extravagant gifts. After being tried for defrauding Mrs Jane Lyon of sixty thousand pounds in 1868, Home staged his most famous feat, the Ashley Place levitation, allegedly floating in and out of a third-floor room.

The slate-writing medium Henry Slade was prosecuted under the Vagrancy Act in 1876. This illustration from *The Graphic* shows Professor Ray Lankester at Bow Street Court, demonstrating how he detected Slade's trickery.

Michael Faraday (1791–1867) devised a series of ingenious trials at the Royal Institution which demonstrated that table moving was due to unconscious muscular action. The spiritualists rejected such 'learned theories', insisting that the tilting of tables was, like mesmerism, most probably due to the agency of a mysterious 'subtle matter which pervades all nature'.

Reverend William Stainton Moses (1839–1892), English spiritualism's most respectable and prolific medium. The full extent of Moses's contact with the spirit world emerged after his death, when notebooks revealed messages from a dizzying assembly of fifty or so biblical sages and ancient philosophers.

The naturalist Alfred Russel Wallace (1823–1903) was one of a number of respected Victorian scientists who lent credence to the 'extraordinary phenomena' witnessed at mesmeric and spiritualist séances. Wallace is here photographed alongside a 'spirit' summoned during a séance with Mrs Guppy.

The Boston-born medium Leonora Piper (1859–1950) remains the most credible and psychologically intriguing of all the mediums that fell under the scrutiny of the English Society for Psychical Research.

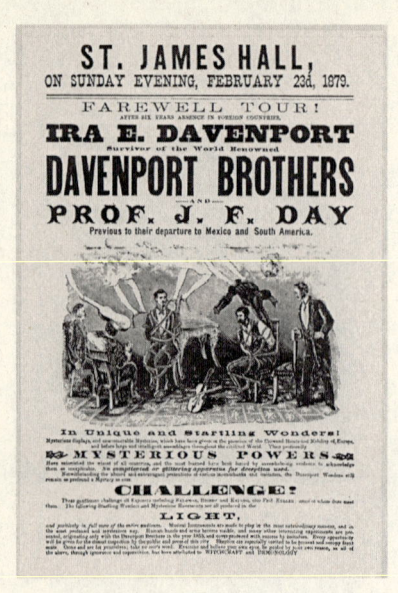

The American mediums Ira and William Davenport brought their cabinet jugglery to English theatres in 1864. After facing hostile crowds in the North, the Davenports left for France, performing for the Empress Napoleon. Returning to England in 1868, they agreed to undertake trial séances for the Anthropological Society but found the conditions in which they were required to work unacceptable.

Spiritualism's most formidable enemy, John Nevil Maskelyne (1838–1917), enjoyed great success at Piccadilly's Egyptian Hall imitating the manifestations produced by mediums such as the Davenports. The cover of Maskelyne's *Modern Spiritualism* (1876) shows Mrs Agnes Guppy, a medium who was renowned for her aerial transportations, being spirited to a North London séance.

Shortly after her fourteenth birthday, Florence Cook (1856–1904) began to materialise into 'Katie King' – the wife of the buccaneering John King, a ubiquitous spirit control who assisted many Victorian mediums – becoming a star attraction at London séances. Florence was eventually exposed at a dark séance in 1880, when two sitters grabbed at her latest alter-ego, 'Marie', and found a flesh and blood medium dressed for the part.

the meanest degradation were not infinitely superior to the annihilation which Man has been consigned to by Philosophers and Atheists.

The séances that Mrs Hayden undertook relied on the alphabetic mode of spirit communication that Isaac Post had deployed with the Fox sisters. A noise similar to that of knitting needles dropping on to marble indicated each letter of a given message, and 'a hailstorm of knitting needles' was sometimes heard when the numerous spirits attempted to make themselves heard simultaneously. This method was sufficient to stimulate the curiosity of a small number of high-profile socialites and intellectuals, including Robert Chambers and Augustus de Morgan, but the majority of Mrs Hayden's sitters appear to have been disappointed by England's first spiritual medium. Arthur Conan Doyle's *History of Spiritualism* offers a simple defence. Writing in the 1920s, Conan Doyle blamed Lewes and other 'pseudo-researchers' for Mrs Hayden's failures. This 'remarkable woman' and 'excellent medium' was, he contended, the innocent victim of an unbelieving press and narrow-minded pulpit: 'Like all true mediums, she was sensitive to discord in her surroundings, with the result that the contemptible crew of practical jokers and ill-natured researchers who visited her found her a ready victim. Deceit is repaid by deceit and the fool is answered according to his folly.'

Discounting the testimony of sceptics who exposed the American medium to 'the crushing force of antagonism', Conan Doyle preferred the evidence presented by the more chivalrous and less discerning sitters. Among these wide-eyed converts was Julian Charles Young, rector of Southwick, whose self-confessed 'weakness for the mystic and supernatural' led him to attend his first séance. Young was 'astounded' by the following communication, solicited during a visit to Mrs Hayden's home in April 1853:

MRS H[ayden]: Have you, sir, any wish to communicate with the spirit of a departed friend?
J.C.Y.: Yes.
MRS H: Be pleased then to ask your question in the manner described by the formula, and I dare say you will get satisfactory replies.
J.C.Y.: (*addressing himself to one invisible yet supposed to be present*): Tell me the name of the person I wish to communicate with.
The letters written down according to the dictation of the taps when put together spelt 'George William Young'.
J.C.Y.: On whom are my thoughts now fixed?
A[nswer]: Frederik William Young.
J.C.Y.: What is he suffering from?
A: Tic Douloureux.
J.C.Y.: Can you prescribe anything for him?
A: Powerful mesmerism.
J.C.Y.: Who should be the administrator?
A: Someone who has strong sympathy with the patient.
J.C.Y.: Should I succeed?
A: No.
J.C.Y.: Who would?
A: Joseph Ries. (*A gentleman whom my uncle much respected.*)

Much to Elliotson's chagrin many of the figures who supplied testimonies to Mrs Hayden's spiritual manifestations were, he barked in the *Zoist*, 'persons qualified for admission into the asylum for idiots or Bedlam Hospital'. Elliotson's close friend John Ashburner, a royal physician who had recently helped found the London Mesmeric Hospital, hurried to Mrs Hayden's defence, insisting that he had 'calmly, deliberately and very cautiously studied' the American medium and obtained 'telegraphic raps' from his father. During their protracted conversation Ashburner's father confirmed the date and place of his death, answering correctly all the questions that were silently put to him. In a letter to Lewes, Ashburner gave notice of his defection to the new spiritualist faith:

> A battle is to be fought for the new manifestations. I have no hesitation in saying, that, much as I have seen of mesmerism and clairvoyance – grand as were my anticipations of the vast amount of good to accrue to the human race, in mental and physical improvement . . . all sinks into shade and comparative insignificance, in the contemplation of those consequences which must result from the Spirit Manifestations . . . Animal magnetism and its consequences appeared marvellous to petty minds. The Spirit Manifestations have, in the last three weeks, produced *miracles*, and many more will, ere long, astound the would-be considered philosophers, who may continue to deny and sneer at the most obvious facts.

This was the second momentous discovery that Ashburner had made since being converted to mesmerism. Around 1850 he had begun to experiment with a magnetoscope, a device that measured the 'vibratory magnetic force', which was believed to be the cause of various séance phenomena. The invention of a Dr Leger, the magnetoscope was essentially a small pendulum that hung over the centre of a series of thirty concentric circles, upon which its rotations and oscillations could be recorded. Designed to register the vibrations that emanated from different subjects (via the middle finger of the right hand), Leger found that the magnetoscope could also effectively measure the forces of the various phrenological organs, thereby applying 'mathematical laws to the functions of the human mind'. Astonished that Elliotson had failed to give the magnetoscope due coverage in the *Zoist*, Ashburner was now doubly aggrieved at his latest attack on spiritualism.

The 'battle' that Ashburner predicted seemed to gain momentum in May 1853, when William Hayden launched Britain's first spiritualist periodical, the *Spirit World*. In its first and only issue, the *Spirit World* attacked 'the gross and unpardonable ignorance' that Elliotson's *Zoist* had exhibited in its account of Mrs Hayden's séances, gave news of spiritualism's progress on its native soil, and issued advice to would-be home circles. Groups of six to eight were instructed to sit for rappings 'in a circle around a table, remaining very quiet for an hour an evening'. Once sounds were heard, the spirits could be asked to nominate the medium who would take the alphabet and ask the spirits to provide further directions. Persons wishing to become writing mediums (a skill that Mrs Hayden had yet to demonstrate) were similarly encouraged to dedicate an hour a day, in silence, concentrating the mind upon the spirit from whom a communication was desired: 'the hand will be moved to write the word as it is impressed on the mind . . . the medium should not doubt, because doubt is what makes resistance.' Frivolity was equally frowned upon. In all cases Hayden advised that 'the medium would do well to concentrate the mind on spirits of that circle, capable of instructing in the knowledge of God and in the wisdom of heaven'.

The *Spirit World* carried a clutch of endorsements from 'persons of rank' and 'high character', all testifying to the spiritual manifestations exhibited in Mrs Hayden's séances. The new converts included Sophia de Morgan, Henry Spicer, Sir Charles Isham, the writer Catherine Crowe and the veteran

Socialist Robert Owen, who would play a crucial role in the dissemination of millenarian-tinted spiritualism to the labour movement. Owen was eighty-three when he paid the first of many visits to Mrs Hayden and her newly arrived compatriot, Mrs Roberts. Having long surrendered belief in the Christian hereafter, Owen's energies remained focused on the moral improvement of the working classes, especially through the trade union movement, which he had done much to foster. Yet as much as Owen had always been open to secular heterodoxies (strangely, he was not averse to the language of phrenology despite its deplorable tendency to 'attribute more to nature and less to circumstances'), few Owenites would have expected their venerable leader to proclaim 'the promised second coming of Truth or Christ to the inhabitants of the earth' after fourteen visits to an American lady medium:

> I asked many of the spirits of my own family, questions to test their identity; also from several of my long departed friends, and from some well-known characters known to me only by their writings, and in all these instances the answers have been true, prompt, and direct, and always rational. Incorrect, and often absurd replies are sometimes given to strangers at the first or more interviews; but from my own experience I am induced to believe that these false replies proceed from the unprepared state of the mind of the enquirers, from their desire, known to the spirits, to deceive, or from the inexperience of the questioners so as to obtain correct replies . . . I am not only convinced that there is no deception with truthful mediums, in these proceedings, but that they are destined to effect, at this period, the greatest moral revolution in the character and condition of the human race.

Although British spiritualists lagged some way behind the 30,000 men and women who were reputed to have become mediums in the United States, the mania for 'tea and table moving' was sufficient to prompt a number of noted scientists and academics to investigate the spirits. Faraday undertook his first experimental trials of table moving at the Royal Institution in June 1853, after being 'greatly startled' by the way in which the public mind had been swayed by 'this purely physical subject'. Aware of the sizeable number of eminent and educated séance goers who ascribed the movement of the table to electricity, magnetism or an as yet unidentified physical force, Faraday advised that they 'suspend their judgement, or acknowledge to themselves that they are not learned enough in these matters to decide'. Certain that mediums and sitters caused the séance table to move by 'ordinary mechanical action', Faraday opened his laboratory to a 'very honourable' party of persons who were keen for the doyen of English science to identify the imponderable force which, they believed, was the *vera causa* of table tilting.

In his first trials, Faraday observed the table move in both circular motions and straight lines, but found no indication of attraction or repulsion, nor any signs of tangential force. He then proceeded to analyse the mechanical pressure that the party of spiritualists were inadvertently exerting, using layers of lined cardboard sheet packed with soft cement to measure any manual displacement of the table. Once the layers of cardboard were lifted, 'it was easy to see by displacements of part of the line, that the hand had moved further than the table'. To establish whether the table or hands moved first, Faraday commissioned a Regent Street instrument maker to construct a levered apparatus that would register downward and oblique pressure. Using a concealed gauge, Faraday surprised the table movers by showing that their hands were applying lateral pressure to the table. Once the gauge was made visible, the movements of the table ceased. Faraday's relatively simple device proved a sobering antidote to the spiritual hypothesis:

> [T]he most valuable effect of this test apparatus . . . is the corrective powers it possesses over the mind of the table-turner. As soon as the index is placed before the most earnest, and they perceive . . . that it tells truly whether they are pressing downwards or obliquely, then all effect of table-turning cease, even though the parties persevere, earnestly desiring motion, till they become weary and worn out.

Faraday's ingenious demonstration of the effects of 'unconscious muscular action' in the séance room were corroborated by other researchers, including James Braid and the physiologist William Carpenter, who had been researching the influence of suggestion in modifying and directing muscular movement before Mrs Hayden set the Hepplewhites and Chippendales clicking. In a series of lectures on mental education at the Royal Institute in 1854 a number of noted scientists, including John Tyndall and William Whewell, joined with Faraday in pouring cold water on table tilting, mesmerism and other marvels.

Invitations to 'tea and table moving' began to dwindle in the capital when Mrs Hayden retired to Boston in the autumn of 1853, but it was around this time that the North of England began to receive its first spirit communications. David Richmond, a Darlington-born craftsman and communitarian who had been resident in America when the Fox girls set the spirits rapping, was chiefly responsible for fanning the flames of spiritualism among the working-class secularists. Returning to

Britain as a missionary Shaker, Richmond toured the secular societies and advised all working men to interrogate the spirits, to glean as much knowledge as they could of the one place that knew no distinction of rank – Heaven's Republic.

Owen's recent conversion to spiritualism ensured that a substantial number of fustian-jacketed Socialists and freethinkers proved highly receptive to Richmond's lectures and demonstrations, and it was in the prosperous mill towns of Yorkshire's West Riding that 'Father David' and the table manifestations were most enthusiastically embraced. In the autumn of 1854 thirteen members of a spirit circle in Keighley attested to the procurement of a four-page sermon. Not long afterwards a circle in Bingley was able to receive messages from the Scottish bard Robert Burns, who became a garrulous confidant to spirit circles across the Aire valley. One of the first Keighley residents to become convinced of the truth of spiritual intercourse was David Weatherhead, a stalwart of the Ten Hours movement and a former Chartist agitator, who attended David Richmond's lectures at the Workingmen's Hall. Weatherhead, a prosperous grocer who had lost a beloved son, bankrolled the *Yorkshire Spiritual Telegraph*, which announced the arrival of a new millenarian credo: a 'working religion' that would overhaul 'the present wretched and disorganised condition of the human race'. Thanks to Weatherhead, Keighley established itself as the cradle of British spiritualism.

The debt this new wave of spiritualists owed to mesmerism was abundantly clear. When Ashburner addressed the working-class followers of spiritualism in a series of essays in the *British Spiritual Telegraph*, he lamented Elliotson's reluctance to accept the facts and reasoning that lay behind 'the mesmeric science of spiritualism', but continued to advise all spiritualists to draw on the rich store of practical lessons that could be found in the

Zoist. (Those who wished to develop their powers as healing mediums were encouraged to 'practise the art of staring with a purpose'.) Plebeian spiritualists would continue to pledge allegiance to mesmerism, while echoing Ashburner's hope for Elliotson's conversion to their greater cause.

In the meantime, the popular press continued to portray spiritualism as a pernicious craze that had led many of its transatlantic adherents to the madhouse. Early in 1854 the *Daily News* reported that the Ohio lunatic asylum counted no fewer than twenty-six persons 'who found their way there by means of spiritual rappings', and went on to list the names of worthy and industrious citizens whose spiritual experiments had terminated in suicide or the murder of family members. Reports of this kind created anxiety and trepidation among the would-be investigators, but the dangers of spiritualism were made even more immediate when the writer Catherine Crowe became Britain's first public victim of the spirit-rapping fancies.

An established writer of plays, children's stories and romantic novels, Catherine Crowe had been among the first of the literary beau monde to attend Mrs Hayden's séances. Best known for the domestic dramas *Susan Hopley* and *Lily Dawson*, Crowe was a seasoned collector of 'that class of phenomena which appears to throw some light on our physical nature and on the probable state of the soul after death'. In 1845 she provided English readers with the first translation of Justinus Kerner's renowned *Seeress of Prevorst* and followed this with *The Night Side of Nature* (1845), a seminal collection of supernatural reports that drew much from 'German authorities'. Crammed with accounts of poltergeists, apparitions, doubles, second sight, prophetic dreams and other strange presentiments, this psychic *Wunderkammer* ran to numerous editions, proving as popular with the general public as it was with the select group of Cambridge graduates who formed the first ghost club. The uneasiness that some reviewers expressed towards Crowe's refusal to regard phantoms as the progeny of nervous illness or excited imagination proved eerily prescient: Crowe's personal journey into spiritualism was destined to provide early critics of spiritualism with striking evidence of the 'diseased fancy' with which ghost seers were thought to be afflicted.

On a sunny February morning in 1854 the spirits instructed Crowe to leave her home in Darnoway Street, Edinburgh, clothed only in her chastity, while carrying a card case in her right hand and a handkerchief in her left. Crowe's 'temporary insanity' was the subject of endless hearsay. The actress Fanny Kemble wrote that Mrs Crowe 'imagined that she received a visit from the Virgin Mary and our Saviour, both of whom commanded her to go without any clothes on into the streets of Edinburgh, and walk a certain distance in that condition, in reward for which the sins and sufferings of the whole world would be immediately alleviated'. According to Owen Meredith, the unfortunate authoress was apprehended 'by certain materialists in the Police Force'. On being asked by the magistrate to account for her 'singularity of costume', Crowe explained that she had received distinct assurances from the spirits that the arrangement of fan and card case would guarantee her invisibility. Evidently, the spirits failed her. Believing that she had descended into permanent insanity, Crowe's family arranged for her to be taken promptly to Hanwell Asylum in Middlesex.

Many female spiritualists would be certified as lunatics in the 1860s and 1870s. Crowe was spared this fate by the intervention of Dr John Conolly, a friend and follower of her Edinburgh neighbour George Combe. As soon as her delirium subsided, Conolly arranged for Mrs Crowe to be transferred to a private house in west London. Shortly afterwards, while recuperating at Dr Wilson's hydropathic institution in Great Malvern, she became aware of the rumours that her seizure had provoked. Finding that the *Daily News* and other London newspapers had been alerted to her spiritual misadventures by the *Zoist*, Crowe wrote to upbraid its editor for his insensitive and ill-informed reports: 'The world has been ready enough to call you mad for your heterodox beliefs, and if I did believe in the spirits it would be no proof of madness . . . I should have thought your own experience would have made you more just and merciful to others. I have always been indignant at the persecution you have suffered; but since you are ready to persecute others, you thoroughly deserve what you have met with.'

Considering it his duty to expose the ignorance and absurdity of 'those poor creatures who believe in spirit-rappings and spirit-table-movings', Elliotson was as intransigent as ever. In July 1854 the *Zoist* reported more instances in which the spiritualists had been led astray by this 'wicked doctrine'. One case brought to his notice concerned a 'beautiful' and 'accomplished' lady, who had been an excellent wife and mother before falling victim to the spirit-rapping imposition:

After reading Mr Owen's pamphlet [*The Future of the Human Race*] she began to have consultations with the spirits; heard them rapping at all hours day and night; neglected her poor little children, and at length became so violent and mischievous that her relatives came forward and insisted upon placing her at the lunatic asylum in Brixton . . . But, before this necessary step was taken, she had brought over the weak husband to her own folly, and, though he goes to work . . . he has communication with spirits, hears them rap around him, has grown 'as pale as a ghost', to use the words of my informant, and sometimes has no sleep all night through the visits and conversations of the spirits. He says they have told him to go to the chief constable of St Pancras and get his wife out and that money is coming from Australia: sometimes he sees his wife coming in at the door and she talks to him.

Elliotson's attempts to expose the 'wicked doctrine' were futile. Following Ashburner's lead, mesmerists who had once dedicated themselves to demonstrate that man's intellectual and moral functions were regulated by 'the living organ called the brain, or other nervous substances' had now been seduced by 'that curse of all true knowledge and moral progress – superstition – supernatural imaginings'. Refusing to accept defeat, Elliotson brought the *Zoist* to a close on 31 December 1855 by claiming that his mission had been accomplished:

We have furnished ample examples of facts in the physiology of the brain which metaphysicians and physiologists are not aware of . . . We have shown that one brain can act silently upon another, and one silently sympathize with another in emotion and in impressions communicated by the organs of sensation; that the brain can experience impressions from concealed or distant objects of sight; receive impressions to which we are habitually strangers; and can be impressed with what has passed or is to come . . . We have detailed almost endless instances of the great curative powers of mesmerism over diseases apparently very different from each other, and shown that it is a mighty adjunct to the restorative power of the living frame . . . We have presented satisfactory proofs that mesmeric phenomena, though they may be produced artificially, may all occur without artificial means, and are due to a peculiar condition, of which we are as ignorant as of the true nature of gravitation, electricity, heat, light, &c. . . . We have proved that mesmeric phenomena are independent of imagination, suggestion, fixed ideas, &c., though every mesmerist should be aware that imagination often plays a powerful part in mesmeric phenomena.

Lessons had been learned but the mesmeric classroom lay abandoned. Few of Elliotson's one-time followers now subscribed to, or remembered, the materialist credo that the *Zoist* had laid out in its very opening article – 'grapple with nature, cease speculating on the unseen'. It would be left to a future generation of researchers to dust down and recatalogue the cabinet of medical and psychological curiosities that Elliotson had dutifully curated.

Chapter Eight

Dark Employments

The sight of a spectral arm in an audience of three thousand persons will appeal to more hearts, make a deeper impression, and convert more people to a belief in the hereafter, in ten minutes, than a whole regiment of preachers, no matter how eloquent, could in five years.
P. B. Randall, quoted in Arthur Conan Doyle's
The History of Spiritualism

While mediums on the east coast of America composed lectures and poetry, delivered trance sermons, levitated, raised 'ponderable bodies', lent voice to absent friends and produced all forms of materialisation, their English cousins retained a decidedly scanty repertoire. Lamenting this shortage of 'new facts' (and the long hours that table rapping required to solicit the most rudimentary of messages) native spiritualists were awaiting the emergence of a medium who could draw Christians and freethinkers, intellectuals and self-taught plebeians, to the séance room – an enigma who would be openly embraced by persons of rank and distinction – a miracle monger who would finally bring incontrovertible evidence of the afterlife into arm's reach.

The man destined to fulfil this exacting role, Daniel Dunglas Home (1833–86), left America in April 1854, intending to allay 'the indurated and materialistic tone of the English mind' with his burgeoning ragbag of spiritual marvels. Within weeks of his arrival, London society was giddy with news of the lanky red-haired spirit rapper who claimed to be the illegitimate grandson of the tenth Earl of Home. Among the first to procure invitations to sit with Home at William Cox's Hotel in Jermyn Street were Lady Waldegrave, Lady Combermere, Baroness Grey de Ruthyn, and the Marchioness of Hastings. London's great hostesses were followed by Bulwer-Lytton, Lord Brougham, Sir Charles Isham and Robert Owen, who left this brief account of his séance with the young Scotsman:

On being seated around a regular full-sized card table, there were raps immediately, and because I do not hear very well, the raps increased until they became very loud, but I heard the first arising raps very distinctly. Many spirits were present, some relatives of my friends, and others, my own relations. My wife and daughters, my son and brother, and also my own father and mother, with all of whom I have had frequent delightful intercourse ... the first new occurrence to me was seeing a lady's silk apron untied, by invisible means.... Next a flower was taken from the table, converted away by invisible means and brought to me ... Next I had my handkerchief out, it was taken from my hands, and in an instant thrown from the opposite side of the table ... Then the spirits came and touched each of us ... An accordion was then placed under the table, and soon the spirit of the daughter of the family played, most beautifully, several pieces of music . . . The table was then lifted from the floor; at first, about a foot, and immediately afterwards three feet. After this the medium was put into a trance, during which he saw beautiful visions of Spirits, and one of them spoke through him while in that state, sentiments that went to the heart of each of us, giving us advice, invaluable in its import, and in language beautifully and eloquently expressed, and calculated to make the deepest impressions on our memories. While reason remains, I shall never forget it.

Sceptical of the powers that were being attributed to Home, Lord Brougham, the great Whig reformer, took the precaution of asking Sir David Brewster to assist him in 'finding out the trick'. Brewster was certainly well qualified for the task. The discoverer of the laws of light absorption, and inventor of the kaleidoscope and lighthouse illuminator, Brewster had employed his knowledge of optics and mechanics to account for apparitions, talking statues and various wonders in his well-known book *Natural Magic*. Yet Brewster's diary account of the séance provided no clues as to how the rappings might have been manufactured; indeed, he was at a complete loss to account for any of the phenomena he had witnessed at Jermyn Street:

We four sat down at a moderately sized table, the structure of which we were invited to examine. In a short time the table shuddered and a tremulous motion ran up all our arms; at our bidding these motions ceased and returned. The most unaccountable rappings were produced in various parts of the table; and the table actually rose from the ground when no hand was upon it . . . A larger table was now produced, and exhibited similar movements... A small handbell was then laid down with its mouth on the carpet; and, after lying for some time, it actually rang when nothing could have touched it. The bell was placed on the other side, still upon the carpet, and it came over to me and placed itself in my hand. It did the same to Lord Brougham. These were the principal experiments. We could give no explanation of them, and could not conjecture how they would be produced by any kind of mechanism.

Sensational accounts of Home's sittings with Owen, Brougham and Brewster soon appeared in the American and English press. Though Brougham chose not to become entangled in a public dispute, Brewster felt it his professional duty to disclaim any belief in the phenomena he had witnessed. In a letter to the *Morning Advertiser*, Brewster maintained that everything he had seen at the séance with Home 'could all be produced by human hands and feet'. When William Cox, the proprietor of the hotel where Home was based, took issue with Brewster's published remarks, suggesting that they were entirely at odds with the impression he had reported in the aftermath of the séance, Brewster supplied a fuller version of his investigations. He had not, he insisted, been allowed to examine the undersides of the tables that were covered with copious drapery. Moreover, he suspected that the violent coughing fit that had prompted the medium to leave the room was merely a pretext for him to equip his lower extremities with the machinery required to perform his feats.

These allegations were vigorously contested by Home's growing circle of London acolytes. Rebuking Brewster for his unkind treatment of 'the orphan Home', they reminded the well-respected scientist that Home had demonstrated his 'ruinous peculiarity of a gift' without the aid of assistants, screens or bulging pockets. But not all of Home's sitters were as eager to vouch for his probity. Shortly after Home had transferred to Ealing, one sharp-eyed sitter claimed to have noticed 'the whole connection between the medium's shoulder and arm and the spirit hand dressed out on the end of his own'. Home's questionable methods became the subject of more open rumour, and scurrilous gossip, when Mr and Mrs Robert Browning drove out to Ealing in July 1855.

The Brownings had heard much of Home from their Boston friends, the Jarveses, who had paid for the young medium's passage to England. Born in Currie, near Edinburgh, Home had been, by his own account, a nervous and sickly child, fond of musical recitations and given to spells of dreamy quietude. At the age of thirteen, while living in Waterford, Connecticut, an apparition of a dead school friend confirmed that he was, like his mother, gifted with second sight. Four years on, after a second wraith foretold the death of his mother, his aunt's home was besieged by flying chairs and sinister rappings. Provoking distrust among his relations, and bitter disagreement among the local ministers, the spirit rappings soon revealed the whereabouts of distant relatives and misplaced items. Tired of being petitioned by curious and disapproving neighbours, the seventeen-year-old prodigy was encouraged to employ his dubious talents elsewhere. Refusing to take fees for his mediumship – 'on the grounds of taste rather than principle' – Home became a social gadfly, a serial house guest, captivating his New England patrons with his easy charm and versatile repertoire. According to the Jarveses, the young medium's integrity was unquestionable: never exposed in any trickery, his séances were a real wonder to behold.

The first English observer to record his impressions of one of

Home's American séances was William Makepeace Thackeray, who, during a visit to New York in November 1852 was ushered into an impromptu sitting. Thackeray was excited by the moving of tables. He urged friends in England to try this 'wonderful thing' – using a circle of six or seven people, and a deal table without castors – and promised that 'in ½ an hour or so it will begin to turn round and round'. As for the spirit messages that Home relayed: 'What pained me was to see good kind people believing – to find what folly satisfied them, what childish ideas of God they have. They call for their relations and Franklin and Washington, and that sort of thing – But the physical manifestations are undoubted.'

Elizabeth Barrett Browning – destined to become spiritualism's most ardent literary convert – was particularly keen to meet Home and more than ready to believe in the strange powers that he was said to possess. Her husband's first impression of Home was of 'a rather handsome and prepossessing' youth, with 'nothing offensive or pretentious in his demeanour' except for the childish endearments that he lavished on Mr and Mrs Rymer, his new 'Papa and Mama'. The phenomena that Home went on to exhibit were altogether more troublesome. The Ealing séance began with the table they were gathered round being suddenly lifted. Elizabeth's dress was then 'slightly but distinctly uplifted . . . as if by some object inside'. Two phantom hands clothed in white muslin now rose and sat at the edge of the table. The larger hand snatched a clematis wreath from the table, moved slowly towards Mrs Browning and dropped it on top of her head. Minutes passed. The spirits explained that they would again lift the table, this time allowing Mr Browning to observe the process in light: 'I looked under the table and can aver that it was lifted from the ground, say a foot-high, more than once – Mr Home's hands being plainly above it.' Browning could no more account for the table's repeated movements than he could explain how an accordion appeared to be played by invisible hands: 'I don't know at all how the thing was done.' For a clematis-crowned Elizabeth, the séance had been 'wonderful and conclusive'.

Throughout the Ealing séance the Brownings had complied with Home's request not to put questions to the spirits, or to ask them to exhibit anything beyond what they chose to. But while Elizabeth left Ealing believing that Home 'was no more *responsible* for the things said and done, than I myself was', her husband's scepticism increased by the day. Soon enough, Browning declared that 'the whole display of "hands", "spirit utterances" etc. were a cheat and imposture', being most probably produced by Home's feet with the assistance of some added mechanical contrivance. Vexed and irritated by his wife's infatuation with the spirit world, Browning's anger exploded when the Rymers brought Home to visit him at his Dorset Street home. Ignoring Home, Browning turned to Mrs Rymer to express blunt dissatisfaction with everything he had seen. When Home interjected, enquiring why he had not said so at the time, Browning became incandescent: 'Mr Browning's face was pallid with rage . . . his movements, as he swayed backwards and forwards on his chair were like those of a maniac.'

Home and spiritualism became taboo subjects in the Browning household. While Elizabeth remained an avid séance goer (despite the exposure of her intimate friend, the Boston medium Sophia Eckley) through to her death in the spring of 1861, Browning would be left to ruminate on his personal failure in allowing 'the regular tests of truth and rationality' to be put aside during his séance with Home. Certain that he had been duped, but lacking the evidence to establish his claim,

Browning could only imagine the kind of snivelling, self-justifying monologue that a medium such as Home, a *Mr Sludge*, might deliver on being detected in his trickery:

> Now, don't sir! Don't expose me! Just this once!
> This was the first and only time, I'll swear –
> Look at me – see, I kneel – the only time,
> I swear, I ever cheated –
> . . .
> I tell you, sir, in one sense, I believe
> Nothing at all, that everybody can,
> Will, and does cheat; but in another sense
> I'm ready to believe my very self
> That every cheat's inspired, and every lie
> Quick with a germ of truth.

Fêted as a wonder worker, denounced as the prince of charlatans, Home embarked on a European tour, giving sittings for Louis Napoleon, the Queen of Holland and Friedrich Wilhelm, the Crown Prince of Prussia. After returning to London with his young wife, Sacha, Home added to his celebrity by introducing a phenomenon that had never before been witnessed in an English séance – levitation. Writing in the *Cornhill Magazine* in 1860, the well-known dramatist and critic Robert Bell described Home making a brief aerial voyage of the drawing room at a Monday sitting at the Hyde Park home of Mrs Milner Gibson: 'Through the semi-darkness his head was dimly visible against the curtains, and his hands might be seen in a faint white heap before him. Presently, he said, in a quiet voice, "My chair is moving – I am off the ground – don't notice me – talk of something else," or words to that effect . . . I was sitting nearly opposite Mr Home, and I saw his hands disappear from the table, and his head vanish into the deep shadow beyond. In a moment or two he spoke again. This time his voice was in the air above our heads. He had risen from his chair to a height of four or five feet from the ground. As he ascended higher he described his position, which was at first perpendicular, and afterwards became horizontal.'

Most literary intellectuals were distinctly unimpressed by such reports. George Eliot, common-law wife of George Lewes, privately expressed deep misgivings about the 'odious trickery', 'degrading folly' and 'impudent impostures' that were being performed in the name of spiritualism. Home was, for Eliot, an 'object of moral disgust' – a charlatan who had fashioned a new market for his juggleries, 'just as if they were papier mâché wares or pomades for the idle rich'. Dickens shared the sentiment. Thomas Trollope had told him how Home had fallen for the 'small test' he had set one afternoon, while walking in his villa garden in Florence. Passing within earshot of Home, Trollope said to his wife that it was the anniversary of a friend's drowning. Later that evening the spirit of the named person contacted Home, supplying information about the fictitious drowning.

As editor of *Household Words* and *All the Year Round*, Dickens ensured that Home and the spiritualist cause were given caustic notice. Declining various opportunities to sit with Home, he was not in the least disposed to 'receive enlightenment' through spirits who expressed themselves through mediums: 'Mr Hume or Home (I rather think he has gone by both names), I take the liberty of regarding as an impostor. If he *appeared* on his own behalf in any controversy with me, I should take the further liberty of letting him know publicly why. But be assured that if he were demonstrated a humbug in every microscopic cell of his blood, the disciples would still believe and worship.'

Convinced that Home's indubitable powers would silence the most entrenched and contemptuous of sceptics, London spiritualists attempted to broker a meeting with Michael Faraday at the Royal Institution. Faraday had grown impatient of the spiritualists. Since undertaking his table-turning experiments, he had been mercilessly lambasted by Home's followers over his failure to investigate the new and startling facts that had emerged from the séance room. In a much-quoted letter, written in 1861, Faraday suggested that he might be prepared to investigate Home's manifestations, providing certain conditions were met: 'Is he [Home] willing to investigate as a philosopher, and, as such to have no concealments, no darkness, to be open in communication, and to aid inquiry all that he can?' But before establishing whether the phenomena occurring in Home's presence were 'glimpses of natural action not yet reduced to law', Faraday required a further disclosure: 'If the effects are miracles, the work of spirits, does he admit the utterly contemptible character both of them and their results, up to the present time, in respect of either yielding information or instruction, or supplying any force or action of the least value to mankind.' A devout Sandemanian who was steeped in apostolic doctrine, Faraday was not afraid to apply a moral yardstick to spiritualism.

Of all the conversions that Home claimed to have had a hand in orchestrating, the most unexpected occurred in Dieppe, in the summer of 1863, when he contrived to meet John Elliotson, 'the martyr of Mesmerism turned persecutor of Spiritualism'. Elliotson was now seventy-two years of age and living with the family of an ex-pupil, Edmund Symes. Two years previously, concerns over his finances and mental health had led Dickens to dash over to Conduit Street, where he found his 'dear old friend' in morbid spirits. Separated from his sisters (after an argument over a cockatoo) and excessively preoccupied with his dwindling income, Elliotson was a ghost of the belligerent cockney professor who had fought to bring mesmerism into mainstream science. According to Home's suspiciously sketchy version of the encounter, he gently ribbed Elliotson for his acerbic attacks on spiritualism and proceeded to purge him of his egregious scepticism. Though Home omitted to mention quite what Elliotson saw in the course of the Dieppe séance, the spiritualist press was only too pleased to report that Elliotson was now 'a thoroughly changed man', humbled by his efforts in promulgating the materialist credo.

The history of spiritualism is littered with pseudo-confessions and post-mortem apologias. Despite corroboration from outside the spiritualist coterie, Home's breezy account of Elliotson's transfiguration does not ring true. The statement that Elliotson forwarded to the *Spiritualist Magazine* in 1864 makes clear that he was by no means immediately convinced of the truth of spiritualism, or led to reject materialism, by what he had witnessed: 'I am not yet prepared to admit that they are produced by the agency of spirits ... The explanations which have been made to account for the phenomena do not satisfy me, but I desire to reserve my opinion on that point at present. I am free, however, to say that I regret the opportunity was not afforded me at an earlier period. What I have seen lately has made a deep impression on my mind; and the recognition of the reality of these manifestations, from whatever cause, is tending to revolutionise my thoughts and feelings on almost every subject.' Elliotson's position was at this time probably closer to that of fellow rationalists such as Charles Bray, Edward Cox and Henry Atkinson, all of whom were inclined to regard séance manifestations as mental emanations, which mediums were somehow able to invest with requisite 'density'.

Elliotson left no record of the investigations that he went on to undertake with Edmund Symes's sons, or the séances that he went on to participate in at the home of Mrs Milner-Gibson. Elliotson's name appears in the 1866 council of the Spiritual Athenaeum (where a beleaguered Home was briefly installed as resident secretary) and, after his death in August 1868, the *Morning Post*'s obituary reported that the once-truculent materialist had become a sincere Christian who 'looked forward to the life hereafter with calm confidence'. Still, Elliotson's conversion to mainstream spiritualism remains as doubtful as his reported progress in the Other World. Speaking through Home, a spirit who identified himself as Elliotson informed Lord Adare's circle of sitters that he had not suffered pain in passing away, and that afterlife was 'very much as he expected it to be'. On 'studying nature', he had arrived at the conclusion that illness is often generated 'by mere presence without actual contact', that the winds are capable of carrying and curing disease, and that persons of unsound mind or body should not be permitted to procreate. Some months later Elliotson (still speaking via Home) belatedly informed Lord Adare that something was amiss in the Other World – the sun was cold.

This blunt indifference that Faraday and his fellow scientists displayed towards 'the so-called supernatural, as developed in the phenomena of animal magnetism, clairvoyance, and modern spiritualism' was anathema to Home's extended circle of followers. William Howitt, a well-known nonconformist and the principal contributor to William Wilkinson's *Spiritual Magazine*, attacked this perceived prejudice with the fiery gusto that he had once channelled in the anti-slavery campaign, poor law reform and the temperance movement. Finding echoes of the spirit world everywhere he looked, Howitt contended that there was 'no part of human history or human literature which does not abound in the plainest demonstrations of this influence'. The neglect of the supernatural by the likes of Faraday, Brewster and Dickens could, Howitt suggested, be traced back to the 'death-creed of Hobbes, Diderot and Co.', and, before that, to 'a certain benumbing modern pyrrhonism, which came in with Protestantism, the direct and avowed product of opposition to miracle in the Church of Rome'.

In his two-volume magnus opus, *The History of the Supernatural in All Ages and Nations* (1863), Howitt went on to argue that the marvels that Home and other mediums had brought to the domestic arena (though 'vastly inferior' to the great and glorious transfigurations found in the New and Old Testament) were genuine miracles that promised to reveal 'the internal nature of man . . . his properties and prospects as an immortal being'. By providing *evidence* of the soul's immortality, Home had helped herald the dawn of a world religion, a faith beyond petty sectarianism:

> Everyone who enters into spiritualism very soon becomes aware how perpetually he is under the observation of invisible eyes and ears, and I have had different persons say that they never realized this in any degree before. The assertion that we had angels and spirits about us, was a sort of indifferent or poetical idea in the mind, but was not a living truth. Spiritualism at once makes it palpable, and awfully real, and people begin to say, 'I can no longer say and do things as I could before. My whole being is open to spiritual realities. A fair outside will no longer do, I see that I must be genuine and pure all through and through.'

The first established scientist to lend credence to the notion that higher and more recondite laws were to be found in the operation of spiritual 'miracles' was Alfred Russel Wallace, explorer, naturalist and co-architect of natural selection. On returning from his travels to the East Indies, in July 1865, Wallace joined friends and family at the séance table. Initially, Wallace was inclined to believe that table moving and rapping was either imposture, illusion or an effect of imponderable forces. When the raps at Mrs Marshall's table conveyed a message from his dead brother, Wallace found his scepticism abating. Some months later he was delighted to find that a shower 'of fifteen chrysanthemums, six variegated anemones, four tulips, five orange-berried solanums, six ferns of two sorts, one *Auricula sinensis* with nine flowers' descended upon the table, 'all fresh, cold, and damp with dew'.

Wallace moved one step closer to embracing the spiritualist credo when a Miss Nichol, a family friend who was living with his sister, developed mediumistic powers. Over a period of weeks, Wallace and his sister had 'constant sittings', witnessing on one occasion the levitation of a heavy table with Miss Nichol seated upon it. Confronted by facts outside the 'existing fabric of thought', Wallace was now led to reflect on their implication for the theory of natural selection, the doctrine he and Darwin independently arrived at in the late 1850s. Apostasy beckoned. Neither natural selection nor the laws of evolution could, he wrote in the *Quarterly Review*, account for the origins of conscious life. Other higher laws could not be ruled out when considering the moral and intellectual progress of man:

> Let us freely admit that the mind of a man (itself the living proof of a supreme mind) is able to trace, and to a considerable extent

has traced, the laws by means of which the organic world has developed. But let us not shut our eyes to the evidence that an Overruling Intelligence has watched over the action of those laws, so directing their variations, so determining their accumulation, as finally to produce an organisation sufficiently perfect to admit of, and even to aid in, the indefinite advancement of our mental and moral nature.

Darwin was taken aback by Wallace's 'little heresy'. Seeing no reason for invoking any additional or proximate cause in regard to man's evolution, he could scarcely believe that Wallace was prepared to defy his own doctrine. Wallace understood Darwin's misgivings and responded with a disarming admission: 'I can quite comprehend your feelings with regard to my unscientific opinions as to man, because a few years back I should have looked at them as equally wild and uncalled for ... My opinions on the subject have been modified solely by the consideration of a series of remarkable phenomena, physical and mental, which I have now had the opportunity of fully testing, and which demonstrate the existence of forces and influences not yet recognised by science.'

Rising public interest in spiritualism could not disguise the fact that séance goers remained, in Dickens's phrase, 'preposterously wanting in the commonest securities against deceit or mistakes'. The advice given to those wishing to acquire 'experimental knowledge' of spiritual phenomena by the indefatigable James Burns, London's leading promoter of 'progressive' spiritualism, was typical in this regard. Between three and ten people were advised to meet in a warm and ventilated room without draughts. Since mental excitement was considered detrimental to the production of spiritual phenomena, 'opinionated', 'crude' and 'dogmatic' individuals were actively discouraged from participation. To 'harmonise' the minds of the sitters, the 'director' of the séance would encourage the circle to engage in singing, reading or prayer, before laying hands at the table. The director, seated opposite the medium, would be responsible for putting questions to the spirits and ensuring that order was kept throughout, while a recorder took notes when the table tilted or raps were heard. Burns recommended using a table that was oval, oblong or square. As regards seating, wooden or cane seats were judged superior to stuffed chairs, since the latter were thought to accumulate 'influences' that might adversely affect the medium.

Spiritualism was subjected to its first 'scientific' inquiry in April 1869, when Home and several mediums of 'good social position' and 'unimpeachable integrity' were examined by the London Dialectical Society, a newly formed body of eighty or so 'persons of Education & respectability' that sought to give unbiased attention to 'important questions, which have at various times occupied the attention of Philosophers & all thinking men'. The committee appointed to investigate séance phenomena was composed of arch believers such as Wallace and the barrister Henry Jencken, sceptics such as Charles Bradlaugh and Dr James Edmunds, a good quota of lawyers, physicians and professionals who had little or no experience of spiritual manifestations, and the ever-vacillating Reverend Charles Davies, who nodded assent to the spirits while nervously clutching his Common Prayer Book. William Carpenter, Thomas Huxley and George Lewes all declined the invitations that were extended to them. 'The only good that I can seen in a demonstration of the truth of "Spiritualism",' wrote the ever-acerbic Huxley, 'is to furnish an additional argument against suicide. Better live a crossing-sweeper than die and be made to talk twaddle by a "medium" hired at a guinea a *séance*.'

England's most celebrated medium had fallen on hard times. Thwarted in his attempts to secure the estate of his deceased wife, Home had spent the last few years giving public readings, while pursuing plans for alternative careers as a sculptor and actor. Though Home's circumstances improved considerably after securing the position of secretary at the Spiritual Athenaeum on Sloane Street, his relationship with a wealthy believer, Mrs Jane Lyon, saw him entangled in a scandal that took him to the High Court, to face charges for extorting upwards of sixty thousand pounds. After the court ordered Home to return the 'gifts' – dismissing spiritualism as 'mischievous nonsense' that lent itself to 'the projects of the needy and of the adventurer' – Home's most faithful supporter, Lord Adare, was especially keen for him to redeem himself before the Dialectical Society.

Home provided the society with 'the fullest facilities for investigation' on four separate occasions. Though subcommittee no. 5 was rather guileless in allowing Home to bring Lord Adare to the séance table, it did at least take the precaution of sitting in a well-lit room and undertaking some checks for concealed gadgetry. The presence of the more sceptical of the society's members appeared to impede Home. During one séance, following a slight disputation over the source of some slight raps, Home started, shrieked 'Ah!' and covered his face with his hands. Aside from a few feeble raps and some slight movement of the table, the subcommittee concluded that 'nothing occurred at any of the meetings which could be attributed to supernatural causes'. No ghostly hands, no flying tables and no messages from the spirit world. 'The members had fully expected that they would have witnessed some of the alleged extra-ordinary levitations of Mr Home, but he explained that the phenomena produced through his agency were of uncertain manifestation and that he had no power whatever to produce them at will.' After his fourth séance Home retired on the grounds of illness.

One of the most eagerly awaited of the thirty or so witnesses that were called on to give evidence was Cromwell Fleetwood Varley, chief electrician to the Electric and International Telegraphy Company. Varley informed the Dialectical Society that he had become interested in spiritualism in around 1850, when he undertook experiments that he believed demonstrated that table moving could not be explained in terms of electrical force. Three years after these experiments, Varley obtained the consent of his future wife's parents to try mesmerism, to cure her of nervous headaches, and received his first intimations of the Other World from his entranced fiancée. After visiting various New York mediums (who accurately described the condition of his health as well as clairvoyantly retrieving information relative to important legal documents) Varley decided 'to see if there was any truth in what was related of Mr Home'.

As impressed as Varley was by the many physical phenomena that presented themselves during his first séance with Home, he was 'too much astonished to feel satisfied'. Later that evening, while alone in his drawing room, he heard raps. 'The next morning I received a letter from Mr Home, in which he said, "When alone in your room last night you heard sounds. I am so pleased!" He stated that the spirits had told him they followed me, and were enabled to produce sounds.' This was the evidence that he was waiting for. In the spring of 1868

Varley made his belief in spiritualism public, testifying to Home's character when he was tried for extortion and undue influence in the High Court. Shortly afterwards Varley informed a committee of the Dialectical Society that he had, over the course of his investigations, gathered a great deal of personal evidence that confirmed that 'spirits of kindred beings do visit us'. He had often seen spirit forms. Mediums had frequently furnished him with information regarding deceased persons. Matters 'entirely forgotten' had been recalled to mind by communicating spirits. Questions posed mentally had been answered by mediums. 'Invisible informants' had told him the truth regarding coming events on several occasions.

Believing that evidence given to the Dialectical Society would remain confidential, Varley was perhaps a little too open in relating experiences of a private nature and a little too ready to confess to a question that had long puzzled him: 'Why have the more intelligent spirits not given us some scientific information in advance of any yet possessed by man?' Varley's only answer was that there were probably only 'one hundred known mediums in the whole kingdom', many of whom were women and artisans who had absolutely no understanding of natural philosophy. Once he had discovered a medium acquainted with science, Varley hoped that real breakthroughs could be made.

Despite the very slight phenomena observed by the four subcommittees of the Dialectical Society, the majority of its members were led to conclude that *'there is a force capable of moving heavy bodies without material contact, and which force is in some unknown manner dependent'*. Bradlaugh and Edmunds dissented, pointing to evidence of fraud employed by some of the mediums who had been examined. Finding that all the manifestations that Home and his fellow mediums had produced could easily be simulated, they chose not to endorse the conclusions of the society's *Report on Spiritualism*. In their eyes, too much weight was given to the opinions of members and to the record of extraordinary facts solicited from witnesses who had been called to give evidence. Since oral and written testimony had been given priority over experimental evidence, the character and respectability of mediums and sitters were the only guarantee that the committee was able to give.

The press greeted the Dialectical Society's *Report on Spiritualism* as 'a farrago of impotent conclusions, garnished by a mass of the most monstrous rubbish'. Apart from the various subcommittees' inability to generate experimental evidence, there was a glaring failure, on the part of those called to give evidence, to consider seriously the question of fraud. Emma Hardinge, when asked to suggest any means of detecting imposture on the part of mediums, was 'unable to give any specific information on that point'. William Howitt insisted that the Davenports were true mediums, despite serial exposure and imitation. And Thomas Trollope was content to cite the authority of Bosco, the great Italian magician, who had personally reassured him that the physical phenomena Home performed fell beyond the resources of his art.

In June 1871, four months before the publication of the Dialectical Society's findings, the Royal Society was pressed to make its position on spiritualism clear. A report on 'crucial tests' undertaken with Home, and 'nine or ten persons who possess psychic powers in various degrees' was sent to its co-secretaries, Professor Sharpey and Professor Stokes. The author of the report, the chemist and physicist William Crookes, had employed a dynamometer to measure the 'psychic force' that Home and other mediums were able to exert remotely on various objects. Working under the 'strictest test conditions',

Crookes believed that he had repeatedly observed and measured the motion of heavy bodies without mechanical contact. Crookes, a rising star of the scientific world, invited Sharpey and Stokes to call on him at his home in Mornington Villas, to see the machine he had devised. William Sharpey, Elliotson's old nemesis at University College Hospital, was dismayed by the claims. No more inclined to believe in the existence of 'a force in nature as yet unknown' than he was when Elliotson began his trials of mesmerism, he politely declined the Crookes invitation. It was left to Stokes to inform Crookes that, owing to the various possible sources of error in the experiments and apparatus, his report was being declined.

Undaunted, Crookes reported new experiments to the *Quarterly Journal of Science*. These second papers came before the council of the Royal Society in December 1871 and were duly rejected by a committee that found 'not an iota of proof in favour of your doctrine of psychic force'. Widely castigated by his peers, especially by William Carpenter, Crookes refused to believe that he had been duped by Home or any of the lesser mediums he had tested. A good experimentalist was in his opinion more than a match for any medium who resorted to tricks. He had taken all the precautions he deemed necessary. The only occasions on which less than full light was employed was when it appeared to exert 'an interfering action on some of the phenomena'.

During three years of intensive experimentation, Crookes saw Home levitate on three occasions. He witnessed countless movements and vibrations of furniture, watched luminous clouds float across his laboratory, saw a disembodied hand picking petals from a flower from Home's buttonhole, and received numerous messages by way of raps, luminous flashes, paper and planchette. Rejecting Carpenter's theory of unconscious cerebral action, and refusing to relate the phenomena to imagination, to delusion, to 'gnomes, fairies, kobolds, elves, goblins', let alone departed human beings, Crookes ascribed all the anomalies to a certain 'something' possessed by mediums but not ordinarily found in 'ordinary human beings'. Pressed to give this something, this 'x', a name, he opted for 'psychic force', a term proposed by Edward Cox, a dissenting member of the Dialectical Society. Finding no proof of the agency of spirits of the dead, Crookes never anticipated that his research would carry him ever closer towards the spiritualist credo.

With Home having effectively retired from the séance room, Crookes turned his attention to a new wave of London mediums, accepting an invitation to join Cromwell Varley in testing Miss Florence Cook, an eighteen-year-old Hackney medium who had dazzled London spiritualists with a wide repertoire of phenomena, culminating in the apogee of all séance-room manifestations: a fully-formed materialised spirit. Bankrolled by various patrons, including William Harrison, the editor of the *Spiritualist*, Cook's materialisations took place in a dark cabinet or side room, which guests were invited to search before binding the young medium into an armchair. With the lights dimmed and sitters gathered at a nearby table, Miss Cook moaned and mumbled, while entering 'a trance'. A few minutes later the curtains would be pulled back to reveal a white-robed figure, with bare arms and feet, and a flowing headdress that framed features not dissimilar to Miss Cook's. Introducing herself as Katie King, the spirit daughter of a seventeenth-century Welsh buccaneer, the diaphanous figure would briefly engage the sitters in conversation, regaling them with tales from the spirit world or recording messages to be taken back, before returning to her cabinet.

Varley and Crookes were approached to assist in performing 'scientific séances' with Miss Cook shortly after a performance that had roused some suspicions as to Katie King's true provenance. In December 1873 William Volkman, one of the more sceptical members of the Dialectical Society, seized Katie King by the hand and waist as she walked back to the cabinet. After an awkward tussle, Katie was rescued from Volkman's marauding grasp by two assistants. Ensuing accounts of Miss Florence Cook's exposé drew a mixed response from the spiritualist community. While James Burns complained that Miss Cook's séances provided no opportunity for reasonable investigation, many prominent believers castigated Volkman for his aggressive and insensitive behaviour. Varley would, they hoped, be able to avoid such unseemly episodes by devising electrical tests that could establish that Katie and Florence were unrelated entities. This would, surely, be indubitable proof of the spirit world?

The test that Varley devised employed 'a regular cable-testing apparatus', comprising a mirror-galvanometer, a weak current supplied by Daniell's cells, and a series of resistance coils and switches. When Miss Cook was seated and bound, the galvanometer's copper wires were extended into her cabinet and attached to electrical contacts on her wrists. Satisfied that it was 'impossible for even a thoroughly experienced electrician to escape from the electric circuit without producing such an alteration of resistance as would proclaim the fact instantly', Varley undertook his first electrical séance with Miss Cook in February 1874. According to Richard Noakes' recent account of the séance:

Groans were soon heard from the cabinet and Varley recorded a gentle flicker and steady fall of the meter reading that he ascribed to Miss Cook's 'uneasiness' and drying electrical contacts respectively. At 7.27 'Katie' looked out from under the curtain and as she moved her hands, Varley remained satisfied with the meter deflection. However, when 'Katie' moved her arms at 7.36 Varley recorded a 'very suspicious fall' in the meter reading by seventeen divisions followed by an increase of twenty-one divisions. But when 'Katie' moved forward into the seance room and touched Crookes's head, he rejected his doubts and noted, 'No movement of the Galvanometer. Excellent Test.'

Having spent three months investigating Miss Cook, William Crookes came to believe that it was impossible that 'an innocent school-girl of fifteen' should be able 'to conceive and then successfully carry out for three years so gigantic an imposture as this'. To establish that Miss Florence Cook and Katie King were not one and the same, Crookes eventually employed five cameras to take numerous photographs of Katie King by the aid of electric light. Using his library as a dark cabinet, Crookes and his assistants remained in an adjacent laboratory, with cameras trained at the curtain:

On entering the cabinet Miss Cook lies down upon the floor, with head on a pillow, and is soon entranced. During the photographic *séances*, Katie muffled her medium's head up in a shawl to prevent the light falling upon her face. I frequently drew the curtain on one side when Katie was standing near, and it was a common thing for the seven or eight of us in the laboratory to see Miss Cook and Katie at the same time, under the full blaze of the electric light. We did not on these occasions actually see the face of the medium because of the shawl, but we saw her hands and feet; we saw her move uneasily under the influence of the intense light, and we heard her moan occasionally. I have one photograph of the two together, but Katie is seated in front of Miss Cook's head.

The electrical and photographic evidence that Varley and Crookes furnished fell short of convincing many spiritualists that Miss Cook and Katie King were not one and the same, or that a confederate had not been employed to play her part. Alerted to the need for greater vigilance by a spate of exposures, stricter conditions were called for by 'scientific spiritualists' such as Edward Cox, who had discovered (via a 'confidential communication' that had been passed to him) that materialising mediums like Florence Cook were given to carrying their spirit costume and veil inside their drawers, and that the figure that remained behind the curtain was nothing more than a gown spread over pillows, with its 'face' wrapped in a shawl. Though Cox was a little naïve in acquitting some mediums of deliberate fraud — he claimed that materialisations might sometimes be performed in a state of somnambulism — he was rightly critical of investigators who had permitted mediums to deny them reasonable light and effective means of detection. 'The lesson to be learned from all this is that no phenomena should be accepted as genuine that are not produced under strict test conditions. Investigators should be satisfied with no evidence short of the very best that they will permit. Why accept the doubtful testimony of one person groping in the dark when the question can be decided beyond dispute and for ever by the simple process of drawing back the curtain while the alleged spirit is outside, and showing the medium inside to the eyes of all present.'

Aiming to draw lessons from the preposterous delusion that the public had been lured into, the physiologist William

Carpenter insisted that only minds 'trained in philosophical habits' were capable of separating the real facts of mesmerism, odylism and spiritualism from overblown inference. Carpenter had investigated séance phenomena for forty years. He had seen Elliotson mesmerise the Okeys at University College Hospital. He had assisted in Braid's hypnotic experiments, investigated the claims made on behalf of electro-biology, the odometer and the magnetometer, accompanied Forbes on numerous visits to Alexis Didier, studied the physiology of table tilting, and made countless visits to professional mediums, waiting 'hour after hour for manifestations, the non-production of which was attributed to "my atmosphere of incredulity"'. While Carpenter was certain that deliberate fraud had often been employed, particularly by Didier and other clairvoyants, he believed that the most outlandish of the séance *bizarrerie*, such as Home's levitations, were due to, or aided by, the state of 'expectancy' that attended prolonged and repeated séances: 'by mere continued monotony of impression, the mind tends towards a state in which the will and discrimination are suspended, and the expected phenomena (such as the rising of a table in the air) takes place *subjectively*.' While paying lip-service to inductive methods of empirical science, Crookes and the spiritualists were oblivious to 'the modes in which fallacies are best detected and exposed'. They had, Carpenter concluded, prosecuted inquiries for which they were educationally and temperamentally unqualified.

Though the spiritualist community was becoming inured to such criticisms, there was one withering attack on its methods that took it completely by surprise. In his much-anticipated book *Lights and Shadows of Spiritualism* (1877), Home unleashed an unexpected broadside, siding with

Carpenter to accuse his one-time supporters of gross negligence and self-delusion in their failure to police trickery in the séance room:

> I must confess that I stand in the position of many parents; being ashamed of my offspring. With me, their father, they were thorough in their investigations, and based conviction only on absolute certainty. Now, they have cast caution aside, and seem to experience an insane pleasure in being duped . . . Their vagaries are often scarcely distinguishable from those beheld in madhouses, or at the wilder kind of revival meetings. The disease manifests itself in a variety of ways. Some of the men attacked by it pin themselves to a particular delusion, with a fanatical tenacity which nothing can affect. Others flit tirelessly from mania to mania. One or more of the class will invariably be found at every 'materialization' séance where the light is too poor to distinguish features.

If Home in reality was a faker and fantasist, a trickster who combined legerdemain with psychological illusion to produce his most celebrated of feats, how had he managed to avoid the kind of exposure that was becoming increasingly commonplace for professional mediums in the 1860s and 1870s? Home's biographers have been generally more inclined to defend his reputation rather than interrogate his methods, but eyewitness accounts of his sittings provide plenty of clues as to the ways in which he would have been able to control the outcome of the séances. Home always insisted that his powers wavered, never being subject to voluntary control: if séance manifestations were not forthcoming – and often they were not – then so be it. Rarely, if ever, performing before more than groups of eight or nine people, he would have been able effectively to select his sitters, using the most zealous of his followers as unconscious confederates. Contrary to the claims made in *Lights and Shadows of Spiritualism*, he often performed in semi-darkness, encouraging his sitters not to pay *direct* attention to any manifestations.

Recurrent illness also provided Home with a useful expedient for cancelling séances at short notice, or for making a spluttering exit from a séance that was already under way, but the most decisive advantage he had over the Davenport brothers, Florence Cook and other professional mediums was the respectable milieu in which he exclusively operated. Never scrutinising his motives or methods, polite society gave Home the latitude to dictate the conditions in which he worked – a privilege that he was, understandably enough, intent on denying his dark-adapted imitators.

Chapter Nine

'Conjurers in Disguise'

To convict the spiritual impostor one must not approach him with theories based on 'recondite principles of modern science', . . . his habits and methods should be minutely and covertly investigated as those of the elusive wild beast, and then at the right moment he may be seized and brought to light 'taken in the act'.

Professor Edwin Ray Lankester, Letter to *The Times*, September 1876

The only mid-century mediums that came close to attracting the level of publicity that Home generated in his pomp were Ira and William Davenport, two young American performers whose cabinet séances were reputed to 'have done more than all other men to familiarise England with so-called spiritualism' during the 1860s. The Davenport brothers gave their first London séance at the Regent Street home of Dion Boucicault, an Irish actor and playwright best known for his hugely popular play *The Corsican Brothers* (whose ghostly effects alarmed Queen Victoria on no fewer than five occasions). Performing before Robert Chambers, Charles Reade and other gathered luminaries, the brothers were introduced by a Nashville preacher, Reverend J. B. Ferguson, 'a decidedly remarkable man' who delivered his stirring appeal while a cabinet was placed on trestles at the far side of the dimly-lit room. The walnut cabinet was six feet square, less than two feet deep, with a bench plank running across its interior. The front of the cabinet consisted of three doors, the central door having a lozenge-shaped aperture. After inviting the audience to examine the cabinet's interior for concealed machinery, the Reverend Ferguson selected two gentlemen to bind the brothers' arms and legs, using a rope that ran through holes in the bench, so as to make it impossible for either prisoner to access the assortment of instruments that was placed between them.

Once Ira and William were secured, their knots fastened with sealing wax and the cabinet doors bolted, the sounds of a 'strange discordant concert held within a wardrobe' began to fill the room. When the concert ended, with instruments appearing to be hurled across the cabinet, the guests were amazed to find the brothers still 'bound head and foot with strong chords like the most dangerous malefactors'. After being released from their ropes, the Davenports seated themselves among the party of guests, inviting them to bind them to their chairs. As soon as the light was extinguished, a tambourine and guitar sailed across the room while a violin gently thrummed of its own accord. 'Sometimes a smart blow was administered, sometimes a knee was patted by a mysterious hand, divers shrieks from the members of the company indicating the side on which the tangible manifestations had taken place.' When a candle was finally lit, the inscrutable Davenports remained bound to their chairs, seemingly oblivious to the commotion around them.

The Davenports' first cabinet séances were widely reported. A *Times* correspondent, nose bloodied from a flying guitar, called on future investigators to ascertain more properly 'whether the brothers are able to release themselves and resume their straitened condition during the intervals of dark'. The *Daily Telegraph* wondered whether the Davenports' spiritualist followers were 'the embodiment of mutual and colossal self-deceit, or the silent heralds of a social revolution which must shake the world'. But Boucicault had no such qualms. Rebutting any suggestion of trickery, he defended the Davenports' penchant for darkness, offering an analogy that was rather less reassuring than he intended:

> Is not a dark chamber essential in the process of photography? And what would we reply to him who would say 'I believe photography to be a humbug; do it all in the light and we will believe otherwise'? It is true that we know why darkness is necessary to the production of the sun picture; and if the scientific man will subject these phenomena to analysis, we shall find out why darkness is essential to such manifestations. It is a subject which scientific men are not justified in treating with the neglect of contempt.

The nightly performances that the Davenports went on to stage at the Court Concert Rooms, Hanover Square, in October 1864 gave many Londoners their first introduction to 'spiritual phenomena'. But when conjurers such as John Henry Anderson, the Wizard of the North, began to imitate the Davenports' séances, the press swiftly turned against the

American duo and their cabinet jugglery. The spiritualist community were intransigent. Richard Burton, having seen the Davenports perform at numerous private séances and read every explanation of their trickery, found in their favour. Burton's opinion was endorsed by the *Spiritual Magazine*, though it did acknowledge that even genuine mediums might sometimes resort to trickery.

The Davenports never personally claimed to be mediums – they kept schtum and let the Reverend do the talking. Pressed to defend wonders of the cabinet from repeated accusations of fraud, their manager offered a reward of one hundred pounds to any person capable of demonstrating the same results by legerdemain. It was a fatuous wager (no working magician would *reveal* a trade secret) and a good publicity stunt. The threat of exposure drew even more substantial crowds, and it was only when the Davenports took their dark cabinet into the hotbed of Northern spiritualism that the strategy backfired. In Liverpool they were confronted by openly hostile audiences and a platform committee that ensured their ropes were secured tightly enough to impair circulation. When Reverend Ferguson cut the ropes, the audience stormed the stage and proceeded to smash the cabinet. Similar scenes unfolded at mechanics institutes in Leeds, Bradford and Hull, where police struggled to contain mobs intent on storming the cabinet. The Davenports returned to the South protesting their innocence.

The secret of the dark cabinet was uncovered by John Nevil Maskelyne, a young watchmaker and amateur conjurer who was destined to become the doyen of Victorian magic. In April 1865 Maskelyne was invited to join the committee overseeing the Davenports' cabinet séance at Cheltenham town hall. Having recently come across a mechanical rapping device employed by a local medium, Maskelyne had good reason to be distrustful of spiritualism. A few minutes into the Davenports' performance, the young magician made a second discovery. As the instruments flew out of the cabinet, the theatre curtains allowed a narrow beam of light to illuminate the interior of the cabinet. Positioned at a favourable angle, Maskelyne descried one of the brothers pressing and handling the instrument with a free hand. Immediately he realised that the act relied on the brothers holding a loop of cord to retain sufficient slack. By pressing forward with their ankles, the brothers were able to loosen their knots and then re-enter using a slip knot. Seizing his moment, Maskelyne brought the performance to a halt, announcing that he had 'by a slight accident' discovered the 'knotty trick'. Four months on, having mastered the requisite techniques, Maskelyne persuaded his friend George Alfred Cooke, a cabinetmaker and fellow cornet player in the volunteer rifle corps, to down tools and embark on a tour of the provincial theatres.

It was a timely career move. Stage magic was now a respectable, middle-class entertainment, offering 'new experiments divested of all charlatanism, and possessing no other resources than those offered by skilful manipulation, and the influence of illusions'. Taking leave of the fairground booth and carnival pitch, Europe's best-known purveyors of 'honest deception' wore tails, published books and memoirs, performed for royalty, secured patents on electrical and mechanical innovations, and, on occasion, offered technical assistance to police. The days of being harassed by clergymen and charged by magistrates were long gone. Using their art to explode the trickery of somnambules and mediums, illusionists were proving to be more wily enemies of the supernatural than any gentleman scientist.

Maskelyne had long dreamed of becoming a professional conjurer. As a child he had spent countless hours rehearsing

Antonio Blitz's famous 'Dancing Dinner Plates' routine, summoning his family to watch as he deftly maintained a line of dishes spinning over the kitchen table. In his teens, while working as a watchmaker's apprentice, Maskelyne went on to master the art of vanishing, constructing his own cabinet with a neatly concealed inner panel and release mechanism. From the very beginning of the partnership with Cooke, Maskelyne took charge of the act, shoehorning new and more complex illusions such as second sight and levitation into the frivolous dramas they enacted. Success came quickly. Drawing glittering reviews for their polished exposés of 'spiritual buffoonery', the moustachioed illusionists were, in January 1870, invited to give a command performance for the Prince of Wales at Berkeley Castle. Not long afterwards the newly-styled 'Royal Illusionists and Anti-Spiritualists' found a permanent venue at London's Egyptian Hall on the south side of Piccadilly.

Richly decorated with scarabs, sphinxes and hieroglyphics, the three-floored Regency exhibition hall had in its time played host to some of London's most alluring oddities, from William Bullock's collection of '16,000 natural wonders' to General Tom Thumb. Taking lease of the Egyptian Hall's smaller theatre, Messrs Maskelyne and Cooke committed themselves to producing 'the most Clever and Amusing Entertainment ever presented to the public', transforming the hall into 'England's Home of Mystery'. Over the next thirty or so years audiences would be captivated by an array of 'modern miracles' (including the famous 'Psycho', a twenty-two-inch-high, whist-playing automaton) but it was the twice-daily performances of 'so-called SPIRITUAL manifestations' that remained the highlight of any visit to the Egyptian Hall.

Although Benjamin Coleman, erstwhile editor of the *Spiritual Magazine*, was adamant that the Egyptian Hall's new leaseholders were actually wayward mediums, 'who find it much more profitable to pander to the prejudices of the multitude by pretending to expose Spiritualism than by honestly taking their proper place in their ranks', most of the London spiritualists found that their 'miserable buffoonery' bore no relation to the genuine manifestations they had witnessed at close quarters. These counterfeit miracles were, they complained, a travesty of the holy work that private and public mediums performed in the séance room.

George Sexton, a well-known secularist who had recently been converted to Christianity and the spiritualist cause, led the attack. Though Sexton had been duped by the Davenports, he had since acquired a very solid grasp of the mechanics of stage illusion that were being performed at the Egyptian Hall and was determined to give Maskelyne a good dressing down. In a lecture on 'Spirit Mediums and Conjurers', delivered at the Cavendish Rooms on 15 June 1873, Sexton aimed his opening salvo at Maskelyne, spotted nestling towards the back of the lecture hall:

> We have in London at this moment several conjurers who night after night attempt by trickery to show the phenomena something like those that take place in the presence of spirit mediums, and to burlesque and ridicule the whole of the subject of spirit communication. If I deal severely with these men – several of whom are present – I do it not out of ill-will that I bear them, but simply to defend the glorious truths of Spiritualism against their miserable burlesque imitations.

Diagram in hand, Sexton proceeded systematically to unpick the trickery employed in Maskelyne's and Cooke's parody of the Davenports' cabinet séance, the 'Enchanted Gorilla Den', revealing the knot employed, the movements of a mirror inside the cabinet and the exact manner in which the 'captive sailor' was able to steal behind the looking-glass. That the illusion relied on an inserted mirror was, Sexton explained, obvious from the tell-tale shadowy light that filled the cabinet once the mirror moved upwards. 'When Mr Maskelyne talks about no one ever having found out the principle upon which this illusion is accomplished, he displays an amount of effrontery that is really amusing. . . . It is exactly the same thing as the Proteus of Professor Pepper [who had engineered the means of projecting the spectral ghosts of Hamlet's father and Jacob Marley on to the stage of Royal Polytechnic], excepting that the glass is arranged differently.' As for Maskelyne's levitation, the performance was, when compared to accounts of Home's remarkable feat at Ashley Place, 'as the ascent of an eagle to an acrobat climbing a rope'.

The kind of spiritual burlesque that Maskelyne and Cooke brought to the Egyptian Hall was, as Sexton rightly inferred, not entirely new to the English stage. As early as 1846, homegrown illusionists had begun to ape the second-sighted exploits of somnambulists such as Alexis Didier, and a host of visiting virtuosi, including Jean Eugène Robert-Houdin Houdin, had also showcased more elaborate feats of 'Mental Conjuring' and 'Pretended Mesmerism' at the St James Theatre. Maskelyne's own portfolio of 'Modern Witchery' drew inspiration from various sources, but his most obvious debt was to John Henry Anderson, 'The Great Wizard of the North', the Scots-born showman and impresario who had used his lavish theatricals to denounce spiritualist mediums as 'conjurers in disguise'.

A second-rate illusionist with a genius for self-promotion, Anderson had, in 1849, famously entertained Queen Victoria and Prince Albert at Balmoral with his extravagant display of 'scientific magic and legerdemain'. During a subsequent tour of America he set about exposing the *diablerie* of spirit rapping, but proved wildly mistaken in assuming that mediums such as the Fox sisters relied on any form of electrical apparatus. After incurring heavy losses in a rather feeble attempt at emulating the Davenports' cabinet séance, the Great Wizard decided that it was time to challenge England's most renowned medium, Daniel Dunglas Home. The confrontation, which took place at Willis's Rooms in St James Street, birthplace of the Liberal Party, was not quite what Anderson had envisaged. Home began his lecture with some consoling words for the gathered converts. Spiritualism's lesson was quite simple: 'it does teach that the pure heart shall see God. He teaches us that he is love, and that there is no death.' To find spiritualism but one step removed from insanity, or to argue that his own powers were due to legerdemain and self-deception on the part of the sitters was, Home intoned, 'fantastic, far-fetched and inadequate'. Anderson, evidently in no fit state to address a public meeting, took this as his cue. Taking off his coat, he began to denounce Home while striding purposefully towards the platform. Before Anderson had a chance to warm to his theme, Home had jumped from the platform and called on the ushers to escort the ruddy-faced unbeliever from the building.

John Nevil Maskelyne was a more sober and mindful critic of Home and his excitable brethren. Home's manifestations were, Maskelyne maintained, 'strong or weak in exact proportion to the abundance or lack of faith in the company he found himself'. Take away 'all that may be trickery, or due to an "excited" . . . or diseased state of the brain, and we shall have few miracles on hand'. To his mind, William Crookes, Alfred Russel Wallace and Cromwell Varley had all been repeatedly duped by errant trickery. Brewster had made a pig's ear of his séance-room investigations. And the London Dialectical Society had not even thought to engage the services of a competent conjurer. To exorcise the ghost of the supernatural from the séance room required hands-on insights into the art of illusion – insights these scientific luminaries patently lacked.

As an expert in the science of illusion, Maskelyne was confident that he could imitate the jugglery of any medium who feigned contact with the spirit world. But this would not be enough to halt the epidemic of spiritualist insanity. To do so, Maskelyne recognised that spirit hoaxers would have to be pursued into the law courts and prosecuted for obtaining monies under false pretences. Mrs Marshall and Mrs Guppy, the Misses Cook, Fairlamb, Fay, Fox, Nichols, Wood and Stokes, Messrs Herne, Williams, Bastian and Taylor – all the metropolitan mediums who charged for their manifestations 'deserved the attention of Scotland Yard'.

The spiritualist press complained that Maskelyne's crusade against these séance tricksters was merely a commercial expedient, a ruse, providing an enticing strap line for the Egyptian Hall's ubiquitous playbills. To a certain extent the complaint was valid: anti-spiritualist puffery certainly made for good business at the box office. Yet Maskelyne's bid to expose séance-room trickery was nevertheless in time with the growing alliance of professional magicians who identified themselves as public enemies of urban tricksters, swindlers and flimflam merchants. England's most renowned conjurer accepted that it was his professional duty to police the scams and tricks that were being perpetrated in the name of spiritualism. And within weeks of taking on the full lease of the Egyptian Hall, he was gifted the opportunity he had been waiting for: the chance to assist in exposing an established medium in a court of law.

Six foot tall, with 'a figure of unusual symmetry' and 'a face that would attract notice anywhere for its uncommon beauty', 'Dr' Henry Slade had forged a reputation as one of New York's most capable and innovative mediums. In 1861, after abandoning his practice as a mesmeric healer, Slade began to beguile his paying sitters with levitations and demonstrations of 'direct writing' from the spirit world. At first Slade's spirit messages materialised only in dark séances, being revealed once the lights were turned up again. As public suspicion of dark séances mounted, Slade, conveniently enough, discovered that the spirits were not averse to scribbling messages on slates that rested on his lap. When Madame Blavatsky was dispatched to New York to find mediums worthy of investigation at the Imperial University, Slade was among the first to be tested by the enigmatic *grande dame* of theosophy. After he had summoned 'real phantoms' and induced the spirits to compose long messages in Russian on blank slates, Blavatsky invited Slade, 'one of the best and least fraudulent mediums ever developed', to perform in St Petersburg. Slade and his manager, Mr Simmons, belatedly accepted the offer but decided to try their luck first in London, where many of their compatriots were already making a tidy living.

English séance goers had for many years sought written communication from the spirit world. In the late 1850s the prospect of direct communication without the intervention of a medium had been raised after reports that Baron de Guldenstubbé, a Scandinavian nobleman who had previously introduced table turning to France, had succeeded in obtaining messages from St Paul, Plato, Cicero and Juvenal, as well as a number of deceased friends. According to de Guldenstubbé, the first of his signed messages had appeared in a small locked box containing pencil and paper, and then on sheets of paper he had strategically placed in the cemeteries of Montmartre and Montparnasse, at the Louvre, the Cathedral of St Denis, the Museum at Versailles, and at various churches and ruins in France, Germany and England. Convinced that this '*phénomène merveilleux*' was indubitable evidence of spiritual agency, de Guldenstubbé's account of '*écriture directe*' provoked a wave of copycat experiments in Europe and America.

Cases of so-called 'psychography' had rarely been reported in England before Slade's arrival in London. Generally speaking, the only written communications that English spiritualists received were those that came from the tremulous hands of entranced mediums (such as one Thomas Slater, to whom Robert Owen turned when he wanted news and counsel from the Duke of Kent and other deceased friends) or by way of the planchette, a small heart-shaped writing device running on castors, which had been manoeuvred round the séance table with varying success since the late 1860s. The prospect of receiving messages direct from the spirit world brought a parade of fashionable ladies and gentlemen rushing to consult Slade in his newly rented rooms in Russell Square. Among the first of the sovereign-paying guests was a journalist from the *World*, who found himself 'inexpressibly puzzled and perplexed' by the wild-eyed American postmaster:

A highly-wrought nervous temperament, a dreamy mystical face, eyes luminous with expression, a rather sad smile, and a certain melancholy grace of manner were the impressions conveyed by the tall lithe figure introduced to me as Dr Slade. He is the sort of man you would pick out of a roomful as an enthusiast. He at once invited me into a back room on the same floor, in the centre of which stood a small table, without a cloth or other covering... I seated myself at one side of the table, he also sitting at it sideways. The corner was between us. The table was about five feet by four, had four legs, no ledge below or covering upon it. It would be difficult to imagine anything simpler or more overboard, as we both placed our palms upon it.

Dr Slade's long, white nervous fingers had scarcely touched mine when a violent knocking began. The doctor became visibly agitated... his excitement, and subsequent exhaustion, impressed me as strongly as anything which happened during this curious interview. 'You are a medium, sir,' he gasped; and I, feeling like the man who had talked poetry all his life without knowing it, smiled feebly, as if to say, 'So you've found me out.' The knocking immediately became more vehement, and the doctor declared the spirit of his wife wished to pronounce on my claims to mediumship. There were a couple of ordinary-looking slates lying near, and taking one of these, and placing on it a tiny piece of common slate pencil, bitten from a stick and about the size of a grain of wheat, the doctor held the slate under the table with one hand, saying at the same time, 'Is this gentleman a medium, Allie?' The words were hardly spoken before there was a sound of writing, followed by two or three vigorous taps. The slate was looked at, and 'He is not', in a flowing hand was written on it. [Later]... messages of various kinds were inscribed rapidly and in different handwritings. One, the longest, was of a religious character, and inculcated the usual religious lessons. Others were in reply to questions in which I pressed hard for a communication on some subject which could be known only to myself. Dr Slade did not discourage this, but said, 'We cannot but try; write the name of the deceased person you wish to communicate with on the side of the slate I cannot see, and we'll ask if he be present.' I did so, and the answer came promptly . . . the name I had written was not present. I tried again, writing another name. The slate was held under the table, and a message came in the first person, signed with Christian name in full and the initial of the surname, saying, 'I cannot write more at present,' or something equally vague.

Within a matter of weeks, Slade's 'long, white nervous fingers' had plied Edward Cox, William Carpenter, Alfred Russel Wallace, William Crookes, William Harrison, Colonel Lane Fox and Lord Raleigh with messages from the spirit world. Some of these visitors took the precaution of bringing their own slates, investigating the underside of the table, and examining Slade's hands and sleeves, but, of course, no evidence of trickery was discovered. The Reverend Stainton Moses, a relatively recent convert to spiritualism and a powerful medium in his own right, was greeted with a performance he would never forget. During his half-hour sitting Moses received several short messages, heard accordion music and was 'levitated, chair and all' a few inches above the ground. Never before had he seen such phenomena 'occur rapidly and consecutively in broad daylight'.

With the exception of Edward Cox and William Carpenter, all of Slade's early sitters appeared to have been taken in by his stock sermons and desultory asides. Alfred Russel Wallace 'saw nothing whatever indicative of imposture' in Slade's séances. Any motion of the medium's arm seemed to him 'involuntary', being due to the state of agitation he had seen so many mediums overcome with. As regards the paucity of actual information carried in the slate writings, Wallace attached significance only 'to the fact that there is writing, not to the subject matter of the writing'. Appearing to have opened a new channel of communication with the Other World, Slade was hailed as spiritualism's daylight saviour. Even sceptical investigators who were highly dubious of physical mediums added their voice to the chorus of hallelujahs in pronouncing slate writing 'A Modern Miracle'. After a month in London, it was little wonder Slade and Simmons agreed that St Petersburg could wait.

In September 1876 the British Association for the Advancement of Science held its annual meeting in Glasgow. Following a controversial call for the formation of a scientific committee dedicated to the study of mesmeric and spiritual phenomena, a number of conference speakers put forward Slade's name as a medium whose powers might be usefully investigated. Edwin Ray Lankester, a young and brash Professor of Zoology at University College, took a deep breath and shook his 'heavy-jawed, pig-like face'. Only days earlier Lankester had made an appointment to sit with Slade. Convinced that he would uncover subterfuge of some sort, the young zoologist was not disappointed. What he had seen of Slade led him to believe that the kind of research that his colleagues were proposing was misconceived:

> The real question to be investigated in this matter is not 'By what strange agency are these Spiritualist marvels brought about?' but 'How is it that apparently sane persons believe that Spiritualist tricks are marvels due to a strange agency?' The answer which all history and experience gives to the latter question is to be found in the existence of an unsuspected amount of credulity and incapacity for observation, and of an unsuspected amount of impudence and mendacity.

During his séance with Slade on 11 September, Lankester had 'most distinctly heard the sound of writing on the slate', while noticing 'a movement showing that his fingers were moving'. When Slade asked him to provide any kind of question for the spirits he wrote: 'Where was I on Saturday afternoon,' turned the slate over and passed it back. 'The slate was soon out of my sight, and I saw him moving. He said, "They are a long time coming." I felt convinced before the slate went under the table that the message was already written. However, the scratching noise was heard, and the following answer was given, "We did not see you on Saturday afternoon."' All of Slade's subsequent messages and manifestations appeared to be equally contrived.

Lankester, a former laboratory assistant to Thomas Huxley, was a staunch Darwinian who would go on to forge an international reputation for his work on the evolutionary understanding of embryology, degeneration and the morphology of spiders, crabs and scorpions. Too young to have played a part in the storming debates that followed the publication of *The Origin of Species*, his talents and tenacity were quickly recognised by Darwin, who predicted that Lankester would 'some day become our first star in Natural History'. Looking to further impress his mentor, Lankester turned his sights on exposing the fakery of the mediums that had made converts of Wallace and Hensleigh Wedgwood, Darwin's cousin and brother-in-law. Out of respect to Wallace, Darwin had refrained from making any public statements on the subject of spiritualism, but most of his inner circle were fully aware of his desire to see its 'clever rogues' exposed.

Lankester was not exactly certain how Slade's messages were composed, but the medium's attempt to divert his attention by way of kicks, raps, convulsive movements and incessant chatter suggested that the only agency that slate writing required was sleight-of-hand. Determined to catch his 'wild beast', Lankester made a second appointment and brought a friend,

Dr Horatio Donkin, to assist. After the usual preliminaries, Slade took a slate under the table and invited Lankester to hold it, so that the spirits might write more distinctly. Seizing his moment, Lankester pulled the slate from his lap:

> I got up from the table holding the slate up, and said, 'You have already written on it. I have watched you doing it each time. You are a scoundrel and an impostor.' These words were already on the slate, 'I am glad to meet you, Edwin Lankester' . . . I then carried the slate into the waiting-room, where there were five persons besides Simmons. Slade said nothing at all. He appeared much agitated, fell back in the chair, and became white. He made no explanation whatever.

After submitting an account of Slade's exposure to *The Times*, Lankester instructed his solicitor, George Lewis, to apply for criminal proceedings. Slade was accused of violating the 1824 Vagrancy Act by 'unlawfully using certain subtle craft, means, and devices to deceive and impose', and both men were alleged to have conspired to cheat and defraud – a charge which, if sustained, would see the case brought before a jury. In a letter to *The Times*, Slade denied all the claims Lankester had made. No message had been found on the slate – 'there were only two, or, at the most, three, words on the upper surface of the slate.' Moreover, he had, at the very moment that Lankester grabbed the slate, apparently announced that the spirits were writing.

Lankester's motives for pursuing his 'wild beast' as far as the courtroom were not quite what they seemed. Though genuinely aggrieved that recent discussions of the British Association had been 'degraded by the introduction of the subject of Spiritualism', he was also preoccupied by his family's interest in séance-room manifestations. Since the death of his father in 1875, Lankester's mother had consulted several mediums, and made numerous attempts to obtain messages from Edwin Snr on the planchette. On the afternoon of 15 September 1876 he had by coincidence met his mother en route to a séance with Slade and failed to dissuade her from keeping her appointment. What Mrs Lankester went on to observe left her less than well disposed towards her son's belligerent materialism. The first message she received was from a spirit called Phoebe – the very spirit that had once signed its name through her planchette. Even if Slade had time to write messages under the table, 'she really did not know what he did. She had heard of clairvoyance and that some people believe that a name in the mind of one of the sitters might be written on the table.' Unable to convince his mother that Slade had used Simmons as a confederate, extracting and passing on information relating to her previous experience of the spirits, Lankester resolved to settle the matter in court. Darwin was delighted to learn that a professional medium would finally be appearing in court. He sent his congratulations and ten pounds towards the cost of prosecution.

The court and bench were crowded to excess when Slade made his first appearance at Bow Street Court on 2 October. Over thirty reporters were on hand to file reports on what would be remembered as 'one of the strangest courtroom cases in Victorian England'. Outside, a rowdy throng of supporters brandished placards proclaiming Slade's innocence. George Lewis opened the case for the prosecution by describing the cruel charade that Slade and Simmons had apparently employed to defraud clients who came to them hoping to contact departed relatives:

'Conjurers in Disguise'

[Mr] Simmons, being seated in an outer apartment, saw the persons who came, with the view of picking up any information he could. Many of the visitors dropped hints, which were duly communicated to Slade, and enabled him to carry on the fraud he practised. Simmons carried on all communications outside the room. If anyone wrote for an appointment, Simmons would make it; and if the case for the prosecution was correct that Slade himself wrote the spirit messages, it was important that his handwriting should be unknown to those who went to see him. ... After visitors had spent a little time with Simmons, they were asked into the adjoining room where Mr Slade was, where no more than two visitors were allowed at a time. ... Mr Slade always kept the visitors well engaged in conversation after the fashion of conjurers generally. Part of a conjurer's business is to keep up conversation, so as to distract at the moment of performing the trick, and this was done by Mr Slade. He also pretended to be very much affected when under the influence of the spirits; he shuddered or shivered, and put himself in various attitudes and seemed to be much alarmed, and in the midst of this visitors received kicks under the table. There was nothing done that was not within the reach of his legs or arms that he could not do with either foot or hand, nothing that a good conjurer could not do more cleverly.

To demonstrate how Slade had produced his more extended communications, Lewis produced an ordinary wooden-framed slate on which he had written, 'I wonder whether the spirits will appear in court before the magistrates to-day.' Taking a sponge that had been moistened with wine, he rubbed the surface clean and told the court that the message would soon be visible. Before the words had a chance to reappear the bench intervened. Indicating that this was not prima facie evidence of an attempt to deceive, the magistrate pointed out that since Dr Lankester and Donkin 'did not believe the pretence of communicating with spirits before the *séance*', it would be difficult to uphold the claim that the defendants had defrauded the doctors. Lewis insisted that the prosecution had been undertaken in the public interest. Evidence that the defendants had conspired together to obtain money by false pretences would, Lewis promised, be provided in due course. Any persons able 'to give testimony on these matters' were invited to contact his Holborn office.

After taking to the witness stand to give evidence relating to his two visits to Dr Slade, Professor Lankester was cross-examined and asked why he had, in his first letter to *The Times*, observed that Slade had produced the messages with a single finger. Realising that he had been a little hasty in committing his early speculations to print, Lankester floundered: 'The writing may have been produced, but I cannot say. I think it was.' A week later, when Lankester returned to give further evidence, he found himself facing a sizeable group of lady spiritualists who stood patiently, 'occasionally giving audible utterance to their view on the evidence being given'. Georgina Weldon, the most vocal of Slade's supporters, was a professional singer who had recently turned her Bloomsbury home into a progressive orphanage. Alongside her stood Mrs MacDougall Gregory, widow of the late professor, and various members of the British National Association of Spiritualists who had heard that John Nevil Maskelyne would today be missing a matinée performance at the Egyptian Hall to give evidence.

Lankester's opening testimony gave Slade's supporters reason to cheer. On being asked to peruse the mahogany Pembroke table, which he had previously described as 'calculated to facilitate the movement of Dr Slade's arms, and legs', the professor stalled and stumbled, unable to give a positive answer. 'It must be the same, or it might not. It looked like it.' To the jeering delight of Slade's supporters the remainder of Lankester's deposition was terse and agitated. Having no precise explanation of the manner in which Slade had produced the messages, Lankester was fast losing his 'calm and superior air'. Casting furtive glances to his side, in the direction of a trim, neatly dressed man with a brush moustache, Lankester merely reiterated the fact that Donkin had detected movement of Slade's flexor tendons.

> At this point a truly dramatic incident occurred. Mr Maskelyne, who had been in court an attentive listener to the proceedings saw that the moment for his interposition had arrived. Professor Lankester . . . was in obvious difficulty, and, briskly stepping across the platform of the bench, Maskelyne came to the rescue. Turning up the table, he adroitly diverted public attention from the point at issue to other features in the construction [of the table].

Maskelyne had made public his intention to expose Slade's trickery in several newspaper advertisements. Inspecting the medium's table, he explained that one or two appendages had been removed since Dr Slade had last used it, and that it was a very convenient table for the 'business' he was engaged in. A small wedge had been inserted for the production of raps, and a movable bar on the underside held the slates, freeing Dr Slade's fingers to compose messages under the table. The trick was, he announced, really quite simple. Returning to the witness box, Maskelyne placed a thimble with a tiny pencil on its apex on one of his fingers, took a wooden slate, and, while holding it with one hand, wrote on its underside, 'The spirits are here.'

Maskelyne was in the midst of explaining the curious appearance and disappearance of writing on the slate, when the magistrate, Mr Flowers, turned to address objections raised by Slade's solicitor. 'Mr Maskelyne, undaunted by these protests proceeded to address the court, and to illustrate his "mysteries", obliterating and reviving the messages written on the slate in a few seconds by the application of a sponge dipped in some chymical fluid.' Ignoring growing protests from Slade's supporters, Maskelyne rattled on, describing the case of a medium who had, while having his arms held either side, contrived to write messages using a piece of pencil held in his mouth. When Slade's manager intervened, to ask if he could examine the slate, Maskelyne barked back, 'Oh, you know all about it.'

Maskelyne's cameo appearance changed the whole nature and course of the trial. 'From that moment on,' observed the Reverend Moses, 'the public mind was possessed with the notion that the table was a trick, and even the magistrate, who knew nothing whatever about it and had never examined it, heedlessly adopting the conjurer's suggestion, pronounced it to be "the most extraordinary table I have ever seen".' As far as the neutral observer was concerned, the evidence submitted by Slade's most prominent supporters only confirmed that spiritualism's leap of faith required a diminished capacity for critical inquiry. Wallace, for example, repeated that he had seen nothing indicative of imposture during his three visits to Slade. When asked to compare a specimen of Slade's own handwriting with the writings that appeared on the slate, Wallace noted the 'general resemblance' but did not think it had any bearing on the question of spiritual authorship.

The newly formed British National Association of Spiritualists had hoped that the Slade trial would expose the scientific community's inability to confront Nature's most opaque secrets, exposing the Lankester-Donkin offensive as an alliance of half-thinking philosophers. The same sentiment was echoed by Helena Blavatsky in the American spiritualists weekly, *The Banner of Light*. The 'experiments' she had conducted with Slade before his departure for England led her to believe that spiritualism's golden hour was imminent. If the courts allowed Slade to summon his spirit council, Blavatsky thought that spiritualism would claim its first public triumph over 'the world of matter'.

A week before the court convened to pass final judgment on Slade, his supporters received some ominous news. Francis Ward Monck, a Baptist minister who was rumoured to have acquired a carriage and yacht since becoming a professional medium, had also been charged under the Vagrancy Act in Huddersfield. Monck had been giving a séance at the home of a local wool merchant when an amateur conjurer insisted on seeing the paraphernalia he carried with him. Monck fled to his bedroom, escaped from the window using a sheet, and left behind three boxes containing gloved spirits' hands, musical boxes and other incriminating items. Here was clear evidence of subterfuge. Even if Slade managed to escape conviction, the spiritualist movement would soon have its first courtroom martyr.

On the morning of 1 November 1876 Slade was found guilty of 'using some subtle agent, means, or device likes palmistry' to 'deceive or impose upon some person' and sentenced to three months' imprisonment with hard labour. Slade's defence gave notice of appeal and, courtesy of a donation from the Spiritualists' Defence fund, paid bail at £400. A few days later a Huddersfield court issued the same sentence to Francis Monck, who, on being dispatched to Wakefield Gaol, allegedly rejoiced at the prospect of suffering for 'the glorious truth of Spiritualism'.

The outcome of the Slade trial not only surprised the medium's more gullible followers. The *Spectator*, a journal that had done spiritualism few favours over the last three decades, expressed bewilderment at the magistrate's handling of the trial. No evidence had been produced to substantiate Lankester's claims of imposture and, while Maskelyne had been allowed free run of the courtroom, the testimony of several defence witnesses had been deemed inadmissible. Two months on the Middlesex Court of Sessions overturned Slade's sentence, ruling that the Vagrancy Act could not be applied to slate writing. Before a date was set for retrial, Slade and Simmons made a hasty retreat, travelling on to Germany and Russia. In 1885, after appearing before the University of Pennsylvania's Seybert Commission (a ten-man committee that had begun to undertake an 'impartial investigation of all systems of morals, religion, or philosophy which assume to represent the truth . . . of Modern Spiritualism'), Slade's methods were again exposed. As one commissioner put it, the only remarkable aspect of his performances was 'the recklessness of the risks which he assumes in his deceptions'.

Back at the Egyptian Hall, Messrs Maskelyne and Cooke lost no time in adding slate writing to their repertoire of spiritualist mockeries. The trick, which Maskelyne had only partially revealed in court, had actually taken him some weeks to figure out. Sitting sideways on from his guests, Slade had, while asking his sitters to inspect the slate, used his left hand to retrieve a flesh-coloured thimble, which he had tied to a piece of elastic on his right arm. The medium had then slipped the thimble on to the middle finger of his right hand and, after resting the slate on a hidden ledge under the table, used its leaded edge to compose a short message. As soon as he had finished he would turn his finger inwards and let the elastic carry the thimble back up his sleeve.

The production of the longer messages and sermons did not, however, rely on the method that Maskelyne and Lewis had so confidently outlined in court. Slade's technique was far simpler. Pre-prepared slates or 'flaps' were housed on the underside of the table, and these were either substituted for the clean slates or inserted directly over them. All in all it was, as the Seybert Commission concluded after observing Slade in action, a 'perfectly transparent' parlour trick, which he 'practiced in the most barefaced manner'.

Chapter Ten

Mental Notes

*I cannot but take exception to such terms as 'psychology',
holding the soul . . . to be the ego of man.*
    Sir Richard Burton, letter to Dr Charles Tuckey, 1889

In November 1872 Edward Tylor, one of the great armchair-bound Victorian anthropologists, left his Somerset home to embark on a fortnight's fieldwork in the outer reaches of Bloomsbury, Mayfair, Islington and Notting Hill. Tylor intended to 'look into the alleged manifestations' that had come to his attention through correspondence with William Crookes and Edward Cox. Now that Home's powers were in decline, he was particularly keen to witness the first wave of spirit materialisations that he had heard so much about, and to meet Kate Fox (of Rochester Rappings fame). Also on Tylor's itinerary was a new and powerful medium who had recently been appointed English master at University College: Reverend William Stainton Moses.

A tall, imposing man with an Old Testament beard, Tylor was inclined to dismiss modern spiritualism as an atavistic delusion: 'a survival and a revival of savage thought, which the general tendency of civilization and science has been to discard'. In his classic study of animism among the 'lower races', *Primitive Culture*, he argued that man in his lowest state of culture is a 'wonderfully ignorant, consistent, and natural spiritualist'. Rapping, spirit writing, levitation and other séance manifestations were, for Tylor, simply latter-day analogues of the superstitions, delusions and trickery that all races wallowed in before the advent of natural science.

Despite these grave misgivings, Tylor's first impressions of the portly, regal-looking Reverend Moses were surprisingly positive. The schoolmaster talked openly about his history of illness and somnambulism – he claimed to have once written a prizewinning essay in his sleep – and described himself as 'sensitive in the extreme', regularly having 'mysterious senses of future things'. Writing to his wife Anna, Tylor observed that Moses appeared to be 'not only honest but not morbid-minded'. Better still, Reverend Moses had 'jumped' at the idea of participating in some 'experimental tests' with Tylor.

In the first of two séances that took place in the darkened library of Edward Cox's home, the sceptical anthropologist heard little more than a few scratching raps coming from the medium's heavy chair. After excusing himself for a short while, and returning to learn that he had missed some quite violent manifestations, Tylor watched Moses yawning and gasping into trance. When paper and pen were placed at his disposal, his twitching hand wrote in large letters: 'We cannot manifest through the medium.' During a later séance Moses again sat in the dark and produced some rappings and occasional movements of the table before making a conspicuously hurried exit.

Two of the ladies who were present at this Russell Square séance, both ardent believers, duly informed Tyler that Moses had sat close up and into the table, and provided its main thrusts. At one point, one of the ladies' hands had been lodged between the table and Moses's leg, and she had distinctly felt the powerful thrust that sent the table towards her. These sitters 'were utterly convinced (while retaining their faith in the manifestations of mediums under other circumstances) that this particular medium had been fraudulently assisting nature'.

Tylor returned to Somerset not knowing what to believe. Frank Herne and Charles Williams, two mediums who anticipated Florence Cook in their materialisation of full-body spirit figures, had failed to show. Neither Mrs Guppy nor Lottie Fowler had produced any positive results. Mrs Jenny Homes, 'a half-educated American with a black bush of curls' had been seemingly possessed by the spirit of an Ojibwa Indian, but her performance suggested nothing more than imposture: 'the most shameful and shameless I ever came across'. Mrs Olive's 'acting of her various characters was superficial, without any insight, and in voice and language pitiable'. And yet Kate Fox's raps (which seemed to emanate from every side and corner of the room) were genuinely puzzling, and the Reverend Moses appeared, despite the testimonies he had received, altogether trustworthy: 'his trance seemed real, & he made out he knew nothing of what he had done.' A well-respected schoolmaster, 'a gentleman and apparently sincere', Moses received no remuneration for his séances – only 'a certain social consideration'.

Moses, the most prominent of the High Church converts to spiritualism, was no ordinary medium. Born in Lincolnshire in 1852, he suffered the first of several nervous breakdowns while studying at Exeter College, Oxford. After travelling to St

Petersburg and spending several months recovering from 'brain fever' in the Byzantine monasteries on Mount Athos, Moses returned to Oxford to sit his finals, being ordained by Bishop Wilberforce in 1863. During his first curacy at Kirk Maughold in the Isle of Man, Moses carried out his pastoral duties with great 'kindness' and 'liberality', but by the end of the decade his health and faith were in mutual decline. Questioning the narrow dogmas of the Anglican Church, and with a persistent battery of ailments ostensibly preventing him from public speaking, Moses preached his last sermon at the age of twenty-eight.

On transferring to London, Moses began his headlong journey into religious heterodoxy in the home of Dr Stanhope Templeman Speer. Unable to follow the freethinkers and agnostics who had elected to become pallbearers at God's funeral, Moses's search for a new faith saw him exploring the Cabbala, astrology and various other occult byways. At the suggestion of Mrs Speer, he finally, and somewhat reluctantly, turned his sights on the new spiritualist credo. *The Debatable Land* by Robert Dale Owen, the social reformer and son of Robert Owen, made a deep impression. Spiritualism was, Owen exhorted, necessary to confirm the truths of Christianity and ensure its future progress. As such, all believers were encouraged to accept that the investigation of spiritual manifestations was nothing less than a 'sacred duty'.

Moses attended his first séance with Miss Lottie Fowler, a regular attraction at James Burn's Spiritual Institution. After falling into trance, Miss Fowler – described by one observer as a 'pasty-faced, long-nosed, ugly creature' – would usually feign possession by a child spirit called Annie who proceeded to describe to each member of the circle the spirits that sat behind them. It was a well-worked routine. Fishing for hints and prompts, Miss Fowler chattered away, making many wild guesses before supplying Moses with 'a striking description of the spirit presence of a friend who had died in the North of England'. Over the next six months, after sittings with other public and private mediums, including Home, Moses became convinced that discarnate spirits were capable of earthly communication.

In the Speers' home circle at St John's Wood, Moses began to exhibit the first signs of personal mediumship. Lights rose from the floor and moved upwards through his body. Heavily perfumed breezes swept around the séance room. Candlesticks, ornaments and precious stones took flight. On returning to his locked room, Moses claimed to have found his clothes arranged in the shape of the cross. More than once, friends reported seeing him gently levitate in his chair. Then, in around August 1872, Moses's mediumship took a new turn – he received, while fully conscious, his first written message from the spirit world:

At first the writing was very small and irregular, and it was necessary for me to write slowly and cautiously and to watch the hand, following the lines with my eye, otherwise the message soon became incoherent, and the result was mere scribble.

In a short time, however, I found that I could dispense with these precautions. The writing, while becoming more and more minute, became at the same time very regular and beautifully formed . . . The answers to my questions (written at the top of the page) were paragraphed, and arranged as if for press: and the name of God was always written in capitals, and slowly, and, as it seemed, reverentially.

To begin with the spirits kept irregular hours, summoning

Moses to write at any moment he might find himself alone and in a suitably passive state of mind. By cultivating the habit of rising early and spending the first hour of the day awaiting the spirits (in a room that was especially reserved for his new 'religious service') Moses increased the frequency of messages. Though he would never be able to command the spirits to communicate at will, he was soon capable of talking, reading or following some unconnected line of reasoning while his hand freely transcribed messages into pocketbooks chosen especially for their 'psychic aura'. 'I could tell at once who was writing by the mere characteristics of the calligraphy. By degrees I found that the many Spirits who were unable to influence my hand themselves, sought the aid of a Spirit "Rector", who was apparently able to write more freely, and with less strain on me.'

Passive writing was an important tool to spiritualists who sought to develop mediumistic powers outside the séance, especially to men and women who were otherwise denied the opportunity to preach or lecture. Andrew Davis Jackson (1826–1910), the most prodigious of the nineteenth-century 'inspired' or 'passive' writers, was an apprentice shoemaker from Poughkeepsie, New York. Over the course of a fifteen-month period beginning in 1845, Jackson, while being mesmerised by a Bridgeport physician, succeeded in dictating serial instalments of an 800-page epic, *The Principles of Nature, Her Divine Revelations, and a Voice to Mankind*. Belying its author's rudimentary schooling, *The Principles* offered a mystico-scientific account of creation, alongside a critical analysis of the Old Testament and a blueprint for a new system of Socialism. Jackson's heady tome was deemed 'one of the most finished specimens of philosophical argument in the English Language'. On publishing the book in England in 1847, John

Chapman gave ringing endorsement to its moral and scientific insights. If *The Principles*' teachings were consonant with recent findings in astronomy and natural history, its philosophy was, according to the freethinking Chapman, deserving of comparison with the best of Kant, Fichte, Schelling and Hegel.

Although British spiritualists would never discover a homespun genius to match the 'Poughkeepsie Seer', aka 'the John the Baptist of Modern Spiritualism', they did eventually find in Reverend Moses (writing under the pen name of MA Oxon) an inspired writer who enjoyed prolific and instructive intercourse with the spirit world. Unlike most practitioners, who professed to be exasperated by the indiscreet gossip, bad language, poor spelling and dubious logic they had channelled, Moses found his spirit informants to be kindly and judicious, providing him with a reliable stream of messages of 'a pure and elevated character, much of it being of personal application'. All in all, Moses would go on to claim that he had received messages from more than eighty manifesting spirits, extending in serial continuity through to 1880. His personal galaxy of spirit guides included Plato, Seneca, Plotinus, Napoleon, John Dee, Benjamin Franklin and Beethoven, an illustrious band of prophets, sages and saints, a score of 'modern spirits' that Moses had known personally and a small number whom he had not.

Towards the end of 1873, the spirit messages of 'MA Oxon', the best-qualified English medium to date, commenced serialisation in William Harrison's *Spiritualist*. Almost all the short, instructive sermons Moses published over the following years were attributed to a spirit who signed himself '+ Imperator', with the 'Rector' acting as amanuensis. (Believing that many of the great and good who spoke to mediums were destitute and vagrant spirits from the borderland, Moses withheld the true identity of his real spirit guides: the prophet Malachi, with St Hippolytus playing the part of faithful scribe.) Courtesy of the 'Imperator', Moses became intimate with the vagaries of the unseen world, learning, among other things, that spirits communicate with each other by 'transfusion of thought', that another rank of spirits was occupied in providing the training and education that children's souls required before passing into the Single Sphere, and that the future life differed from our present 'only in a very slight degree'. Leading him towards a natural religion that found 'no saviour outside of himself', the messages purged him of all doubt. There was no heaven and hell, no devil, no material resurrection: 'man stands alone in his responsibility for his deeds, and must work out his own salvation, and atone for his own sin.'

Edward Cox, lawyer, publishing magnate and founder of the Psychological Society, had serious doubts about Moses's spirit brethren. For Cox, the messages Moses 'received' were displaced directly from the author's subconscious mind: they were fragments of his buried thoughts. Moses admitted giving 'this interesting subject for speculation' serious thought. Throughout his adult life he had been hostage to what he called 'special moods'. He was apt to 'do things one day, and especially say things, of which I have no remembrance ... When I come to myself, I know nothing of what has taken place; but sometimes I gradually recollect.'

Given his protracted history of somnambulism and dissociation, it might seem surprising that Moses so strenuously rejected the possibility that he himself might have been the unknowing author of the writings that would become 'the bible of British Spiritualism'. And yet, almost twenty years after having channelled the first of the Imperator's sermons, Moses continued to rebuff all psychological speculation as to the inner source of his *Spirit Teachings*: 'Spirits these people call themselves . . . and as such, I accept them.' In fairness, this was not a delusion that Moses entered into lightly or unquestioningly. He found several reasons to reject the 'recondite' theory of unconscious authorship: many of the opinions expressed in his spirit writings were at odds with his personal convictions; the prose style was most unlike his own; the handwriting was manifestly dissimilar; and while he wrote he was aware of being propelled by an external force.

Evidence of a different kind ultimately convinced Moses that he had become a veritable 'gas pipe' for communicating spirits. Towards the end of 1874, during a séance with the Speers, the table spelled out a message from a spirit that gave his name as Abraham Florentine and identified himself as a veteran of the Second War of American Independence. Moses published these scant particulars in *Light*, calling for information to verify the spirit's identity. Sure enough, a New York lawyer who had come across the name on a list of army 'claimagents' applied to the US Army and received official confirmation of Abraham Florentine's army service. Further enquiries led to an interview with his widow, who confirmed that he died, aged eighty-three, on 8 June 1874. This was the proof Moses was waiting for. Overlooking the rather more mundane explanation – that he might have read or peripherally scanned Florentine's obituary in an American newspaper – Moses's self-deception reached new heights.

Over the next six or so years Moses maintained almost daily contact with the Imperator and his band of spiritual advisers. These messengers confirmed that they had come 'to demonstrate to man that he is immortal, by virtue of the soul which is a spark struck off from the Deity itself'. The spirit world was, Moses found, a benign and welcoming place, a republic of universal love governed by higher and wiser spirits who atoned for the errors of the past, while providing moral instruction to ensure passage through the seven spheres of contemplation. Degraded or debased souls who had yielded to animal desires gravitated through the six lower spheres, remaining subject to 'the attempted influence of missionary Spirits, until desire for progress is renewed'. Every question Moses posed regarding modes of spiritual transport, communication and diet, as well as the weightier matters of damnation and salvation, was answered with commanding authority. It was a heart-warming preview of the future life, a blessed reminder of the 'infinite possibilities that are within your grasp', and the spiritualist community embraced it with open arms.

Shortly before collecting and revising his *Spirit Teachings* for publication in 1883, Moses, an inveterate club and committee man, joined two organisations that were in very different ways concerned with gathering evidence of the supernatural. The Ghost Club, an elite dining club that Moses resurrected with his poet friend Alaric Watts, met monthly for informal discussion on all kinds of ghostly manifestations. Here, Moses revealed that his knowledge of the spirit world was no longer derived solely from the Imperator's writings: 'I communicate now by voice. I hear the voice as of a distant person, borne on a breeze, always calm and passionless, as of one mot stirred by human gusts. I can in special moods "sense him" and his thoughts, and am conscious of a transfusion of them direct.'

The Society for Psychical Research (SPR), to which Moses was elected as vice-president in the same year, had a far more ambitious remit. Headed by an impressive trio of Cambridge intellectuals – Frederic Myers, Edmund Gurney and Henry

Sidgwick – it aimed to encourage 'persons of culture and good social position' to give exacting attention to 'that large body of debatable phenomena designated by such terms as mesmeric, psychical and spiritualistic'. Though Moses had, in the wake of the Slade prosecution, warned spiritualists not to expose themselves to the scrutiny of outsiders, he had enjoyed friendly relations with Myers and Gurney, and had dined with the SPR's president, Henry Sidgwick, on several occasions.

Like Moses, Sidgwick had felt the first stirrings of religious doubt in the early 1860s. Unimpressed by the desperate clerical attacks on Darwin's *Origin of Species* (which famously provoked Huxley to retort that he would prefer to have a miserable ape as a grandfather over any Right Reverend Prelate) Sidgwick's reading of Ernest Renan's *Life of Jesus* led him to study the historical and textual origins of Christianity. Finding no evidence of transcendental intervention in the biblical miracles, his deconversion was sealed. His surrogate faith, 'the morality of common sense', was the godless and utilitarian philosophy to which Martineau and Eliot had gravitated. Yet, unlike these mannish prophets of atheism, Sidgwick remained open to the possibility of the afterlife. In the early 1870s he and his future wife Eleanor began to seek out mediums in Cambridge and London. Sharing notes and observations with Myers, Gurney and other Trinity fellows, the Sidgwicks were soon convinced that all the scientific investigators of spiritualism and allied phenomena, from Faraday to Lankester, had been blind to its essential mysteries.

In his presidential address to the SPR in 1882, Sidgwick bemoaned the climate of scepticism, leading Moses and his fellow spiritualists to believe that the society would act as a forceful advocate:

We believed unreservedly in the methods of modern science, and were prepared to accept unreservedly her reasoned conclusions, when sustained by the agreement of experts; but we were not prepared to bow with equal docility to the mere prejudices of scientific men. And it appeared to us that there was an important body of evidence – tending *prima facie* to establish the independence of the soul or spirit – which modern science has simply left on one side with ignorant contempt; and that in so leaving it she had been untrue to her professed method, and had arrived prematurely at her negative conclusions.

While Frederick Myers and Edmund Gurney went on to carry out a prodigious amount of work on behalf of the SPR's committees on thought transference and mesmerism, the literary committee dispatched up to fifty letters a day in its attempt to collect and verify testimonial evidence of thought transference, haunting and crisis apparitions. As the SPR's membership swelled to over 300 (Tennyson and Carroll, Gladstone and Balfour were some of the more illustrious subscribers), its official *Proceedings* were supplemented by a monthly journal, local societies were consolidated in Oxford and Cambridge, and an American sister organisation was inaugurated in 1885. Owing largely to Sidgwick's astute presidency – not to mention his deep pockets – it was an object lesson in the formation of a vibrant scientific society.

But Moses soon had reason to regret his involvement with the SPR. Only a few months into his vice-presidency, many of the members whom he had helped steer towards the SPR were complaining that Sir William Barrett's work on telepathy – 'the nature and extent of any influence which may be exerted by one mind upon another, apart from any generalised mode of perception' – was being advanced to supplant the spirit hypothesis. Others complained that the research strategy that the SPR had embarked on was akin to that of 'a firm of solicitors preparing a case for trial', leading one angry correspondent to suggest: 'instead of evoking shadowy reminiscences of what occurred many years ago, why not test the alleged intervention of the spiritual universe in occurrences of today?'

The SPR appeared to have careered into a cul-de-sac. Having committed itself to a policy of eschewing the services of paid mediums, it found limited opportunities to intrude on private circles; and on the rare occasions that spiritualists did open their homes and families to SPR observers, investigators tended to return empty-handed. Thankfully, news from the American Society for Psychical Research (ASPR) was altogether more promising. The Boston-based ASPR had discovered a mental medium who was destined to become 'the most important figure in the history of psychical research' – or, as the philosopher and psychologist William James preferred, 'the one white crow that proves that all crows are not black'.

Born in New Hampshire in 1859, the 'modest' and 'matronly' Mrs Piper was married to a Beacon Hill clerk whose father was a keen spiritualist. In 1884, shortly after the birth of her first daughter, Mrs Piper, a sometime Methodist who was no longer attached to any Church, was advised to consult J. R. Cocke, a blind clairvoyant, for advice on her ovarian tumour. On first joining Cocke's circle, Mrs Piper's hands twitched and she was overcome by an unpleasant sensation of drowsiness. Weeks later, 'Dr' Cocke placed his hands on her head, causing her to see a flood of light and a sea of strange faces, before sending her unconscious. During subsequent sittings Mrs Piper entered a trance characterised by pronounced muscular unrest and fell under the control of an Indian girl called 'Chlorine'. An array of spirits, including Bach, Luther, Lincoln, Cornelius

Vanderbilt and an Italian signorina called Loretta Ponchini, soon took hold, but Mrs Piper's principal 'control' would be 'Dr Phinuit', a long-winded and often incomprehensible spirit who showed a talent for medical diagnosis, a poor grasp of his personal history and native tongue, and a 'startling intimacy' with the personal affairs of her sitters. Though Dr Phinuit bore a conspicuous resemblance to Dr Cocke's principal control, Albert G. Finnett, he was coarse, boastful and evasive: 'when he failed notoriously, as happened repeatedly, no one could be more ingenious in framing excuses than he.'

William James first learned of Mrs Piper from his mother-in-law, Mrs Gibbens. During her visit 'Mrs Gibbens had been furnished with a long string of names, together with facts about the persons mentioned and their relations to each other, the knowledge of which was incomprehensible without supernormal powers'. The following day Mrs Gibbens's daughter was equally amazed when Mrs Piper was able to describe the 'circumstances' of the writer of a letter she had brought with her. After playing the *'esprit fort'*, explaining to his in-laws that Mrs Piper had most probably drawn on mundane sources during their sittings, James made his first visit to Boston's latest medium, in the company of his wife:

> The names of none of us up to this meeting had been announced to Mrs P, and Mrs J and I were, of course, careful to make no reference to our relatives who had preceded. The medium, however, when entranced, repeated most of the names of 'spirits' whom she had announced on two former occasions and added others. The names came with difficulty, and were only gradually made perfect. My wife's father's name of Gibbens was announced first as Niblin, then as Giblin. A Child Herman (whom we had lost in the previous year) had his name spelt out as Herrin. I

think that in no case were both Christian and surnames given on the first visit. But the *facts predicated* of the persons named made it in many instances impossible not to recognise the particular individuals who were talked about. We took particular pains on this occasion to give the Phinuit control no help over his difficulties and to ask no leading questions.

Phinuit, despite 'every appearance of being a fictitious being', appeared to James 'a definite human individual, with immense tact and patience, and great desire to please'. Although Mrs Piper might conceivably have had access to James's family affairs through her servant's sister – who was employed by a family where Mrs Gibbens was a frequent visitor – James rather quickly ascribed the medium with powers 'as yet unexplained'. Over the following year James paid a dozen or so visits to Mrs Piper and arranged for friends and members of the ASPR to sit with her. Twelve of the sitters, who usually sat singly, got nothing from the medium but unknown names or trivial talk; fifteen of the sitters were surprised at the communications they received, names and facts being mentioned at the first interview that it seemed improbable should have been known to the medium in a normal way. In James's own case it was Mrs Piper's knowledge of 'intimate' or very trivial details that impressed him most:

> She said that we had recently lost a rug, and I a waistcoat. (She wrongly accused a person of stealing the rug, which was afterwards found in the house.) She told of my killing a gray-and-white cat, with ether, and described how it had 'spun round and round' before dying. She told how my New York aunt had written a letter to my wife, warning her against all mediums, and then went off on a most amusing criticism, full of *traits vifs*, of

the excellent woman's character. (Of course no one but my wife and I knew the existence of the letter in question.) She was strong on events in our nursery, and gave striking advice on our first visit to her about the way to deal with certain 'tantrums' of our second child, 'little Billy-boy', as she called him, reproducing his nursery name. She told how the crib creaked at night, how a certain rocking chair creaked mysteriously, how my wife had heard footsteps on the stairs, etc., etc. Insignificant as these things sound when read, the accumulation of a large number of them has an irresistible effect. And I repeat again what I said before, that, taking everything I know of Mrs P into account, the result is to make me absolutely certain as I am of any personal fact in the world that she knows things on her trances which she cannot possibly have known in her waking state, and that the definitive philosophy of her trances is yet to be found.

James was eager to know if Mrs Piper's trance state was analogous to the ordinary hypnotic trance that he had studied in his Harvard laboratory. His first attempts at hypnosis failed and it was only with the assistance of Phinuit – who kindly agreed to this indulgence – that James was able to induce some 'muscular phenomena' and 'automatic imitation of speech and gesture'. This semi-hypnotic state was, however, very different from her mediumistic trance: while the séance performances were accompanied by great physical agitation, the lassitude that overcame Mrs Piper under hypnosis impaired her ability to respond verbally or physically to suggestions. Furthermore, James found that Mrs Piper showed not the slightest intimation of thought transference under hypnosis, which might have explained her trance recourse to the intimate details regarding her sitters.

Satisfied that he had uncovered a 'genuine mystery', James returned to the more urgent business of finishing his *Principles of Psychology*, already six years past its promised delivery date. Before doing so, he fired off a short report to the ASPR, dropping a strong hint to his fellow psychical researchers as to the best way forward with Mrs Piper:

> If a good trance subject could be obtained for the society at the outset of her career, and kept from doing miscellaneous work until patiently and thoroughly observed and experimented on, with stenographic reports of trances, and as much attention paid to failures and errors as to successes, I am disposed to think that the results would in any event be of scientific value, and would be worth the somewhat high expenses which they would necessarily entail.

With no American researchers able to spare the time or financial investment that James recommended, the English SPR appointed Richard Hodgson, its only salaried researcher, to act as executive secretary to the ASPR, thereby assuming direct control of the Piper case. An athletic, bearded, chain-smoking Australian with a penchant for poetry and brown suits, Hodgson arrived in Boston maintaining that nearly all professional mediums were 'vulgar tricksters who are more or less in a league with one another'. Having already provoked a considerable stir within the SPR by exposing the occult phenomena associated with Madame Blavatsky, Hodgson had further alienated its spiritualist contingency by laying bare the mechanics of fraudulent slate writing, and by demonstrating the extent to which séance testimony was contaminated by malobservation and flawed memory. Inclined to believe that Mrs Piper would prove the author of a cleverly perpetrated fraud, his first sitting, carried out anonymously, gave him food for thought:

> Phinuit began, after the usual introduction, by describing members of my family.
>
> 'Mother living, father died, little brother dead.' [True.]
>
> Father and mother described correctly, though not with much detail. In connection with the enumeration of the members of our family, Phinuit tried to get a name beginning with 'R', but failed. [A little sister of mine, named Rebecca, died when I was very young, I think less than eighteen months old.]
>
> Phinuit mentioned the name 'Fred'. I said that it might be my cousin. 'He says that you went to school together. He goes on jumping frogs, and laughs. He says he used to get the better of you. He had convulsive movements before his death, struggles. He went off in a sort of spasm. You were not there.' [My cousin Fred far excelled any other person that I have seen in the game of Leap frog, fly the garter, &c. He injured his spine in a gymnasium in Melbourne, Australia, in 1871, and was carried to the hospital, where he lingered for a fortnight, with occasional spasmodic convulsions, in one of which he died.]

To exclude the possibility that Mrs Piper was deploying information culled from informants, Hodgson hired a private detective to tail Mrs Piper and intercept her household mail. Finding no evidence of suspicious journeys, indiscreet questioning, or agents being used to gather leads on Mrs Piper's behalf, Hodgson spoke to James and decided that to impose more stringent conditions on her sittings it would be best to remove Mrs Piper from her native milieu.

In November 1889, after spending two nights in Liverpool with Professor Oliver Lodge, Mrs Piper and her two children were taken to Leckhampton House, the Cambridge home of Frederic Myers. Mrs Myers could not contain her surprise: 'Why, Mrs Piper, you are not at all like I had expected. I thought you would wear your hair in frizettes and be dressed in magenta.' Lady Lodge, who had initially opposed her husband's foray into psychical research, was even more taken aback: 'When Mrs Piper came to us and I saw her beautiful face and realised the utter refinement of the woman, I became interested in my husband's investigation in spite of myself.'

Mrs Piper remained in England two months longer than anticipated, giving a total of eighty-three sittings for the SPR. Before her arrival in Cambridge, Myers took the precaution of selecting a servant from a nearby village who was 'quite ignorant of my own or my friends' affairs' to attend to Mrs Piper, and made sure that sitters were brought to her under false names. Lodge hired an entirely new set of staff, locking away the family bible and albums, and requesting permission to search her luggage for directories or biographies that might provide any information on her sitters. Though neither investigator was inclined to endorse the notion that Dr Phinuit – with his deep manly voice that mingled Negro patois, American slang and sub-schoolboy French – was a real person, both were shaken by communications that were purportedly conveyed by deceased friends and family. In his autobiography, Lodge recalled being greatly moved by his first sitting with Mrs Piper:

> The result was quite astonishing. Messages were received from many subordinate people, but the special feature was that my Aunt Anne . . . ostensibly took possession of the medium; and in her own energetic manner reminded me of her promise to come back if she could, and spoke a few sentences in her own well-

remembered voice. This was an unusual thing to happen, but was very characteristic of her energy and determination. The sitting continued till midnight, a great deal more was said, and Myers and I were both exhausted.

Lodge, Professor of Physics at the University of Liverpool, initially thought that much of the 'bare information' might have been acquired by mind reading. However, in later sittings in Liverpool, Mrs Piper's access to certain 'facts' that were 'in good faith asserted never to have been known' by the sitters came to the fore. None of the ordinary methods known to physical science, Lodge wrote in his report to the SPR, could explain the means by which she acquired such information: 'some hypothesis which goes as far as thought-transference from the minds of distant living persons is demanded.' Myers, the SPR's chief theorist, broadly agreed. Mrs Piper's ability to transfer her mental centre of perception to the spirit world seemed to indicate that 'telepathy and the cognate faculties' were inherent in the 'subconscious strata of human intelligence'.

The notion of subliminal consciousness that Myers outlined in a string of essays, and in his posthumous book *Human Personality and its Survival of Bodily Death*, proposed that 'the stream of consciousness in which we live is not the only consciousness which exists in connection within our organism'. Myers thought it perfectly possible that 'other thoughts, feelings, and memories, either isolated or in conscious connection, may now be actively conscious, as we say, "within me" – in some kind of co-ordination with my organism, and forming some point of my total individuality'. Drawing on studies of hypnotism, hysteria, thought transference and various séance phenomena, this 'gothic psychology' not only attempted to highlight the shifting and multiplex nature of consciousness: Myers, 'a man of wide scientific imagination' and rarefied sensibility, also sought to register seismic shifts in human intelligence, sudden increments in man's mental powers. To him, Mrs Piper appeared as a butterfly on the cabbage leaf of evolution, a trailblazer on the 'pathway through which the human mind gropes upwards into full light'.

After writing to William James to obtain a full record of his experiences with Mrs Piper, Myers asked William's novelist brother Henry, who had made his home in London, whether he might read William's report at a meeting of the SPR in October 1890. Much to Myers's delight, Henry agreed. The short paper, which he went on to deliver at Westminster Town Hall at one of SPR's best-attended meetings, vouched emphatically for Mrs Piper's bona fides. Having renewed his contact with Mrs Piper in 1889, James insisted that she was an 'absolutely simple and genuine person', and that he was quite prepared to stake his reputation on her honesty. James had not kept notes of any of his sittings, however. He had no evidence or 'scientific theory to offer', only the abiding impression that this white crow was somehow tapping into a vast, cosmic repository of human memory.

Back in Boston, Mrs Piper agreed that Hodgson and the SPR should manage her future sittings, thereby ensuring herself an annual income of around one thousand dollars. The relationship between medium and investigator was often troubled (Hodgson's dealings with Mrs Piper were, James observed, characterised by a pronounced *'brusquerie'*, which she was clearly sensitive to) but enormously productive. In March 1892 Hodgson observed the appearance of a communicator who would gradually take over from Phinuit, producing 'a notable evolution in the quality of trance results'. The new control identified himself as George Pellew, a young writer and former member of the ASPR, who had died some weeks earlier following a riding accident. Speaking through Phinuit, Pellew spoke with 'a fullness of private remembrance and specific knowledge' that left around thirty sitters unable 'to resist the conviction that they were actually conversing with their old friend'.

Having had some contact with Pellew after he had sat anonymously with Mrs Piper, Hodgson concurred. In spirit, Pellew seemed to retain all 'the keenness and pertinency which were entirely characteristic of G. P.'. Seduced by the intimate information that Pellew transmitted via Mrs Piper, Hodgson now insisted that 'talk about the subliminal self in the usual sense, secondary personality and all that, simply won't do'. But while Hodgson was ready to sign up to the spirit hypothesis, Mrs Piper was not. Her personal views on the nature of her trance insights, as later reported in the *New York Herald*, seemed to lean towards telepathy as 'the most plausible and scientific solution'. This statement was later retracted by Mrs Piper, but even then she insisted that she remained uncertain of the true nature of her powers.

William James's ambivalence towards Mrs Piper became increasingly pronounced in the late 1890s. Bored 'to extinction' by the Piper investigation, James complained that the time and energy that Hodgson had expended were excessive, and that not one of the hundreds of reports that had been collected (arguably the first substantial records of the interaction between scientific observers and a subject in a trance state) could begin to convey the sense of wonder experienced by Mrs Piper's sitters:

The whole talk gets warmed with your own warmth, and takes on the reality of your own part in it; confusions and defects you charge to imperfect conditions, while you credit the success to the genuineness of the communicating spirit . . . These consequently *loom* more in our memory, and give the key to our dramatic interpretation of the phenomenon. But a sitting that thus seemed important at the time may greatly shrink in value on a cold rereading, and if read by a non-participant, it may seem thin and almost insignificant.

But there was another reason for James's diffidence. The SPR, as Mrs Piper's employer, was incurring a 'pecuniary responsibility for her old age'. Whatever he thought of Mrs Piper as a medium, this was not a responsibility he was willing to share.

James was called on to renew his investigation of Mrs Piper after the spirit of Richard Hodgson, who died suddenly during a game of handball in 1905, became the medium's new control. After sitting with Mrs Piper on half a dozen occasions, and studying the transcripts of seventy or so séances, James amassed a wealth of evidential information regarding Hodgson, much of it being quite personal to the sitters. How could Mrs Piper have known about Ella Densmore, the woman to whom Hodgson had secretly proposed marriage? How could she have supplied such detailed accounts of the times Hodgson had spent at Bar Harbor, as a summer guest of George Dorr? James did not think that Hodgson would have confided these and other personal incidents to Mrs Piper, but, once again, he had no definite answers to the Piper mystery. The content of the most telling communications was, he concluded, 'no more veridical than is a lot of earlier Piper material' and 'vastly more leaky and susceptible of naturalistic explanation'.

The journal *Science* echoed the sentiments of many prominent psychologists when it accused James of having lent himself to a grand hoax, and of 'doing much to injure psychology' through his endorsement of the Piper investigation. For Stanley Hall, a former student and colleague of James, this ill feeling was even more pronounced. Hall, an outspoken critic of psychical research, had visited Mrs Piper with James in the late 1880s and attempted to initiate some experiments of his own. James's serial reports on Mrs Piper's supernatural powers were everything that he expected from 'an *impressionist* in psychology'. The portrait that James had painted of Mrs Piper was, in Hall's mind, testament to one thing alone: 'an inveterate lust for evidence of the independent post-mortem existence of souls'.

Almost all the recorded transcripts of the Piper sittings were, Hall rightly noted, of little to no value in establishing the case for survival or telepathy. There was hardly 'any full record kept of what her interlocutors said . . . and even the full and exact form of questions is rarely, if ever kept'. While this failure was partly due to Mrs Piper's growing reluctance to permit stenographers into her sittings, a more fundamental fault was the investigative presumption of total unconsciousness in the medium. As soon as Mrs Piper fell into trance, observers were 'thrown completely off their guard, so that they at first whisper then talk *sotto voce*, and perhaps finally in their natural tones . . . feeling that she is out of their social circle'.

In the spring of 1909 Mrs Piper's new 'manager', George Dorr, agreed to allow Hall and his colleague Amy Tanner access to America's most famous medium. Over seventy-five thousand dollars had now been expended on Mrs Piper, with over two thousand pages of reports published in the SPR *Proceedings* alone. Hall set out to investigate Mrs Piper as 'an interesting case of secondary personality with its own unique features'. A battery of physiological and psychological tests would be administered over the course of six sittings to assess the extent to which the Hodgson control's knowledge and personality were contiguous with Mrs Piper, to gauge his suggestibility, and to see whether the fictitious ghost of Richard Hodgson might be induced to betray himself.

At their first meeting Hall introduced himself under his own name, which Mrs Piper 'seemed somewhat impressed by'. After only a few minutes of conversation her eyelids dropped, her breathing became heavy and her face 'worked convulsively'. As she fell forward into the pillows that were placed on the table before her, Mr Dorr raised her head and positioned himself close to her writing hand, so that he might help Hall decipher any words that he could not make out. Mrs Piper's hand lost no time in announcing the arrival of 'Rector, servant of God', one-time control to the Reverend Moses. Following the usual protocol of addressing all questions to Mrs Piper's hand, Dorr asked the rector whether Dr Hodgson might come and conduct the sitting. Almost immediately, Piper wrote to acknowledge Hodgson's presence. Curious to know how Hall was progressing in solving 'the problems of life', Hodgson accepted every fake memory and invented character with which Hall plied him. Always vague and elusive, constantly pressing his 'old friend' to talk, Hall thought that Hodgson appeared to be learning far more of this world than he was of theirs.

Though the SPR had been keen to present Mrs Piper as a healthy and well-balanced individual, Hall found that illness and depression had loomed large in the life of the widowed medium. The short interviews he went on to conduct with Mrs Piper prior to her falling into trance suggested that psychical research was unconscious of the ways in which it had sustained and directed her mediumship. The 'personalities' of all four of her dominant controls – Phinuit, Pelham, Imperator and Hodgson – had, Hall observed, been shapeless and fragmentary in their first incarnation:

> But by degrees, in response to the questionings of the sitter or of the person's own self-consciousness, the secondary personality gives itself a date of birth, and sometimes a birth place and family history, and when confronted with falsities and contradictions in its account of itself it shifts, evades, etc. very much as Phinuit did. But the point of especial importance here is, that the form which the personality takes depends upon the environment into which it has come, the attitude taken towards it by the person and her friends, etc.

Raised as a puritan, and holding that spiritualism was 'the common enemy of true science and true religion', Hall believed that Mrs Piper might, if isolated from 'spiritistic influences', be divested of her secondary personalities. Believing that he had been given carte blanche to perform any experiment, Hall attempted to secure a confession of deception from the Hodgson control. The ensuing interrogation, which he hoped would lead to a ghostly *felo de se*, spawned some unexpectedly comical exchanges:

> HALL: Now, Hodgson, I want to talk to you a little. Now I am going to be honest with you and tell you that you have not convinced us that you are Hodgson. You are just Mrs Piper's idea of Hodgson ... Mrs Piper is a remarkable woman to make you seem so lifelike and vivid, but nevertheless I am sure you are not Hodgson.

HODGSON: Look here, Hall, you ought to be ashamed to talk like that.

HALL: No, Hodgson, I am not ashamed. I am honest in this, and I want you to know just what I think before we say good-bye.

HODGSON: I U[nderstan]D, and I have been the same as far as it has been possible.

HALL: Very well, Hodgson, you are honest, too, so which shall I call you, Borst or Mrs Piper Second?

HODGSON: You can't call me either and be a comrade of mine.

HALL: Now, I want you to humour me, and let me call you one or the other.

HODGSON: I am neither. I am Hodgson, and I am perfectly sure of my own identity.

HALL: I wish I was. But I'm going to call you Borst.

HODGSON: Don't. Don't do that.

HALL: Why not?

HODGSON: Because I have felt so keenly, I have felt so keenly.

. . .

HALL: Now just as matters of repetition, to oblige me, repeat the words, 'I am not Hodgson.'

HODGSON: No. I am Hodgson.

HALL: Very well, this ends it then. You can't convince me, and I'm going to say good-bye forever.

HODGSON: I didn't expect to convince you in the least.

Despite its botched attempt to resolve 'the malady of a bifurcated personality', Hall's and Tanner's *Studies in Spiritism* offered a telling account of the genesis of Mrs Piper's trance mediumship. The medium's personations were, Hall surmised, readily assembled fictions or confabulations that fed on audible prompts of her sitters and on information already known to the medium. But if Mrs Piper's thaumaturgy could be explained in terms of the psychology of suggestion – and the capacious storehouse of personal memory that trance allowed her to retrieve – the social opportunities that psychical research offered this ambitious and clever Boston housewife were altogether more obvious.

Mrs Piper had no contact with Boston's lively subculture of spiritualism. She did not belong to any circle, sniffed at the *Banner of Light* and other journals, and 'seemed somewhat indignant that Dr Hall should suppose that she would connect herself with the common level of Spiritists'. A voracious reader, she made a point of reading every published report of her sittings, all the *Proceedings* of the SPR, and particularly enjoyed James's *Varieties of Religious Experience*. Hall's account of his investigations did not make for happy reading. According to Mrs Piper's daughter, his experiments were sufficient to cause a temporary withdrawal of her powers. Though she continued to work fitfully over the next decade, uncertainty as to the motive and intentions of her sitters made her resistant to trance.

Predictably enough, it was exactly as Hodgson had forecast twenty years previously. Refusing Professor Hall's request to conduct psychological tests with Mrs Piper, he explained that 'a man of uncertain purposes might mar her work'.

Epilogue

In his classic study of mystical anarchism in the Middle Ages, *The Pursuit of the Millennium*, Norman Cohn observed that 'in situations of mass disorientation and anxiety, traditional beliefs about a future golden age or messianic kingdoms come to serve as vehicles for social aspirations and animosities'. For the thousands of High Church deserters who were shaken and dizzied by the rational assault on biblical truth, the séance clearly provided a similar form of supernatural refuge, granting spiritualism's domestic front line of female mediums the power and authority to undertake direct communication with the Other World.

Want of faith and the search for positive evidence of the afterlife are nevertheless only partial explanations for the rise of the Victorian séance. Many of the oddities that came to life in the séance room were, as we have seen, also a by-product of secular preoccupations. The paucity of medical treatments for hysteria, epilepsy and other nervous conditions, rife among the charitable poor, provided the initial impetus for the first trials of mesmerism undertaken by Elliotson and his contemporaries. A nascent culture of popular science, promulgated through cheap print and affordable lectures, played its part in fostering domestic and public trials of mesmerism, clairvoyance and kindred 'sciences'. The failure of Owenite Socialism brought new purpose and direction to the spiritualism in the Northern counties. And the lack of effective communication in the decades that saw the Crimean War and the far-flung expansion of the British Empire sustained the demand for news from clairvoyant mediums.

Beginning in the 1850s, an ad hoc alliance of scientists, physicians, stage magicians, writers and lawyers sought to halt the epidemic of séance-room trickery and charlatanism, turning the spotlight on the underhand methods employed by Daniel Dunglas Home, the Davenport brothers, Henry Slade and a host of physical and mental mediums. With the advent of psychical research and the anti-spiritualist entertainments of Anderson and Maskelyne, the séance became an increasingly more unreliable form of social machinery, liable to stall and misfire, generating confusion and disenchantment among its clammy-palmed sitters, yet its scientific demise was only sealed after a new generation of parapsychologists, led by John B. Rhine, undertook controlled experiments in telepathy and clairvoyance, which were designed to eliminate the possibility of subjects acting on sensory cues.

While the parapsychological laboratory found no significant statistical evidence of paranormal powers in the general population, the sixties counter-culture went on to unleash a tide of psychical hoaxes, lending credence to phenomena that mesmerists and spiritualists had testified to over a century earlier. Today's New Age ministry of 'Mind, Body and Spirit' has spawned countless paperback meditations on the power of

Epilogue

'cosmic consciousness', a myriad of subcultures that claim to channel the wisdom of aliens and angels, and an unseemly procession of TV ghost hunters, faith healers and paranormal tricksters.

One of the most caustic critics of this 'supernatural flimflam', the Canadian-born illusionist James Randi, has followed in the footsteps of John Nevil Maskelyne, exposing the deceptions employed by various high-profile clairvoyants, psychic surgeons, spoon benders and mind readers. Randi continues to provide useful insights into the probable sources of séance trickery, but his inveterate urge to debunk falters when confronted with what I take to be the one genuine anomaly that Victorian séance goers discovered – trance. On the subject of hypnosis, Randi's *Encyclopaedia of Claims, Frauds, and Hoaxes of the Occult and Supernatural* at once holds that it is 'a mystic-sounding but ineffective therapy' and 'a valuable tool in psychology'. Insisting that no standard definition of the hypnotic trance has been arrived at, Randi warns that psychics and spirit mediums 'often claim to be "in trance" when they work'.

To my mind the history of the séance room provides compelling evidence that many mental mediums and somnambules feigned trance, that others were psychologically primed to behave *as if* they were entranced, and that a small minority were genuine trance mediums. While the precise nature of the trance state is still disputed by practising hypnotists and psychologists (most behaviourists favour a role-enactment theory, suggesting that trance subjects do not enter an altered state but simply respond to the 'demand characteristics' of the hypnotic milieu) a recent cross-cultural study undertaken by Erika Bourguignon, Professor of Anthropology at Ohio State University, has found that the kind of dissociated possession practised by Mrs Piper and other mediums is widespread, being most usually associated with the most subservient members of a society. Individuals who are socially, economically and psychologically adrift are, Bourguignon observes, universally likely to use trance 'to act out their own needs for assertion', availing themselves of 'an opportunity to manipulate others and their own real life situations'.

In their search to understand the enigma of trance possession, the first wave of psychical researchers looked elsewhere. Finding a parallel between the garbled speech of aphasic patients (who had incurred damage to the left-hemisphere's language centres) and the coarse and broken wordage produced by most automatic writers, Frederic Myers, the SPR's intellectual powerhouse, was quick to moot the enfeebled right-brain as a possible source of paranormal phenomena such as telepathy and clairvoyance: 'An external intelligence wishing to use my brain, might find it convenient to leave alone those more educated but also more preoccupied tracts, and to use the less elaborated, but less engrossed, mechanism of my right-brain.'

Myers's ruminations on the right-brain as the wellspring of a hidden, subliminal consciousness were almost immediately undermined by a new wave of hypnotic experiments. While Charcot, 'the Napoleon of Neuroses', was insisting that *la grande hypnotisme* was peculiar to the hysterics that he paraded in his twice-weekly lectures at the Salpêtrière, the Nancy school, headed by Liebault and Bernheim, found that hypnosis did not require a pathological personality to be effective. When placed before a physician in a clinical environment, the vast majority of people would succumb to a heightened state of suggestibility, the keynote of the hypnotic trance. The highly theatrical performances given by Charcot's patients were a direct result of mimicry. Not one of the hundreds of Nancy patients who had been cured of various nervous and organic conditions by way of hypnosis (using only verbal cues) demonstrated symptoms of this sort.

When William James published *The Principles of Psychology* in 1890, the suggestion theory of hypnosis had eclipsed Charcot's physiological theory. Hypnosis had now revealed the extent to which the conscious mind could be split into *several* parts or 'personalities', which coexisted but remained mutually ignorant of each other. The trance state had 'no particular outward symptoms of its own'. Amnesia, paralysis, compliance, anaesthesia, hyperaesthesia, illusions and hallucinations, selective awareness of the immediate environment and all the other effects that had been so far noted, were artifacts of social interaction, fashioned from the expectation of operator and subject.

Select Bibliography

Much of my primary material has been drawn from articles and notices in *The Times*, *Lancet*, *Medical Times*, the *Zoist*, *Household Words*, *Punch*, the *Phreno-Magnet*, the *Spiritualist*, *Light* and the *Proceedings* and *Journal of the Society of Psychical Research*.

Frank Podmore's *Mediums of the Nineteenth Century* (New York, 1963; originally published as *Modern Spiritualism* 1902) is an invaluable treasure trove of information on professional and amateur mediums, and the oddities they brought to the Victorian séance room. I would also highly recommend Logie Barrow's *Independent Spirits: Spiritualism and the English Plebeians* ΩΩΩΩΩΩΩΩΩ (Manchester, 1986), Janet Oppenheim's *The Other World: Spiritualism and Psychical Research in England*, ΩΩΩΩΩΩΩΩΩ (Cambridge, 1985), Alex Owen's *The Darkened Room* (Chicago, 1989) and Alison Winter's *Mesmerized: Powers of Mind in Victorian Britain* (Chicago, 1998).

Chapter One **Bodies Electric**

Clarke, John Fernandez, *Autobiographical Recollections of the Medical Profession* (London, 1874)
Coburn, Kathleen (ed.), *Inquiring Spirit: A Coleridge Reader* (London, 1968)
Coleridge, Samuel Taylor, *Collected Letters of Samuel Taylor Coleridge*, 6 vols, ed. E. L. Griggs (London, 1956–71)
Darnton, Robert, *Mesmerism and the End of the Enlightenment* (Cambridge, Mass., 1968)
Dupotet de Sennevoy, Baron J., *An Introduction to the Study of Animal Magnetism* (London, 1838)
Ellenberger, Henri, *Discovery of the Unconscious* (New York, 1970)
Fara, Patricia, *An Entertainment for Angels: Electricity in the Enlightenment* (Cambridge, 2002)
Forrest, Derek, *Hypnotism: A History* (Harmondsworth, 2000)
Gauld, Alan, *A History of Hypnotism* (Cambridge, 1992)
Kerner, Justinus, *The Seeress of Prevorst*, trans. Catherine Crowe (London and Edinburgh, 1845)
Korte, Anne-Marie (ed.), *Women and Miracle Stories* (Leiden, 2001)
Porter, Roy, *Quacks: Fakers and Charlatans in English Medicine* (London, 2000)
Shelley, Percy Bysshe, *The Poems of Shelley*, eds Geoffrey Matthews and Kelvin Everest, 2 vols (London, 1989)
Southey, Robert, *Letters from England* (London, 1951, first published 1807)

Select Bibliography

Chapter Two **Magnetic Mockeries**

Bourne Taylor, Jenny and Sally Shuttleworth (eds), *Embodied Selves: An Anthology of Psychological Texts ΩΩΩΩΩΩΩΩΩ* (Oxford, 1998)

Cooter, Roger, *The cultural meaning of popular science: Phrenology and the organization of consent in Nineteenth-Century Britain* (Cambridge, 1984)

De Giustino, David, *Conquest of Mind: Phrenology and Victorian Social Thought* (London, 1975)

Elliotson, John, *Human Physiology* (London, 1840)

Godwin, Joscelyn, *The Theosophical Enlightenment* (New York, 1994)

Kaplan, Fred, *John Elliotson on Mesmerism* (New York, 1982)

Mackay, Charles, *Extraordinary Popular Delusions and the Madness of Crowds* (Ware, Herts, 1995, first published 1841)

Merrington, W. R., *University College Hospital and its Medical School* (London, 1976)

Miller, Jonathan, 'A Gower Street Scandal', *Journal of the Royal College of Physicians*, 1983, 17, pp. 181–191

Trollope, Thomas, *What I Remember* (London, 1887)

Chapter Three **London Trance**

Chambers, Robert, 'A Visit to Dr Elliotson's', *Chambers Edinburgh Journal*, 1839, no. 396, pp. 249–250 (pirated in the 1842 chapbook 'A Full Discovery of the Strange Practices of Dr Elliotson')

Dickens, Charles, *American Notes* (London, 2000, first published 1842)

—— *Hard Times* (Harmondwsorth, 2004, first published 1842)

—— *The Nonesuch Dickens*, eds Arthur Waugh et al (London, 1938)

Elliotson, John, *Numerous Cases of Surgical Operations without Pain in the Mesmeric State* (London, 1843)

Esdaile, James, *Mesmerism in India and its Practical Application in Surgery and Medicine* (Madras, 1989, first published 1846)

Kaplan, Fred, *Dickens and Mesmerism* (Princeton, 1975)

Kemble, Frances, *Records of Later Life*, 3 vols (London, 1882)

Townshend, Chauncey Hare, *Facts in Mesmerism* (London, 1840)

—— *Mesmerism Proved True* (London, 1854)

Wallace, Alfred Russel, *My Life*, 2 vols (Farnborough, Hants, 1969, first published 1905)

Chapter Four   'Lecture Mania'

Capern, Thomas, *The Mighty Curative Powers of Mesmerism* (London, 1851)

—— *Mesmeric Facts* (London, 1870)

Carlyle, Thomas and Jane Welsh, *The Collected Letters of Thomas and Jane Welsh Carlyle*, 28 vols, ed. R. C. Sanders (London, 1970)

Hall, Spencer, *Mesmeric Experiences* (London, 1845)

Howitt, William, *The History of the Supernatural* (London, 1863)

Lang, William, *Animal Magnetism, or Mesmerism* (New York, 1844)

Parsinnen, Terry, 'Mesmeric Performers', *Victorian Studies*, 1977, pp. 21, 87–104

Reynolds, G. W. M., *The Mysteries of London*, ed. Trevor Thomas (Keele, 1996)

Select Bibliography

Sandby, George, *Mesmerism and its Opponents* (London, 1844)
Waite, Arthur. E. (ed.), *Braid on Hypnotism* (New York, 1960)
Winter, Alison, *Mesmerized: Powers of Mind in Victorian Britain* (Chicago and London, 1998)

Chapter Five   **The Infidel in Petticoats**

Atkinson, Henry and Harriet Martineau, *Letters on the Laws of Man's Social Nature* (London, 1851)
Deleuze, Joseph, *Practical Instruction in Animal Magnetism* (New York, 1879, first published 1825)
Ellenberger, Henri, 'Mesmer and Puységur: From Magnetism to Hypnotism', *Psychoanalytical Review*, 1965, pp. 52, 137–53
Martineau, Harriet, *Life in the Sick-Room* (London, 1844)
—— *Letters on Mesmerism* (London, 1845)
—— *Autobiography*, 3 vols (London, 1877)
Pichanick, Valerie, *Harriet Martineau: The Woman and Her Work* (Ann Arbor, 1980)
Wheatley, Vera, *The Life and Work of Harriet Martineau* (London, 1957)

Chapter Six   **News from Nowhere**

Besterman, Theodore, *Crystal Gazing* (New York, 1965)
Dingwall, Eric, *Some Human Oddities* (London, 1947)
Gregory, William, *Letters to a Candid Inquirer on Animal Magnetism* (London, 1851)
Haddock, Joseph, *Somnolism and Psycheism* (London, 1851)

Chapter Seven Tea and Table Moving

Braude, Anne, *Radical Spirits: Spiritualism and Women's Rights in America* (Boston, 1989)

Crowe, Catherine, *The Night Side of Nature* (Ware, 2000, first published 1848)

Goldfarb, Russell and Clare, *Spiritualism and Nineteenth-Century Letters* (New Jersey, 1978)

Owen, Robert, *The Future of the Human Race* (London, 1853)

Chapter Eight **Dark Employments**

Brewster, David, *Natural Magic* (London, 1833)

Browning, Robert, *Dramatis Personae* (London, 1855)

Buranelli, Vincent, *The Wizard from Vienna* (London, 1976)

Burton, Jean, *Heyday of a Wizard: Daniel Home the Medium* (London, 1948)

Carpenter, William, *Mesmerism, Spiritualism, &c., historically and scientifically considered* (London, 1877)

Conan Doyle, Arthur, *The History of Spiritualism* (London, 1926)

Crookes, William, *Researches in the Phenomena of Spiritualism* (London, 1874)

Hardinge, Emma, *Modern American Spiritualism* (New York, 1870)

Home, Daniel Dunglas, *Lights and Shadows of Spiritualism* (London, 1877)

Home, Mme Daniel Dunglas, *D. D. Home: His life and Mission* (London, 1888)

London Dialectical Society, *Report on Spiritualism* (London, 1873)

Miller, Betty, 'The Séance at Ealing', *Cornhill Magazine*, 169, 1957, pp. 317–24

Noakes, Richard, 'Telegraphy is an occult art: Cromwell Fleetwood Varley and the diffusion of electricity to the other world', *British Journal of the History of Science*, 1999, 32, pp. 421–59

Porter, Katherine, *Through a Glass Darkly* (Lawrence, 1958)

Raby, Peter, *Alfred Russel Wallace: A Life* (London, 2002)

Steinmeyer, Jim, *Hiding the Elephant: How Magicians Invented the Impossible* (London, 2005)

Tyndall, John, *Fragments of Science* (London, 1871)

Wallace, Alfred Russel, *The Scientific Aspect of the Supernatural* (London, 1866)

—— *Miracles and Modern Spiritualism* (London, 1874)

Chapter Nine   'Conjurers in Disguise'

Anderson, John Henry, *The Fashionable Science of Parlour Magic* (London, 1850)

Christopher, Milbourne and Maurine, *The Illustrated History of Magic* (New York, 2006)

Cook, James, *The Arts of Deception: Playing with Fraud in the Age of Barnum* (Cambridge, Mass., 2001)

Goldston, Will, *Secrets of Famous Illusionists* (London, 1933)

Houdin, Robert Jean-Eugène, *Secrets of Conjuring and Magic* (London, 1878)

MA (Oxon) [Revd William Stainton Moses], *The Slade Case: Its facts and lessons* (London, 1877)

—— *Psychography* (London, 1878)

Maskelyne, John Nevil, *Modern Spiritualism: A Short History of* its Rise and Progress, with Some Exposures of So-called Spirit Media (London, 1874)

Porter, Roy et al (eds), Women, Madness and Spiritualism (London, 2003)

Seybert Commission, Preliminary Report of the Commission Appointed by the University of Pennsylvania to Investigate Modern Spiritualism (Philadelphia, 1887)

Chapter Ten **Mental Notes**

Cerullo, John, The Secularization of the Soul (Philadelphia, 1982)

Gauld, Alan, Founders of Psychical Research (New York, 1968)

Hardwick, Elizabeth, The Selected Letters of William James (New York, 1961)

James, William, The Principles of Psychology (New York and London 1950, first published 1890)

MA (Oxon), Spirit Teachings (London, 1883)

Murphy, Gardner and Robert O. Ballou, William James on Psychical Research (New York, 1960)

Myers, Frederic, Science and a Future Life (London, 1893)

—— Human Personality and its Survival of Bodily Death (London, 1905)

Sage, Michel, Mrs Piper and the Society for Psychical Research (London, 1903)

Stocking, George W. Jnr, 'Animism in Theory and Practice: E. B. Tylor's Unpublished "Notes on Spiritualism"', Man, vol. 6, no. 1, March 1971, pp. 88–104

Tanner, Amy [with Stanley Hall], Studies in Spiritism (New York, 1910)

Select Bibliography

Taylor, Eugene, *William James on Exceptional Mental States* (Princeton, 1996)

Theobald, Morell, *Spiritualism at Home* (London, 1884)

Acknowledgements

I am indebted to Paola Bertucci, Joscelyn Godwin, Rhodri Hayward, Amy Lehman, Richard Lines, Ronnie Sandison, Alison Winter and Fred Kaplan for responding to questions and queries, and to Jason Burdon for additional material. Staff at the Reading Room of the British Library at Boston Spa, York University Library, the British Library, the Wellcome Institute, the Society for Psychical Research, Special Collections at the Leeds University Library, John Rylands University Library and the Templeman Library at the University of Kent provided invaluable assistance in locating and copying recherché tracts, playbills and ephemera. A special thank you to Ravi Mirchandani for commissioning a second book, and to Gail Lynch, Caroline Knight and Alban Miles at Random House for their editorial input.

Antonio Melechi
York, ΩΩΩΩ

Index

Abernethy, John 42–3
Académie des Sciences 1–9
Adare, Lord 1–42, 190, 195
Adolphe (somnambule of Paris) 108
Albert, Prince 214
Alexis (German somnambule) 84–6
All the Year Round 187
Ambleside 132, 133–4, 135
American Society for Psychical Research (ASPR) 245, 247, 249, 254
Anderson, John Henry 209, 214–15, 262
Anglesea, Marquess of 60
animal magnetism
   charges levelled against 24–5
   Chevenix's interest in 31–2
   Coleridge's interest in 25–8
   cult of 18–19
   demonstration of 7–10
   as form of faith healing 21–3
   Hauffe's involvement in 29–31
   Mesmer's work on 11–18
   name changed to mesmerism 47
   occult followers of 23–4
   ridiculed 10–11, 19
   scientific validity of 45–7
   and treatment of patients 35–41
   versions of 19–21
Anna M 82–3
Antwerp 82
Arnott, Dr 62
Arrowsmith & Co (Messrs P.R.) 152
Arrowsmith, Jane 121–2, 127, 128, 133, 145–7
Arrowsmith, Mrs 146
Ashburner, John 166–8, 172–3, 176
The Athenaeum 54, 128–9
Atkinson, Henry George 88, 118, 125, 131–2, 134, 142, 189–90
   Letters on the Laws of Man's Social Nature (co-authored with Martineau) 134–5
Auxerre 18

Baden, Grand Duke Karl of 48
Baillière, Henri 100, 142
Bainbridge, Richard 58
Balfour, Arthur 244
Balmoral 214
The Banner of Light 229, 260
Barrett, Sir William 244
Bastian, Mr 216
Bath 22
Bavaria 20
Belcher, Sir Edward 159
Bell, John 21
Bell, Robert 186
Berkeley Castle 212
Berlin 26
  Mesmeric Hospital 58
Bernheim, Hippolyte 265
Berny, Madame de 15
Bertrand, Alexandre 100
Blackwell, Elizabeth 36
Blackwood's Magazine 54, 164
Blavatsky, Madame Helena 217, 229, 249
Blessington, Lady 85, 86, 142, 159
Blitz, Antonio 212
Blumenbach, Johann, *Institutions of Physiology* 25, 42, 43
Bosco (Italian magician) 198
Bostock, Dr 62
Boucicault, Dion 207–8, 209
  The Corsican Brothers 208
Bourguignon, Erika 264
Boyle, Lady Carolina Courtenay 149–50
Bradford 210
Bradlaugh, Charles 194, 197
Braid, James 110–13, 114, 116, 171
Braude, Anne 162
Bray, Charles 189
Brewster, Sir David 181–2, 191, 215–16
  Natural Magic 181

Brissot, Jacques-Pierre 19
Bristol 22
Britannia steamship 87
British Association for the Advancement of Science 113, 221, 223
British Cyclopaedia 10–11
British and Foreign Medical Review 143
British National Association of Spiritualists 226, 228–9
Brodie, Benjamin 76
Brontë, Charlotte 135
Brooks, Henry 110
Brougham, Lord 59–60, 180, 181, 182
Brown, Dr 146
Brown, John 109
Browning, Elizabeth Barrett 80, 129, 183–5
Browning, Robert 183, 184–5
Buchanan, Dr 87
Bullock, William 212
Bulwer-Lytton, Edward 125, 159, 180
  Strange Story 3
Burlington, Earl of 60
Burns, James 193–4, 201, 236
Burns, Robert 172
Burton, Isobel 156
Burton, Richard 90, 210
Byron, Lord George Gordon 43

Cagliostro, Count 24
Cahagnet, Alphonse 155
Cambridge 83
Canning, George 65
Capern, Edward 116
Capern, Thomas 116–17
Carlyle, Jane 100, 129
Carlyle, Thomas 76, 92, 124

Index

Carpenter, William 143, 171, 194, 199, 203–5, 220
Carroll, Lewis 244
Catlow, Joseph 113–14
cerebral physiology *see* phrenology
Chambers, Robert 78–80, 104, 165, 208
   Vestiges of Creation 78, 134
Chambers's Edinburgh Journal 78, 79
Chandler, Thomas 57
Chapman, John 135, 238–9
Charcot, Jean Martin 264–5
Chastenier, Benedict 23
Cheltenham 210
Cheltenham Examiner 108
Chevenix, Richard 31–2, 45
chloroform 96–7
The Christian Lady 128
Christian Observer 69
Ciudad Rodrigo 140
clairvoyance
   claims made for 138–45, 147
   denouncements of 145–7
   practitioners of 139–45, 147–56
   prize offered for evidence of 137–8
   researches into 157–60
   and the spirit world 154–6
   and tracking of Franklin's expedition 153–4
   well-known endorsements of 156–7
Claremont, Claire 26
Clarke, John Fernandez 66, 70
Clarke, Lucy 49
Cocke, J.R. 245
Cohn, Norman, *The Pursuit of the Millennium* 261
Coldstream Guards hospital 32
Coleman, Benjamin 212–13

Coleridge, Samuel Taylor 25–8, 32, 42
   An Essay on Scrofula 25
Collins, Wilkie 156–7
Collyer, Dr 87
Colquhoun, John Campbell 139, 158
   Hints on Animal Magnetism 99
   A Short Sketch on Animal Magnetism 99–100
Combe, George 44–5, 89, 104, 134, 174
   The Constitution of Man 45
   System of Phrenology 45
Combermere, Lady 180
Comic Annual 54
Connolly, Dr John 174–5
Cook, Charlotte 56–7
Cook, Florence (aka Katie King) 200–3, 206, 216, 235
Cook, James 101
Cooke, George Alfred 211, 212, 213–14, 230
Cooter, Roger 105
Copland, Dr 93
Cornhill Magazine 186
Cox, Edward 189, 200, 203, 220, 233, 234, 240
Cox, William 180, 182
The Critic 147
Crookes, William 198–203, 204, 215, 220, 233
Crowe, Catherine 168, 173–5
   Lily Dawson 173
   The Night Side of Nature 173
   Susan Hopley 173
   The Night Side of Nature 4
Cruikshank, George 53, 60

Daily News 173, 175
Daily Telegraph 209
Daniell, John Frederick 201

Dannemark of Hungary, Rabbi Professor 148
Darling, Dr (American electrobiologist) 114–15
Darwin, Charles 3, 192, 193, 224
  The Origin of Species 136, 222, 243
Davenport, Ira 2, 198, 206, 207–10, 213, 215, 262
Davenport, William 2, 198, 206, 207–10, 213, 215, 262
Davey, William 116
Davies, Reverend Charles 194
Dawson, Ellen 148–51
De La Rue, Augusta 90–2, 156
Deleuze, Joseph 35, 100
Densmore, Ella 255
Denton, George 49
Deslon, Charles 17, 19
Devonshire, Duchess of 23
Dickens, Catherine 87, 91–2
Dickens, Charles 4, 53, 60, 72, 85, 86–7, 90–2, 156, 163
  Bleak House 164
  and spiritualism 187, 189, 191, 193
Didier, Adolph 148
Didier, Alexis 139–45, 147, 204, 214
Dieppe 188, 189
Dilke, Charles Wentworth 128
Donkin, Dr Horatio 223, 226, 227, 229
Donovan, Cornelius 109
Dorr, George 256, 257
Dove, John 107
Doyle, Arthur Conan 2–3
  The Adventure of Silver Blaze 6
  History of Spiritualism 2, 165
Drayson, General 2

Dupotet de Sennevoy, Jules 45, 68, 75, 99, 101
  and claims for clairvoyance 138
  and Elizabeth Okey 40–1, 66
  first trials of magnetism 7–10, 35–7, 71, 137
  séances conducted by 49–52, 76
  supported by Stanhope 47–9

Eckley, Sophia 185
Edinburgh 101, 133, 174
Edinburgh University 42
Edmunds, Dr James 194, 197
Electric and International Telegraphy Company 196
electrobiology 114–16
Eliot, George 135, 187, 243
Ellenberger, Henri 15
Elliotson, Dr John 7, 8, 86, 87, 159
  and belief in clairvoyance 138–43
  as champion of mesmerism 3, 76–82, 85, 101, 103–4, 115, 117, 131, 199, 262
  and closure of *The Zoist* 176–7
  education of 42
  as free-thinking secularist 43
  Human Physiology 57, 71
  Numerous Cases of Surgical Operations without Pain in the Mesmeric State 94
  and the Okey sisters 38–9, 41, 47, 53–5, 60–74, 79–80, 82, 204
  and painless mesmeric operations 93–7
  and phrenology 45, 88–90
  and spiritualism 166, 175–6, 188–90
  support for and belief in magnetism 46–7

Index

trials and demonstrations of
magnetism 32–3, 37, 40–2,
52–71
Elliotson, Thomas 43
Emerson, Ralph Waldo 124, 163
Emma L. 151–6
Encyclopaedia Metropolitana 25
Engledue, William 88–9
  'Cerebral Physiology and
  Materialism' 89
Esdaile, James 94–6
Examiner 101
Exeter Hospital 117

Fairlamb, Miss 216
Faraday, Michael 3, 32, 55, 60,
170–1, 188, 190, 191
Fay, Miss 216
Ferguson, Reverend J.B. 208, 210
Fiske (American electrobiologist)
114
Flixton 118
Florence 187
Flowers, Mr 228
Flush (dog) 129
Forbes, John 143–7
Fowler, Lottie 236–7
Fox, Colonel Lane 220
Fox, Kate 161–2, 165, 215, 216,
233, 235
Fox, Margaret 161–2, 165, 215,
216
Franklin, Sir John 153–4, 159
French Academy of Medicine
137
French Royal Academy of Science
21
Friedrich Wilhelm, Crown Prince
of Prussia 186
Froude, James Anthony 135

Gall, Franz Jozef 43–4

Gébelin, Antoine Court de, *Monde
Primitif* 17
The Ghost Club 242
Gibbens, Mrs 246
Gillman, Dr 28
Gladstone, W.E. 244
Glasgow 221
Godwin, William 21
Goyder, David 103
Grant, Professor 62
Greatrakes, Valentine 117
Greenhow, Thomas 124, 125–6,
130, 136
  *Medical Report of the Case of H—
  -M—*. 130
Gregory, Mrs MacDougall 226
Gregory, William 133, 157–9
  *Letters to a Candid Inquirer on
  Animal Magnetism* 157–8
Grey de Ruthyn, Baroness 180
Grey, Lord 50
Guldenstubbé, Baron de 217–18
Gully, Dr 156
Guppy, Mrs 216
Gurney, Edmund 242, 243, 244
Gurwood, Colonel John 140

Haddock, Dr Joseph 151–2, 153–6
  Somnolism and Psycheism 154–5
Hall, Spencer 101–5, 117, 121,
126–7, 130
Hall, Stanley 256, 257–60
  Studies in Spiritism (with Amy
  Tanner) 259
Hands, Dr William 148–9
Hanwell Asylum (Middlesex) 72,
174
Hardinge, Emma 52, 198
Harrison, Dr Richard 117
Harrison, William 220, 239
Hastings, Marchioness of 180
Hauffe, Friedericke 29–31, 155

283

Hauser, Kaspar 48–9
Hayden, Maria 163–9
Hayden, William 163, 168
Hell, Maximillian 11
Herne, Frank 216, 235
HMS *Erebus* 153
HMS *Terror* 153
Hockley, Frederic 90
Hodgson, Richard 249–50, 253–4, 255, 257–9
Holland, Queen of 186
Hollis Hospital 101
Holyoake, George 134, 136
Home, Daniel Dunglas 2, 215, 237, 262
  investigations into 195–200
  Lights and Shadows of Spiritualism 204–5, 206
  mixed responses to 182–9
  reputation of 205–6
  retirement of 200
  séances of 180–2, 184–5, 195–6
Home, Sacha 186
Homes, Jenny 235
Hooghly Charity Hospital (Bengal) 94–6
Hospital of Incurables (Dublin) 32
Household Words 163, 187
Howitt, William 101, 103, 190–1, 198
  The History of the Supernatural in All Ages and Nations 191
Huddersfield 229
Hull 146, 210
Hungary 12
Hunter, Hannah 54, 55
Huxley, Thomas 3, 194, 243
Hygiaean Society 21
hypnosis 113, 263–5

Irving, Edward 69
Irvingites 69–70

Isham, Sir Charles 117, 168, 180
Isle of Man 236

Jackson, Andrew Davis 155, 238
  The Principles of Nature, Her Divine Revelations, and a Voice to Mankind 238–9
James, Henry 253
James, Henry Snr 164
James, William 245, 246–50, 253, 254–6
  The Principles of Psychology 265
  Varieties of Religious Experience 260
Jarves family 183
Jencken, Henry 194
Jesus College (Cambridge) 42

Keighley 172
Kemble, Fanny 85–6, 174
Kent, Duke of 218
Kerner, Justinus 29–30
  History of Two Somnambules 29
  Seeress of Prevorst 173
Kiernan, Mr 62
King, Katie *see* Cook, Florence (aka Katie King)
Kluge, Carl Alexander 26, 28
Knowles, Jane 108–9
Kuzeluch, Leopold 12

La Belle Assemble 150
Lafontaine, Charles 101–2, 111
  Mémoirs d'un Magnétiseur 101
Lake Constance 11, 19
Lake District 130
Lambton, John George, 'Radical Jack' 50
Lamport Hall (Northamptonshire) 117

Lancet 9, 40, 54, 59, 61, 62, 63, 64, 67, 69, 76, 93, 111
Lankester, Edwin Ray 221–7
Lankester, Edwin Snr 224
Lankester, Mrs 224
Lardner, Dionysus 55
Lassaigne, August 140
Lausanne 82
Lawrence, William 42–3
Laycock, Thomas 70
The Leader 135, 156–7, 164
Leamington Spa Courier 109
Leeds 210
Leger, Dr 167
levitation 186–7, 199–200, 214
Lewes, George 135, 157, 164, 165, 167, 187, 194
Lewis (American electrobiologist) 114
Lewis, George 223, 224–6, 228
Leyden 16
Liebault, A.A. 265
Liston, Robert 56, 59, 94
Liverpool 210, 250
Lodge, Lady 251
Lodge, Oliver 250–2
London 21–2, 24, 32
   Cavendish Rooms 213
   Court Concert Rooms (Hanover Square) 209
   Egyptian Hall 212–14, 216, 226, 230
   Hanover Rooms 112
   Royal Polytechnic 214
   St George's Hospital 32
   St James Theatre 214
   St Thomas's Hospital 43
   Willis's Rooms 215
London College of Physicians 93
London Dialectical Society 194, 195, 196–8, 200, 201, 216
   Report on Spiritualism 198

London Magazine 16
London Mesmeric Hospital 117, 166
London Phrenological Association 89
London Phrenological Society 45, 131
London Tavern 112
Louis Napoleon 186
Louis XVI 19
Loutherbourg, Lucy 24
Loutherbourg, Philip de 23–4
Lyon, Mrs Jane 195

MA Oxon (pseud. of Reverend Moses) 239
McKay, George, *Extraordinary Popular Delusions* 76
Macready, William 71–2, 87
Macreight, Dr. 57
magic
   cabinet séances 208–11, 215
   illusionists 211–16
   and slate writing 230–1
Mainauduc, John Benoit de 21–3
Maldeghem, Countess von 30–1
Malmaison, Comtesse de la 15
Malthus, Thomas 124
Manchester 101, 111, 112, 113, 114
Manchester Guardian 153
Marcillet, Monsieur 140–2, 144
Marlborough, Duke of 90
Marshall, Mrs 216
Martineau, Harriet 4, 243
   Autobiography 131
   belief in mesmerism 127–34, 146–7
   and clairvoyance 152
   death of 136
   faith in science 134–6
   ill-health 123, 124–5

Illustrations of Political Economy 124
as journalist 123–4
Letters on the Laws of Man's Social Nature (co-authored with Atkinson) 134–5
Letters on Mesmerism 128–30, 145–6
Life in the Sick-Room 124
treated by mesmerism 121–3, 125–7
Martineau, James 125, 135
Maskelyne, John Nevil 210–14, 262, 263
Massachusetts's General Hospital (Boston) 96
Mayo, Herbert 36, 37, 55, 62, 63, 68, 112–13
Medical Gazette 147
mediums 245–60, 262
Medwin, Captain 26
Melhuish, Emma 77
Meredith, Owen 174
Mesmer, Franz Anton 11–18, 20, 21, 22, 23, 25, 27
  The Influence of the Planets on the Human Body 11
Mesmeric Infirmary 97
Mesmeric Mania of 1851 114–15
mesmerism 3–4
  and anti-mesmerists 110–14
  connection with phrenology 87–90
  diatribes against 101
  enthusiasm for 76–8, 82–6, 86–7, 90–2
  experiments and trials 52–74, 261–2
  female interest in 122–36
  introduction of term 47
  lectures on 100, 101–18
  and painless operations 93–7
  popularity of séances 49–52
  practical guides to 100
  psychological aspects 81
  supernatural aspects 82
The Mesmerist 100
Meyer, Johann Georg 48
Middlesex Hospital 32, 37, 47, 55
Mills, George 61, 62, 63–4
Milner-Gibson, Mrs 186, 190
Milnes, Richard Monckton 50, 86
Mitford, Mary 80
M'Neile, Reverend Hugh 101
Monck, Francis Ward 229–30
Montagu, Mr and Mrs Basil 125
Monthly Repository 123
Montlosier, Comte de 18
Montpelier 35
Moore, Thomas 62
More, Hannah 23
Morgan, Augustus de 165
Morgan, Sophia de 168
Morning Advertiser 182
Morning Post 55, 190
Morpeth, Lord 104, 122
Morrison, Lieutenant Richard 51, 159–60
Moses, Reverend William Stainton 220, 228, 233–8
  Spirit Teachings 240–1, 242
Musschenbroek, Pieter van 16, 17
Myers, Frederic 242, 243, 244, 251, 264
  Human Personality and its Survival of Bodily Death 252–3
Myers, Mrs 251
The Mysteries of London (penny magazine) 109–10

Nancy school 265
New York 196, 238
  Barnum's Hotel 162
  Imperial University 217

Index

Newcastle 126
Nichol, Miss 192, 216
Norwich, Bishop of 62
Nottingham 114, 131
Nuremberg 48

occultists 51–2
Ohio lunatic asylum 173
Ohio State University 264
Okey, Elizabeth 37–41, 46, 47, 53–5, 58–65, 66–74, 75, 78, 79–80, 86, 94, 117, 204
Okey, Jane 38, 39, 55, 62, 63–4, 68–9, 71–2, 73, 75, 78, 79–80, 94, 117, 204
Orphic Circle 51–2
Owen, Robert 124, 134, 169, 172, 180, 182, 218
Owen, Robert Dale, *The Debatable Land* 236
Owens, Dr 108

Paget, Sir Charles 60
Paradis, Joseph Anton von 12, 13–14
Paradis, Maria Theresia 12–14
parapsychology 262–3
Paris 8, 14–15, 18, 101, 138, 217–18
   Hôtel Bulliôn 15, 21
   Hôtel Dieu 36
passive writing 238–42
Pellew, George 254
Pepper, Professor 214
Phipps, Edmund 142
The Phreno-Magnet 100, 103
phreno-mesmerism 100, 103–7
Phrenological Almanac 103
phrenology 43–5, 87–90, 135
Pierce, Ambrose, *Devil's Dictionary* 3
Pigeaire, Léonide 138

Pinel, Philippe 19
Piper, Mrs 245–60, 264
Pisa 26
Post, Isaac 162, 164
Pratt, Mary 24
'The Prophetic Lady' 148
'Psycho' (automaton) 212
psychography *see* spirit messages
Psychological Society 240
Punch 3, 147
Purland, Theodosius 97
Puységur, Marquis de 19–21

Quain, Richard 48, 56
Quarterly Journal of Science 199
Quarterly Review 54, 192
Quillinan, Edward 135

Race, Victor 20
Radclyffe, Charles 93
Raleigh, Lord 220
Randi, James 263
   Encyclopaedia of Claims, Frauds and Hoaxes of the Occult and Supernatural 263
Reade, Charles 208
Reichenbach, Baron von 158–9
   Researches on Mesmerism 159
Renan, Ernest, *Life of Jesus* 243
Reynolds, George 109
Rhine, John B. 262
Rhu (West Highlands) 69
Ricard, J.J. 140
Richardson, Dr 66
Richmond, David 171–2
Robert-Houdin, Jean Eugène, 214
Robert Owen 236
Roberts, Mrs 169
Robinson, Henry Crabb 127, 129
Rochdale 112
Roget, Dr 62
Ross, Anne 64

Royal College of Physicians 25
Royal College of Surgeons 42
Royal Institution 188
Royal Medical and Chirurgical Society 93
Royal Medico-Botanical Society 48, 57
Royal Society 32, 36, 54, 64, 76, 198, 199
  Physiological Committee of 62
Royal Society of Edinburgh 71
Rumball, J.Q. 110
Rymer, Mr and Mrs 184, 185

St Albans 117, 118
St Luke's Hospital for the Insane 72
Salieri, Antonio 12
Salisbury, Lady 23
Salpêtrière 21, 265
Samson, Catherine 36
Sandby, George 118
Schelling, Friedrich 29
Science 256
séances 76, 261, 262, 263
  cabinet 208–11, 215
  popularity of 49–52
  spirit messages 217–31, 237–42
  spirit possession 235, 236–7, 239, 240–2
  table rapping 234–5
Sennevoy, Baron Jules Dupotet de 7–10, 35–8
Sexton, George 213–14
Sharpey, William 56, 59, 198, 199
Shelley, Mary 26
  Frankenstein 43
Shelley, Percy Bysshe 26–7, 33, 43
Sidgwick, Henry 242, 243, 244
Simmons, Mr 217, 224–5, 230
Simpson, James 96
Slade, Dr Henry 2, 217–30, 262

Slater, Thomas 218
Société Royale de Médecine 19
Society for Psychical Research (SPR) 2, 242–5, 249, 251, 252, 253, 255, 256, 257, 260, 264
Society of Universal Harmony 18, 19
Somnambule Jane 148
Southey, Robert, *Letters from England* 23
Spectator 230
Speer, Dr Stanhope Templeman 236, 237
Spencer, Herbert 90
Spicer, Henry 168
The Spirit World 168
Spiritual Athenaeum 195
Spiritual Institution 236
Spiritual Magazine 210, 212
spiritualism 2, 4
  American introduction of 161–2
  attacks on 204–6
  British experiments in 170–1
  exposés of scams and tricks concerning 213–16, 221–31
  female practitioners of 162–9
  and levitation 186–7, 199–200
  link with mesmerism 172–3
  North of England movement 171–2, 210
  practitioners and converts 180–90
  scientific indifference towards 190
  scientific inquiries into 194–204
  support for 190–3
  victims of 173–7
Spiritualist Magazine 189, 190, 200, 239
Spurzheim, Johann 44
Stanhope, 3rd Earl, 'Citizen

Index

Stanhope' 47
Stanhope, 4th Earl, Philip Henry
   36, 47–9, 58, 97, 122, 159
   Tracts relating to Caspar Hauser
   48
Stanhope, Lady Hester 48
Stockport 112
Stoerk, Professor von 13, 14
Stokes, Miss 216
Stokes, Professor 198, 199
Stone (American electrobiologist)
   114
Stone, William 163
Strauss, David 31
Swedenborg, Emanuel 147, 155
Switzerland 12, 20
Sylvester, Professor 62
Symes, Edmund 140, 188, 190

Tanner, Amy 256
   Studies in Spiritism (with Stanley
   Hall) 259
Taylor, Mr 216
Tecmen, San Milan (aka Madame
   Tecmen de Mexico) 147–8
Temperance Hall, Newport 105–6
Ten Hours movement 172
Tennyson, Alfred, Lord 244
Teste, Alphonse 138
Thackeray, William Makepeace
   184
   Pendennis 3
Thompson, Colonel Peyronnet 8,
   9–10
Thornton, Dr 39
Thumb, General Tom 212
The Times 41, 49, 54, 101, 142,
   163, 164, 223
Tonna, Charlotte Elizabeth 128
Topham, William 93
Townshend, Reverend Chauncey
   Hare 82–6, 90, 97, 138, 139,
   158
   Facts in Mesmerism 84, 99
trance possession 235, 236–7, 239,
   240–2, 263–4
Trinity College (Cambridge) 83
Trollope, Fanny 80
Trollope, Thomas 50–1, 77–8, 187,
   198
   What I Remember 77–8
Two Modern Doctors (theatrical
   farce) 19
Tylor, Anna 234
Tylor, Edward 233–5
Tyndall, John 171
Tynemouth 121–2, 124, 130, 133,
   136
Tyneside 146

University College 74, 76, 221,
   233
University College Hospital 3–4,
   7–10, 37, 48, 52, 55, 59, 111,
   117, 137, 199
University of Dillingen 11
University of Edinburgh 96, 110,
   157
University of Ingolstadt 11
University of London 45
University of Pennsylvania,
   Seybert Commission 230, 231

Vagrancy Act (1824) 223, 229,
   230
Varley, Cromwell Fleetwood
   196–7, 200–2, 215
Vernon, William 107–8, 148
Vials, Anne 117–18, 125, 131
Victoria, Queen 36, 208, 214
Vienna 11, 12, 14, 44
vitalism 43
Volkman, William 201

Wakefield Asylum 32
Wakefield Gaol 229
Wakley, Thomas 59, 62, 65–70, 76, 94
Waldegrave, Lady 180
Wales, Prince of 212
Wales, Princess of 23
Walker, George 115
Wallace, Alfred Russel 97, 104–5, 192–3, 215, 220, 222, 228
Waterhead 132
Watts, Alaric 242
Weatherhead, David 172
Wedgwood, Hensleigh 222
Weldon, Georgina 226
Wellington, Duke of 140
Wesley, John 16, 147
Weston-Super-Mare 157
Whatley, Bishop 97
Wheatstone, Professor Charles 55, 62
Whewell, William 171
Wilberforce, Bishop 236
Wilkinson, Dr J.J. Garth 90, 164
Wilkinson, William 190

Williams, Charles 216, 235
Wilson, Dr 36, 175
Winter, Alison 107
Wolfart, Karl 26, 58
Wombell, James 93
Wood, Miss 216
Wood, Mr 52, 56, 59, 61
Wordsworth, William 129, 132, 135
World 218
Wynward, Mrs 123, 127, 128, 133, 146

Yorkshire Spiritual Telegraph 172
Young, Julian Charles 165–6

The Zoist 89–90, 93, 94, 100, 103, 130, 131, 139, 140, 143, 145, 147, 166, 168, 172, 175, 176–7